ALLY
FOR
LIFE

TANIA ROBERTS

ALLY FOR LIFE
First published in New Zealand in November 2022 by
Red Rose Publishing, New Plymouth

This novel is a work of fiction. The persons and events in this book may have representations in history, but this work is entirely the author's creation and should not be construed as historical fact.

A catalogue record for the book is available from the National Library of New Zealand.

Format: Print on Demand
ISBN 978-1-99-117462-8
Format: EPUB
ISBN 978-1-99-117461-1

Cover Design: Kura Carpenter Design, thebookcarpenter.co.nz
Cover Image: Arcangel Images Limited,
Back Cover Image: Alamy

ALLY

FOR

LIFE

CHAPTER

1

"You can do this," Alice whispered to herself.

The dirty facade of the factory loomed ominously in front of her and she knew she must conquer her fear. Every dark place held a threat, but what would she find this time? Another boss demanding more than she was prepared to give?

Gingerly, she wrapped her fingers around the worn brass door handle, polished gold by all the hands that had gone before hers. It required all her strength to turn. She could hear the rumbling of the machines as the door edged open. A wall of heat carrying the oily stench of equipment rushed to escape the confines of the factory into the cool morning air. Alice recoiled, the cloying combination of heat and odour stuck in her throat.

"Get a move on, there's work to be done," a baritone voice bellowed orders from the darkness. Alice couldn't see the man behind the command, didn't want to imagine his towering stature or what else he would demand of her. That which she hadn't been able to willingly give to any man.

"Do I have to drag you in here?"

The early morning sun, rising at her back, cast a wedge of light across the concrete floor like an arrow pointing the way. Alice had no choice but to follow its direction and step over the threshold of what was to be. She was only here because of men. Men on the other side of the world whose power struggle had resulted in another global war. Men from the plains of Canterbury who'd enlisted, voluntarily or otherwise, and been taken from the land that was their lifeblood to fight a battle that wasn't theirs. And men much closer to home, who had decided that she, after training in the basics of farming, should be assigned to a factory. Her resentment at men, for all these reasons and more, was a load that sat heavy in the pit of her stomach like the bowels of this factory.

Alice tried to turn back; her attempts were futile. She felt constrained, unable to escape her fate. She wanted to run from her future, to return to Bella and Lizzy, the lambs she'd been feeding. A movement to the left caught her eye. She shrieked with fright. A beady-eyed rat stared defiantly at her before it scampered away behind the metal shroud of a machine, its tail leaving the only evidence of its presence, a slithery spoor through the flax dust on the floor. Alice's heart thundered in her chest, echoed by the pounding of the machinery. A drumbeat, allegro in its tempo, sounded at her ear. It was so close Alice was too frightened to look for its source, but the banging continued, increasing in volume and urgency.

"Alice! Alice!"

The female voice was familiar. Alice found herself drawn to it, knowing that it would offer comfort. The call rang out again and she recognised Grace's voice, but what was Grace doing at the factory? Hadn't she been assigned to Orari Estate?

"Alice! Open the door." Grace thumped her fist on the bedroom door.

"It's open," Alice replied in her semi-awake state. She'd just walked through the door, of course it was open.

Grace rattled the handle. "No, you've locked it. I can see the key blocking the keyhole."

Alice stirred and opened her eyes to the familiar surrounds of the tiny bedroom that had been hers for the last three months. The sun shone through the lace curtains in the dormer window letting her know the day was ready for her. The patchwork quilt of her single bed, which she snuggled under on the cool autumn nights, was now as dishevelled as she felt, scrunched up and twisted around her legs.

"Just a minute," she called to Grace, unravelling herself from the bedding and rearranging her white cotton nightie to a respectable length. The wooden floorboards were cold to her bare feet as she tiptoed across to turn the key.

"Are you alright?" Grace rushed into the room and took Alice by the shoulders. "You screamed so loud. I thought someone must be attacking you."

"No." Alice looked around the room, reassuring herself that there was no intruder. She realised the thoughts of the factory that seemed so real and terrifying must have been nothing more than a nightmare. She shuddered.

"It's alright." Grace wrapped her arms around Alice. "You're safe now."

The warmth of the blonde woman's embrace was like the heat beneath a mother bird incubating her eggs in a nest. Like a hatchling, Alice was going to have to break out of her shell. She felt safe but she couldn't stay there forever. Just as she did when she'd signed up for the land girls, Alice was going to have to rise, to stand as tall as her petite frame would allow and face the world. She broke free from the hug.

"I'll be alright," she said as much to herself as to Grace.

"Whatever scared you?" Grace led Alice to the edge of the bed where they both sat.

"The factory," Alice answered matter-of-factly. "The linen flax mill where I've been assigned. I don't want to go."

"We're supposed to leave today. Moira is going to drive us in Bill's truck."

Alice thought again of the lambs she'd been feeding; like her, they had been abandoned by their mother. Together they had been able to nurture one another and give affection unconditionally. Then Alice pictured Lulu, the first lamb she had named. Just as Duncan, the farm manager and everyone else had warned, Lulu was weaned, returned to the flock and Alice was forgotten. She'd be forgotten by Bella and Lizzy too; perhaps the factory was a good solution, the machines were bolted to the floor.

"I know," Alice replied despondently. "But we've been trained for farming. I've come to love the animals: Jess, Patch, Lulu, Bella and Lizzy."

Grace chuckled. "I knew you'd taken a liking to the animals, but I didn't realise you'd named an entire family of them."

"There won't be any animals at the factory." Alice pictured the beady eyes of the rat and shuddered again; she wouldn't count vermin as a friendly animal. It wasn't just the lack of animals that had her fretting, it was more the abundance of men in the factory who may behave like animals.

"There might be a dog or perhaps you could get a pet cat. There's bound to be some wild kittens around the factory that will need feeding," Grace suggested.

Even the thought of a pet kitten couldn't wipe the dejected look from Alice's face or lift her slumped shoulders.

"Is it just the lack of animals or is there something else bothering you?" Grace asked.

"Duncan's not happy. All his time training me wasted. Perhaps he could complain to the placement officer."

"Maybe. It might be too late for anything to happen today though. You might have to give it a go for a week and apply for a transfer."

Tears fell freely from Alice's eyes. She was exhausted; physically from the work she'd done ploughing fields, fencing paddocks, drenching sheep, and feeding pigs; emotionally from the images of the factory that plagued her nightmare.

"What is it, Alice? What's really wrong? I can't help you if I don't know what has you so upset."

Alice looked into her friend's big blue eyes. They were the colour of the sky on a sunny day, a day that made you feel that anything was possible. She contemplated revealing everything, a vague childhood memory told her a problem shared was a problem halved. She looked away, fidgeted her hands in her lap and picked at a callus on her palm. When she turned back to look, Grace's blue eyes stared kindly and without judgement. Alice took a deep breath, filling her lungs with courage.

"I'm scared the factory will be just like before."

Quietness filled the room. Holding Alice's hand, Grace stroked her thumb gently around and around Alice's palm in small comforting circles. Alice sucked in another breath.

"There will be men at the factory," she blurted.

"Not many." Grace lifted her thumb and wiped a tear away. "Only those essential to keep the factory running."

"It only needs one." Alice swallowed hard, eager to dissipate the bitter tang in her mouth.

"What only needs one, Alice?" Grace's voice was but a whisper as if to contain Alice's secret.

Again, the room sat quiet until Alice found the strength to continue.

"To corner me. To touch me. To take from me what wasn't his to take." Alice spat the words out. She stared at Grace but did not see, looking straight past into a void that held the memories she'd tried hard to suppress.

"Oh, Alice." Grace pulled her petite friend back into her arms. "What happened? Who hurt you?"

"My boss … He …"

"He raped you?" It was Grace who was now tense, anger rising, colouring her cheeks in a red rage.

Rape. A strong and ugly word that Alice didn't know the legalities of in terms of a crime, but what had happened to her that day, a day that was imprinted in her mind forever, was most certainly an offence against her very being. An invasion of her body in the confines of a changing cubicle that had left her feeling violated, dirty, and used.

"At Orari? While we've been here? Duncan?" Grace's rapid-fire questions gave Alice no time to respond. "When? When did he have an opportunity to commit such an horrendous act? We'll have to move quick. It won't be safe

6

for Betsy to stay or for the new recruits who are due to arrive today."

"Not Duncan. My ex-boss," Alice muttered, the image of his ugly face pervading her memory.

"How can any man do such a thing?" Grace's nostrils flared. "At the department store?"

"Yes." Alice spoke slowly, deliberately and with vehemence, but once the words were said her spine lost its rigid stance and she slumped, exhausted into Grace.

"What did you do? Did you complain to the police?"

"No, I just left. He was older, respected in the community."

"Did you tell anyone?"

"I was just a woman working in a department store. Who would have believed me? Nobody!"

"Your mother? A family member or friend? My brothers would have marched straight around and given him what for if it had been me. No-one should have to go through what you've been through, Alice."

Grace was the first person Alice had revealed her secret to and she decided she might as well tell all.

"My mother is an alcoholic. There was no point telling her. She had a drunken argument with our landlord, and we got kicked out of our flat. Jobless and homeless all in one week. That's why I'm here. That's why I joined the land girls. I needed something to do and somewhere to live."

"Oh, Alice." Grace rocked Alice gently backwards and forwards, patting her back like a mother trying to relieve her new-born's wind. Eventually, Alice's breathing slowed and the tension in her shoulders eased.

"Are you two coming?" Betsy called from the passage. "Nel's cooking a special farewell breakfast. We'd better get over there."

Alice jumped up; she may have revealed her secret to Grace, but she wasn't ready to let anyone else know. The movement was too sudden, she wavered unsteadily on her feet while stars circled her head.

"Coming," Grace replied on their behalf. She stood and pulled Alice back into her arms. "Don't worry, it'll be alright. I don't know how but I'll find a way to make it alright."

Alice had only known Grace for the three months of their training. Where Alice was small and childlike, Grace was tall and slender, her fingers long and elegant. Alice only came up to Grace's shoulder, but she was determined her size wouldn't stop her from doing anything the other land girl could do, tasks which in normal times would have been done by a much larger and stronger male.

"Right then." Grace broke away and reached into her pocket for a handkerchief. "Wipe your eyes. You'd better pack up your things. There are more land girls coming today so we have no choice but to leave."

Alice needed more than a hankie to soothe her red-rimmed eyes and ruddy cheeks.

"I promise, everything will be alright." Grace repeated her pledge.

❦

Moira left for Bill's as soon as breakfast was over and was still smiling when she arrived back at Captain Boyle's house to collect Grace and Alice.

"You're looking happy," Grace remarked. "All is well then at your new posting?"

"It will be," Moira replied with a chuckle. "Right, where to first?" she asked when the bags were stowed on the back and the three of them were side by side in the cab, Alice, being the smallest, wedged in the middle, a small posy of pansies clasped tightly in her hand.

"I think we should go to the flax mill," Grace suggested. "Then we will all know where it is."

Alice shivered, she wanted to delay the inevitable as long as possible but the idea that the others would know where she would be, was comforting. Someone would know where to rescue her from.

"I think Orari Estate is on the way so we can see where you'll be too," Moira said.

They were five minutes out of Orari when a sign on a gatepost signalled the entrance to Orari Estate. Two cherry trees, each backed by a large copper beech marked the beginning of a winding driveway. Sheep grazed the paddocks on either side and a dark brown brick house rose from behind a tall hedge of camelias several hundred feet from the road.

"It looks lovely." Alice's desire that this be her new home infused her voice with longing. "You're so lucky, Grace."

Grace squeezed Alice's hand. "It'll be alright. You'll see."

Alice couldn't see anything but a beautiful house that she wouldn't be living in. The images of the factory that had pervaded her sleep tried to seep into her mind. She closed her eyes and inhaled deeply, banishing all thoughts that brought discomfort.

It took another ten minutes to get to the flax mill. To one side, several long paddocks had row upon row of criss-cross stacks of flax, with wispy fibre heads drying in the sun. The factory, the outbuildings and the houses that were home to some of the mill workers were all an off-white colour. It was difficult to discern if this was the original paint or the accumulation of dust and grime from the factory. The houses were adjacent to the road and the factory buildings behind, separated by a dusty metal track. Moira turned the truck off the road and followed the track to what appeared to be the office, part of the main building but with windows and an open door. No-one came to greet them.

"Looks deserted," Moira joked. "Maybe its abandoned and you don't have to come here after all, Alice."

Alice hoped so but a plume of smoke rising from the chimney signalled otherwise.

"It is Sunday. Perhaps they've gone to church." Moira continued her flippant comments unaware of the impact they were having on Alice.

"We'll just have to go and have a look." Grace opened the truck door and climbed out. She poked her head in the office door. "Hello, anyone there?"

There was still no reply by the time the others were at her side.

"I can hear machines. They must be through that door." Moira pointed to a door on the far side of the office.

The door, like the one in Alice's nightmare, led to the factory. Grinding, thrashing, and whirring machinery muffled by the door, filled the office with noise once Grace opened it. Alice poked her fingers into her ears. She felt like sobbing, how was she ever going to manage? Why couldn't she have been assigned to another farm? She needed the peace and quiet of the countryside, not this deafening cacophony.

"Aah! You must be the new worker." A wiry man came out of the darkness and extended his sinewy arm to shake Grace's hand. "Come back into the office … phew, that's better," he said as he closed the factory door. "Sorry about that. Bit noisy in there. I was meant to be looking out for you but we're so short of staff, I had to go and check on the machines." The man took off his hat, ran a hand through his greying hair and sat down behind the only desk in the room. "Welcome aboard. Are we getting all three of you? I thought they'd only been able to assign me one at this stage. Three would be great."

"No, just me," Grace replied.

Alice gasped. Grace turned around, her back to the man to hide the silencing finger she raised to her lips.

"Well, one is better than nothing. It's been a boomer year for production and the demand for the war effort is huge. Sorry, I forgot to introduce myself. I'm Mr Cresswell. I've been factory manager for a couple of years now. And you are? Sorry, I should know, I've got your paperwork here somewhere." Mr Cresswell waved an arm over the mishmash piles of paper strewn across his desk. "Anyway, it'll be Miss McPherson you'll be reporting to in the first instance. She looks after all the female workers. She's just away at church at the moment." Mr Cresswell glanced at the clock on the wall. "She'll be back in an hour. You can go and wait in the women's lunchroom if you like. She can show you around when she gets back. The other women are having a long overdue day off."

"That will be great. Thank you," Grace said.

Mr Cresswell led the women to an oblong building standing off to the side of the main factory.

"This is the women's lunchroom. Make yourself a cuppa if you want," he said, before turning to leave. "I'd better get back to the factory."

As soon as Mr Cresswell was out of earshot, Alice grabbed hold of Grace's arm.

"What are you doing?"

"Yes, what are you doing?" Moira chimed in.

"They were assigned a worker. They're getting a worker," Grace said matter-of-factly.

"Yes, but it is supposed to be me."

"But it is going to be me." Grace was adamant. "I'm much more suited to this work than you. You're much better with animals."

It all sounded logical to Alice, but she was worried about the consequences, if and when the swap was discovered.

"Won't we get in trouble?"

"By the look of the mess on Mr Cresswell's desk it will be a while before they even notice. By then it will be too late, I'll be such a good worker, they won't want to lose me."

"Oh, Grace." Alice was on the verge of tears again, tears of relief this time. She hugged Grace. "Thank you so much. You are a wonderful friend."

"Right then." Moira cleared her throat. "We'll leave you to it and I'll get Alice back to Orari Estate."

"Thanks, Moira. We'll catch up again soon."

"Yes, we'll see you at the races in a fortnight."

CHAPTER

2

Moira drove the truck down the winding tree-lined driveway into Orari Estate, stopping when she reached a fork in the track. Across the paddock, in one direction, farm sheds all painted in matching ochre lined up. In the other direction stood the impressive homestead.

"I guess I'd better drop you at the house."

Moira stopped the truck outside the back door. She pulled on the handbrake and climbed out, grabbing Alice's bag off the back.

"There doesn't seem to be anyone here." Nerves churned Alice's stomach, as they always did when she faced the unknown.

"Best you knock on the door," Moira suggested.

Alice stepped up to the large dark green wooden door and timidly knocked.

"For goodness' sake." Moira stepped up beside Alice. "Nobody's going to hear that." She thumped the door with her fist, then stood back.

Fear gripped Alice. The footsteps were loud. They couldn't possibly belong to a woman, unless she was very large indeed. Alice looked skyward, closed her eyes, and silently prayed, 'please don't let it be a man.'

"Morning there." A tall, weathered man opened the door, wiped his hands on a floury apron and stood aside to welcome them in. "You must be the new land girl. Come on in."

"Not me." Moira gave Alice a not-so-gentle push towards the door. "Just Alice, here."

Alice had no choice. She couldn't back out. She looked up at the man, he was as tall as she was short, but obviously unaware she was supposed to be Grace. His eyes looked friendly enough and his smile appeared genuine, but Alice had learned that looks could be deceiving.

"Alice, it's nice to meet you. Name's Stanley Brown." He extended his arm, engulfing Alice's tiny hand in his and shook with all the gusto you'd expect from a giant. "Everyone calls me Brownie though. Let me take your bag."

Moira handed the bag over. Alice wanted to hang onto it, like a well-cuddled security blanket, but all she had was her posy of pansies whose faces were as downcast as hers.

"You'll be right then, Alice?" Moira asked. "I'll be off."

Before Alice could protest, Moira turned her back, climbed into the truck and drove off, leaving Alice alone to face whatever Orari Estate held for her.

It was cool in the kitchen. A small window above the sink let in the only natural light and a single lightbulb hanging from the ceiling in the centre of the room made little impact. Brownie told Alice to have a seat at the table. He made a pot of tea, placed it and two china cups with a blue floral design

14

and a matching plate in front of her. He retrieved a battered cake tin from the sideboard and added several slices of fruitcake to the plate.

"There, help yourself," Brownie said, taking the seat opposite. "You look like you need feeding up."

Alice was as scared for the delicate china as she was for herself, but Brownie handled everything with care. She hoped that boded well for her. His gentle actions seemed incongruous with his stature.

"So, Alice, tell me about yourself, what brings you to Orari Estate?"

Alice took a bite of fruit cake. She needed time to formulate an answer that wouldn't involve lying. She settled on, "I signed up for the land girls. I've been at Whipsnade Farm for the past three months, getting trained by Mr McKnight."

"Duncan, good man, Duncan. And what did Duncan teach you? Three months isn't long."

"We milked the cows and fed the pigs," Alice replied. "It was my job to get the cows in each day with Jess."

"Jess? Is Jess one of the other land girls?"

"No. Jess was the horse."

"Mmm." Brownie rubbed his bristled chin. "We don't have cows or pigs at Orari but it's good that you can ride a horse."

"We drenched sheep, made hay, I had to be the crow on top of the stack." Alice felt the need to defend herself and didn't mention her panic when it was time to get down. "I was the rousie when we shore the sheep." She neglected to add that it was only because she was too small to manhandle the animals. "I fed lambs who'd been abandoned."

15

"Well, I'm certain there'll be something for you to do. The lads will be back soon, and you can tag along with them. First, we'd better sort your room out."

Alice didn't hear anything past lads. She was stuck on the thought that 'lads' were men and there were more than one of them. She had a foreboding dread that she might have been better off at the linen flax mill under the careful supervision of Miss McPherson.

"I'm not really sure where we should put you," Brownie continued. "Can't really have you sharing with any of the lads."

"Pardon?" Alice shook her head. Tiny trembles of fear started in her toes and crept up until her knees were shuddering under the table. She clenched them together and pressed her feet firmly on the floor.

"There's a little room up in the attic or there's the whare out the back." Brownie relayed the options oblivious to Alice's terror. "Finish your cuppa and we'll take a look. See where you'd rather be. I've got to get this pastry rolled and the pie in the oven if it is going to be ready for lunch." Brownie downed his cup of tea in two mouthfuls and stood ready to leave. "Leave your bag here. We can fetch it when you decide which room you'll take."

Alice reluctantly left her bag on the kitchen floor and the wilting posy of flowers on the table to follow Brownie.

The kitchen door led into a short passageway that joined the main entrance, stained glass windows either side of the front door diffused the sunlight into a kaleidoscope of colours on the wall. Alice hoped the rainbow pattern would lead to a pot of gold, instead it fell at the bottom of a wooden staircase. She clung to the polished wooden balustrade supported by ornately carved spindles and gingerly followed Brownie up the stairs.

"Who are the photos of?" Alice was curious to discover who the finely-clad men and elegant women looking down at her were. The black and white images, arranged in what appeared to be date order, all had stern faces.

"They're the McDonalds." Brownie didn't give the portraits a second look and continued up the staircase as if he had more important matters to attend to. "This property has been in the family since 1854."

Alice wanted to ask why they weren't here now, but she had to hurry to catch up to Brownie. She hoped that everything in this house would be right and proper, just as they appeared to be.

Brownie turned left at the first-floor landing. Open doors on both sides of the hallway revealed bedroom after bedroom, mostly the beds were unmade. Clothing dumped on the floor and shaving equipment left on a dresser indicated the rooms were used by men. In one room the curtains were still drawn, and it was left in darkness. Alice didn't want to imagine what else that space held.

Brownie continued to the end of the passage and opened a small door, he pulled on a cord suspended from the ceiling and the light revealed a steep, narrow staircase.

"I'm not sure what state it is in sorry, I was meaning to get it sorted but I clean forgot about you coming today. I always bang my head when I try to go up there. You have a look and see what you think." Brownie stood to the side and ushered Alice forward.

Slowly, one step at a time, Alice climbed. There was no handrail, but the stairwell was so narrow that she could easily touch the walls on either side. Halfway she stopped and glanced back to be certain that Brownie was true to his word and remained at the bottom. She breathed a sigh of relief.

At the top of the staircase, the multitude of eyes of a large brown spider, stared blindly at her from an intricate web, hanging from the ceiling. The spider, like Alice, wanted to prevent any intrusion into its private space. Alice stopped short, she had no desire to have the arachnid or its web on her. The single lightbulb cast an eerie glow around the small attic room, sufficient light to see a fine layer of dust coated every horizontal surface. At least it was a comforting signal that nobody had been in the room for some time.

Pinpricks of sunlight etched their way under the eaves. The roof's steep pitch only allowed for a single bed in the middle and a small table either side; one with drawers and one with open shelves. Alice thought of her bag, it contained all her meagre belongings; they would be easily accommodated in the room. There was no dormer window like her room at Whipsnade Farm, but Alice decided she would only be here to sleep; each day she would work until she was exhausted and then sleep.

"I think this will do fine," she called to Brownie as she made her way back down the staircase. Alice hoped she sounded more confident than she felt.

A door slammed and the rumble of men's voices increased in volume as Brownie and Alice descended the stairs.

"Sounds like the lads are back. I'd better put the kettle on." Brownie strode ahead.

Alice stopped; her knuckles whitened as she clung to the bottom of the balustrade. Perhaps, she could climb back up to the attic room and begin cleaning. Confronting the spider would be easier than the men in the kitchen.

"You'd best come meet them all." Brownie held the kitchen door ajar, leaving her with no option. Alice needed to retrieve her bag anyway.

"We thought you must be entertaining a dolly bird." The largest of the men laughed at his own humour, his ruddy face colouring still further. "Got the fancy china out, aye Brownie?"

"Hmm mmm!" Brownie cleared his throat. "Now, now, there will be none of that. This is Alice. Alice is the new land girl who has been assigned to help on the farm."

Six heads turned; twelve eyes all looked directly at Alice. She wished the floorboards would part and swallow her. She felt their scrutiny, imagined they would be judging her, assessing her capabilities without giving her a chance; or worse still ogling her womanly features with ungentlemanly intentions. Alice thought of the linen flax mill: would it be too late to change her mind, to run from this assignment? That option would probably result in her and Grace both being expelled from the Land Girls. Alice couldn't risk that. She had no home and no job to return to. This was her only alternative. She knew Grace had only been trying to help, as she always did, but this time Alice may have been better off without Grace's attempt to fix things.

If she couldn't run, then Alice had to start out how she meant to carry on. She was damaged but she was not broken. Determined to show no sign of weakness, to not let any man take advantage of her, Alice squared her shoulders and looked from one man to the next, scrutinizing each one. The man on the far left was short, wider but no taller than her. His dark hair was slicked back and held in place by a gallon of oil. Alice imagined the army had rejected him because of his height. His wide grin appeared friendly despite a missing front tooth. Alice's heart thundered in her chest, but she pulled her shoulders back and looked him straight in the eye, painting her face with the practiced veneer that kept her emotions hidden.

"Hello, lass," he stepped forward and nodded. "Jack's the name. Pleased to meet you."

There was a smell about him that seemed familiar and not in a good way, but his demeanour held no challenge and Alice's heartbeat slowed a fraction. The man next to Jack was a lot taller, so tall that he'd probably have to duck to go through doorways. Alice wondered if the army also refused to enlist those who were too tall. He was much younger than Jack, probably of an age similar to Alice's. His curly blonde hair flopped down over his forehead, and he held his head on an angle as if to see around the fringe and make himself appear shorter.

"Danny, ma'am." Danny bobbed his head and stepped forward with a thump. The reason for his presence on the farm instead of the battlefield became apparent. A wooden leg protruded from baggy trousers occupying the space where his left kneecap, calf and foot should have been.

Alice's heartbeat was returning to normal.

"Rangi," the next man stepped forward to introduce himself. "Pleased to meet you, miss."

Alice sucked in a breath. Rangi was dark, his jet-black mop of curly hair hung untidily down over his face. It was a face that Alice could hear her grandfather describing as typical Maori; broad nose, wide mouth, big lips. She imagined the whites of his eyes and teeth would be the only signal of his presence in the dead of night. A big Maori family had lived down the road from Alice's grandfather. There must have been ten children living with their parents and grandparents in an old house with rotting weatherboards, but Alice wasn't allowed to go near them. Her grandfather, who was usually such a kind man, said they were trouble. He didn't elaborate, just told her in no uncertain terms to stay away. That repeated command had instilled a wariness in Alice that stirred as she looked at Rangi trying to deduce why he wouldn't be at war. He had no prosthetic or missing limbs that she could see. Alice had heard Duncan speak of the much-revered Maori Battalion, so it wasn't because of his race.

"I'm colour blind, miss." Rangi answered her unspoken question like it was a line he'd been reciting since the war began.

Alice reddened. She had just been judging Rangi because of his colour when he was likely unable to discern hers. She'd seen people sneer and heard them whisper behind their hands in judgement. She didn't want to be like that. She felt guilty and turned to meet the next man. What hair he had left was short and grey, his face was weather-beaten from many years on the land. Unlike the other men, he extended his hand—as if she too were a man—and she had no option but to shake it. His hand was tough and callused. It felt like sandpaper as it gripped hers, squashing her tiny fingers, signalling that he wasn't about to proffer her any kind of friendship.

"Lou," he said, his deep voice was as rough as the rest of him. "I'm foreman. I decide who does what. We'll be drenching the wethers this afternoon. All of us."

Alice gulped. The man who appeared the least friendly was the one in control of her future. She'd have to try her hardest to not disappoint him. At least she'd drenched sheep before and knew what was involved. She gave a silent nod of acknowledgement.

"And last but not least," the remaining man announced himself with a drum roll from his hands on the table. "Fergus at your service." He laughed, bowed slightly, and smiled at Alice.

A giggle escaped before Alice had time to stop herself. Lou cleared his throat and Fergus obeyed the cue, stepped back into line, and swapped his smile for a serious downcast face. Any possibility of an ally amongst the group was banished. It was a timely reminder to Alice not to let her guard down. She'd have to prove she was just as capable as them, if not more so, of her own volition.

"Right then, introductions over. Alice, you take your bag and get settled in."

Alice bent down to pick up her bag and came face to face with Fergus who had done the same.

"I'll carry that for you, Alice," he said with a wink and a smile.

Alice collected the wilting posy from the table and turned to leave the kitchen.

"No, you won't," Brownie interrupted. "Alice can carry her own bag. You'll find a jar for the flowers in the washroom off the back porch," he said to her. "You men,

22

have a seat. All of you," Brownie ordered, looking directly at Fergus.

Alice took her bag and left the room but lingered behind the closed kitchen door to hear the ensuing discussion.

"Rule number one: you'll not extend Alice any favours and nor will you take any from her or you will have me to answer to."

It sounded as if Brownie set the rules. Was he her ally? Was he going to keep her safe? If he didn't let them help her with anything though, she was going to have to work extra hard. She heard Brownie begin to announce rule number two, but she didn't wait to hear it. Alice crept away quietly to the tiny room at the top of the house which she hoped would be her new safe haven.

Alice spent the rest of the morning dusting, sweeping, and organising her clothes in the drawers and on the shelves. Except for Brownie, who was toiling away at the bench, the kitchen was empty as she made her way out to find the washroom. Her pansies appreciated the jar of water she arranged them in and perked their heads up to smile at her once again. Alice gathered up the bedspread, carried it outside and hung it on the clothesline at the back of the house. She gave it a good thrashing until dust particles no longer escaped from its threads. Pleasantly surprised that free of dust it was a pretty rose colour, she took comfort in the knowledge that another female had slept in the bed that was now hers.

Adjacent to the clothesline was a small square building Alice assumed was the whare Brownie had referred to. Sacking hung in the tiny window preventing any view of the interior. Curious, Alice left her bedspread on the line to air in the easterly breeze and tried the handle on the single door at the front. The hinges protested loudly at her intrusion and the darkness within the squat building held its contents in secrecy. Like déjà vu, the daylight behind her cast an arrow across the wooden floor of the whare, an arrow pointing the way. Unlike the arrow into the factory, Alice was happy to follow the prompt and step inside. When her eyes adjusted to the darkness, she saw a single crib in the corner. Beside the crib, a copper candle holder sat on a wooden table that could have doubled as a stool, trails of wax suspended from the candle evidence that once someone had called this whare home. Its low roof felt comforting to Alice, she decided then and there that she'd return soon with some matches to light the candle and inspect the whare further. Turning to leave she noticed another reassuring feature. Unlike her attic bedroom the only door had a lock; a strong metal shaft to slide into a catch on the wall. The whare plunged into darkness when Alice shut the door to test the lock. It worked. She returned to the clothesline happy in the knowledge that she had options.

CHAPTER

3

Brownie's pie tasted delicious, almost as good as Nel's. Fergus insisted Alice sit next to him. Alice didn't want to get too friendly. She didn't know him, and she didn't know what his intentions were, but the only other seat was next to Lou, so Fergus's offer was taken.

"Right, everyone over to the woolshed," Lou instructed as the last slice of bread was being smothered with plum jam by Danny. "We'll get stuck into the drenching."

"Can you use a shepherd's whistle?" Lou asked Alice as the group walked across to the woolshed.

"No, sorry," she replied. "I can ride a horse though," Alice added, noticing the paddock full of horses.

"No need for that, we've got the sheep in." Lou's answer and tone were short and abrupt. "Best you stick with Jack then, he'll show you how to open and shut the gate."

Alice stepped back, affronted by Lou's remark.

"Don't mind him," Fergus came up beside her and whispered. "He's grumpy with all of us."

Alice feigned a smile at Fergus. She appreciated his concern but was wary of having to prove herself to Lou.

"Fergus!" Lou said gruffly as if he had heard the whisper. "You can be on the drench trough."

Fergus shrugged his shoulders and moved off to take up the position assigned to him.

Lou flicked the catches on the dogs' kennels and pulled the doors open. The dogs eagerly escaped their pens and jumped up at their master to get a pat on the head.

"Gidday boy," Alice said to the Huntaway that bounded over to her, eager to sniff out the newcomer. She gave him a pat and ruffled his ears, hoping she may have found a canine friend.

"Get in behind, Joe!"

The Huntaway heard its name and was gone in an instant, knowing there was work to be done. Alice's shoulders slumped, it appeared Lou wanted the dogs to be working dogs and nothing more.

The wethers jostled restlessly in the pens and bleated when the group reached the yards. The dogs eyed the sheep, eager to follow their master's commands and hustle the wethers into the race.

"We don't open the gate until we're sure the animal has been in the drench for long enough to get a good dose," Jack explained as he stood beside Alice. "They'll be all blue from the dye in the drench."

"Really," Alice retorted, the sarcasm in her voice too subtle for Jack to detect. She felt her body temperature rise, her anger with the man's patronising manner threatened to boil over. It was one thing for Duncan to prefer male workers over females but at least he never treated the land girls as complete numbskulls like Jack was doing.

The first of the sheep came into the trough and Danny thumped his wooden leg on the concrete edge to scare them along while he and Fergus made sure the animals stayed under the water to get a decent drenching.

"Here they come," Jack yelled as the first of the animals made its way up the ramp.

He leaned out over the railing to open the gate, the bulk of his frame blocking any view Alice had of the proceedings. She felt useless. How was she going to prove her worth when she'd effectively been put out of the way? Alice glared resentfully at Jack's back. Tell-tale sweat stains already coloured his spine and armpits. She decided to bide her time and take over when he was exhausted.

"Keep a count of them, Alice." Lou appeared on the other side of the race. "It's a good opportunity to get a tally."

Alice jumped; she hadn't noticed Lou and guilt coloured her cheeks. She nodded, brought her attention back to the sheep, and climbed onto the bottom railing of the fence to start counting the wethers as they passed through the gate. At least Lou had given her a purposeful task.

Once everyone had settled into their assigned job and the drenching was going to plan, Fergus and Danny, happy in their work, began whistling a tune. It was a cheerful ditty that Alice thought she recognised. She wanted to concentrate on the song so she could remember its title but couldn't risk losing count of the sheep.

By mid-afternoon, the count was up to 131. Alice climbed down from the fence rail and took a moment to blow dust from her nose with a now dirty hanky she had in her pocket.

"Watch out!"

"Grab it!"

"Alice!"

Alice's head jerked back, and her arms raised up, a spontaneous barrier over her body as she heard the warnings yelled in her direction. Wide-eyed, she sought the source. Who had yelled at her and why? Within a matter of seconds, she knew. A blue-stained woolly beast had mounted the top rail and was heading in her direction.

Alice fell back, grabbing at whatever she could as she crashed to the ground. She landed with a thud; the air forced from her chest. A second thud echoed the first, as the wether, whose front legs Alice had a firm hold of, landed on top of her.

The ensuing skirmish resembled a bar brawl. Despite the pain, Alice was determined not to let go of the sheep, as it righted itself, dug its rear hooves into her belly and attempted to escape. Alice's groans competed with the sheep's bleats of battle. She took a deep breath, gritted her teeth and with all the strength she could muster foisted the sheep onto its side; rolled herself over so her weight was now on the animal's shoulder. The wether threshed about, writhing to be free. Alice grabbed its front feet in one hand, dug her elbow into the sheep's rear flank and grabbed hold of the back legs with her other hand. It took all her might but Alice managed to still the wether for a few seconds so she could catch her breath.

She looked up. Fergus, Danny, and Rangi stood around her, clapping and cheering. Alice felt triumphant and smiled.

"Well done, Alice," Fergus congratulated her. "Let me help you with that." He grabbed a handful of wool in each hand and lifted the wether back into the race to join the others leaving the yards, then reached back to extend a hand to Alice to help her up.

She accepted the offer and for a moment thought that Fergus and her could be good friends.

"What number was that?" Lou asked, walking up to the group.

"What number? Ah … um." Alice's jaw dropped. In the confusion, the headcount had gone completely from her own head.

"She just caught one that was about to escape," Fergus said in Alice's defence.

"All very well but Alice's job was to count them, not catch them and now it appears she hasn't managed that."

"Sorry." Alice recited numbers in her head, testing them, trying to determine if one felt more familiar than the other. As her anger at her forgetfulness rose, the likelihood of remembering faded.

"You'd best get over to the tap and clean up," Lou ordered.

Alice looked down at herself. Blue dye from the sheep covered her from head to toe. She soon discovered that tap water was ineffective in removing bluestone. She had to return to her duties beside Jack with her hands, her clothes and one side of her face and hair an indigo blue.

It took another couple of hours before the last of the wethers had been put through the drench trough. Fergus and Danny resumed their whistling and singing. Alice didn't know if it was her imagination, or she was being over-sensitive, but their repertoire did seem to include a number of songs with the word 'blue' in them.

Back at the house, Brownie gave Alice a scrubbing brush and a bar of Wonder Soap.

"Best you head down to the river and have a good scrub up," he suggested. "Can't risk staining the upstairs bathroom. I'll tell the lads to stay clear, so you'll have some privacy."

Alice headed off in the direction Brownie had pointed, nervously glancing back to check nobody was following her. She found a patch of Kanuka bushes close to the river and checked once again that the men had stayed away as instructed. The Kanuka wasn't in flower at this time of the year but still provided plenty of cover for her to undress. She was grateful the dye hadn't soaked through to her bra and underwear, so she was able to leave them on.

A shallow pool at the edge of the river, provided Alice with some rocks to lay her overalls and shirt on and a safe place to sit while the current rushed by. It was late afternoon, and the winter sun was already disappearing behind the hills in the distance. She remembered the river being near freezing when the land girls had bathed after crutching. That was a month ago, the thought of getting in now held no attraction. Alice gingerly dipped in her big toe. The frigid water jolted her like an electric shock, sucking the air from her lungs. Wind whistled down the river, skimming across the chill of the water to hit her body like a punch. If she didn't hurry, it wasn't only her face and clothes that would need attention. Her body would succumb to hypothermia.

Alice scrubbed and scrubbed until her hands, and she imagined her face, were more red than blue. The dye in the clothes had faded but not disappeared, she hoped time and sunshine would take care of the rest or she would be forever labelled with evidence of her mistake.

Still angry with herself for forgetting the head count, Alice lost awareness of her surroundings while her thoughts raged a battle, one moment telling her to buck her ideas up or she would be fired on the first day; the next complimenting her on a job well done to catch the sheep.

A shrill whistle stilled both movement and thoughts. Alice sat bolt upright, alert to whatever had made the sound. She dropped the soap and raised her hands to cover her body. Her eyes bulged, scanning the area – searching for the source, wanting, needing, to know that the noise was from a bird and not a man. Alice's nostrils flared; her heart pounded in her chest while her ears strained to hear. There was nothing but the rushing of the river. Alice thought perhaps she had imagined the whistle.

Several seconds passed before the noise came again. Alice thought she was ready for it, but a primal scream escaped as she flinched at the sound. She leapt out of the water, grabbed her wet clothes and ran for the shelter of the Kanuka bushes. Hurriedly, she tried to dress but the sodden clothes stuck together and clung to her trembling wet limbs. The more she tried to hurry the harder getting dressed became.

It had been a bird's call, she was certain, not definite but reasonably certain. The longer she thought about it the greater her doubt became. Fergus and Danny had been whistling at the yards. If they could whistle a song, could they mimic a bird?

Finally dressed, Alice crouched under the bushes and from her hiding place hunted for a weapon. The first stick she picked up snapped when she poked it at the ground. Silently she cursed, hoping the noise wouldn't give away her position. She retrieved another branch from the undergrowth and held it aloft, ready to poke at her assailant.

Alice had a good view of the river. She could see the bar of soap, wedged between some rocks where she had dropped it. She shook her head, disappointed that a bar of soap would reveal her whereabouts, as she nervously waited for whatever was to come next.

The muscles in her thighs protested at her crouching position, aching to stand upright again. Alice decided she'd count to thirty seconds and if nothing happened in that time, she would leave the shelter of the Kanuka.

"One thousand and one, one thousand and two, one thousand and three …" slowly she counted in her head. "One thousand and twenty, one thousand and …"

"Rark, rark," the harsh raspy screech of two magpies pierced the sky above Alice's head as they flew from the Kanuka bush to land on a rock in the middle of the river.

"Bloody hell," she cursed, startled by the noise again. Alice's expletive almost turned to laughter when she realised the birds were the source of the whistle. She couldn't believe she'd been so jumpy about a pair of birds. She had heard stories though, of territorial magpies attacking people, so she quickly grabbed the soap and headed back over the paddock to the house.

Alice had no option but to join everyone in the kitchen for supper. She'd rather have taken a sandwich up to her bedroom, but Brownie insisted there was to be no food upstairs. He had enough trouble doing the laundry and cleaning the bathroom, he didn't need the extra burden of crumbs and dirty dishes left where they shouldn't be.

Supper was a delicious beef stew with rich brown gravy and diced carrots and parsnips from the garden. Brownie served Alice a small portion first.

"There won't be much left, once this lot help themselves," he said with a laugh, "and come back for seconds."

Alice sat quietly between Rangi and Fergus, hoping she was inconspicuous, her petite frame overshadowed by their broad shoulders. She thought Rangi, with his colour blindness, would be unaware of the still blue tinge to her hands and relied on Fergus, as a friend, to not say anything about the day's events either. But, as luck would have it, her position at the table was opposite Lou. She daren't look at him. She could sense him staring, his eyes boring into her head as she focused on the bowl of stew in front of her.

"Are you any better at ploughing than you are at counting?" he asked.

Alice stopped, her mouth open, a spoonful of stew paused. Lou hadn't said her name, but she knew the question was directed at her. She remembered the ploughing she had done at Whipsnade. Yes, she could plough was the answer to Lou's question. Her hands and feet were only just recovering from the blisters, and she'd didn't have Grace to help her but that wouldn't be what he wanted to hear. Alice put the spoonful in her mouth and slowly chewed, using the time to ponder her response. She thought Lou was issuing a challenge, one that if she failed would mean the end of her time at Orari Estate. She had no option but to take it on.

"I did some ploughing at Whipsnade," she answered, looking directly at Lou.

"Good, we'll get you to do some more tomorrow." He clapped his hands and rubbed his palms together.

Alice wasn't sure if Lou was happy that she could plough or the smile she glimpsed was more a malevolent sneer that would widen when Alice failed at the task and Lou was able to fire her. Either way, she was going to have to do her best.

"How many acres are there to plough?" she asked, hoping to sound like she had some farming knowledge.

"About twenty."

"And what crop will we be sowing?"

"Don't worry your pretty little head about that, I'll get one of the lads to put the seed in."

Alice bristled. She sat upright, inhaled long and slow. If she lost her patience with this man who seemed to hold her fate in his hands, then her time at Orari Estate would be over before it barely began. She remembered Duncan's talk about setting up the plough for the different crops and chose her words carefully.

"Yes, but won't I still need to know what it is you're going to plant, so I can set the spacing of the furrows?"

Lou coughed, splattering spots of gravy over the table from his half-eaten mouthful of stew. His cheeks reddened and his eyes bulged as he glared at the land girl opposite him.

"About a foot apart will be good," he replied after gulping down a glass of water. "That's twelve inches, not one of your feet."

Alice didn't react to his sarcasm. "A foot it is then," was all she said and continued with her supper.

Silence engulfed the room. Eventually, it was Brownie who broke the hush.

"Who's for bread-and-butter pudding then?"

"Yes, please."

"Great, thanks Brownie."

"A double helping for me please."

Alice had had enough. She slipped away from the table and retreated to the quietness of her room. She'd need a good night's sleep if she was to spend tomorrow ploughing.

CHAPTER

4

Alice's day had been physically exhausting and her apprehension at what tomorrow would bring was emotionally draining. There was a comfortable hollow in her worn single mattress that she felt cocooned in, her bedding pulled up snug under her chin. With the door at the bottom of the stairwell closed and the light switched off, the attic room was plunged into darkness and Alice easily slipped into a deep sleep.

She awoke with a start several hours later, sweat beading her brow, her heart thumping in her chest. There had been a scraping but whether the noise was real or imagined, Alice couldn't decide. Had she been dreaming again? She tried to retrace her thoughts but there was no memory of a fantasy woven into her sleep. Perhaps it was morning and the noise had been one of the men getting ready for work. Alice opened her eyes, seeking the reassurance of daylight but the room remained as dark as it had been when her eyes were closed. She willed her heartbeat to slow. She needed to be able to hear more than her own organs resonating from within. She keened her ears, listened for the wind outside, maybe the noise had merely been a tree rustling on a stormy night. Each time she'd moved as a child she had sheltered under the sheets until sounds of a new house became familiar and discernible as to their source.

Tonight, in this new place, she had to make her home, only the distant howl of a lonesome dog echoed into the darkness and Alice began to believe she must have imagined the disturbance that woke her. She rolled over and lay in the darkness facing the stairwell. It was the only way into or out of the room. If someone or something was in or trying to get in, she'd be ready. Cautiously, she reached down beside her bed, picked up one of her shoes and clasped it tight under the bed covers. It wasn't much of a weapon, but it was better than none.

In the chill of the night, the chime of the grandfather clock reached Alice's attic room as it announced the hour. She waited; her breathing suspended to count the strikes of the gong. What was the time? She still felt tired. How many more hours of sleep could she have before the day's challenge would be upon her? When Alice only heard two strikes, she was both disturbed and relieved. Disturbed that she still couldn't work out what had made the noise that had woken her, and relieved that, if she could only manage to put it out of her mind, she could get several more hours of restorative slumber.

Time elapsed and Alice's eyelids grew heavy. There were no more strange noises and she told herself not to be silly and go back to sleep or she wouldn't have the energy she needed for ploughing. She relaxed her grip on the shoe and started to drift off. The grandfather clock chimed the quarter hour, the half hour and then again at quarter to, Alice heard each melodic peal, fainter than its antecedent. She even thought, she counted to three or was it four, she wasn't sure.

What Alice did know, when she awoke again to the sound of men's voices and daylight forcing its way under the door and through the roof cracks, was that her body felt like it had been trampled. Tenderly, she touched her stomach and chest. She pulled the covers aside hoping that whatever was causing her such pain would be obvious. Her shoe lay discarded and squashed into the mattress, the only evidence of the disturbed night but not enough to cause the pain she felt. Lifting the hem of her nightie revealed patches of purple and blue. It wasn't the indigo of the bluestone dye as there had been no staining on her torso yesterday. The painful splotches were bruises. Alice wondered again whether someone had been in her room. Had her brain somehow suppressed any memory of the intrusion or the intruder? Surely not. Her recollection of the attack by her boss at the department store was as real as if it was yesterday. Even his smell assaulted her nostrils if she dared let it. No, nothing like that would ever happen again. Alice wouldn't let it.

Then she remembered the escaping wether, its hooves had rammed into her as they'd tumbled together to the ground. She admonished herself. If only... if only she'd let the sheep run away. She wouldn't be aching black and blue, and she wouldn't have forgotten the head count. Alice didn't want any more 'if only's' today. She needed to put her aches and pains aside and prove she could plough as good as any man, so with that in mind she climbed out of bed, dressed, and went downstairs to face the day.

❧

Lou assigned Fergus the task of showing Alice what to do. Keen to get her instructions and be left to get on with the job, they left the house straight after breakfast. It took three of Alice's tiny steps to keep up with Fergus's long strides and she was almost at a run. There was a dampness in the air, the morning mist still hung low waiting for the ground temperature to rise.

"What are the horse's names?" Alice asked as they approached the horse paddock on the way to the sheds. Three Clydesdales all came to the fence, anticipating the delivery of a ration of hay.

"Barnaby, Trigger and Misty." Fergus reeled off the names but didn't elaborate further as he continued walking.

Alice hoped for more information. If she was going to spend the day with a horse, she wanted to at least know its name, to begin to build the relationship that would ensure they completed their task. The first of the horses to approach the fence was a jet-black beast, it towered over Alice and was several hands taller than the others. It stood defiantly, head high and ears pricked forward. Alice imagined this would be Trigger. He didn't appear at all friendly and she wondered if his name was indicative of his nature. She'd have to be careful if it was Trigger who became her work horse for the day.

A dappled grey mare gave a friendly whinny, making Alice hope this was the horse she'd be ploughing with. Assuming its name would be Misty, Alice imagined what a day walking through dirt would do to the white silky

39

feathering on its legs. She silently promised to clean and brush her back to pristine at the end of the day. That left the chestnut who must be called Barnaby. It seemed a friendly enough name if not a little mischievous. Misty or Barnaby, Alice would be happy working with either.

"Which one do we use for ploughing?" she called after Fergus.

"What?"

Alice repeated her question. She thought it simple enough but perhaps Fergus hadn't heard her correctly.

"Which one do we use for ploughing?"

"Which what?"

"Which horse?" Alice was beginning to wonder at Fergus's level of intelligence.

"We don't use horses for ploughing."

"What?" Alice stopped, she stood still, mouth agape and digested Fergus's statement. If they didn't use horses for ploughing, then what did they use? Was she going to fail Lou's test before she even began? She had no knowledge of any other method of ploughing.

"Why would you use horses when you've got a perfectly good tractor?" Fergus laughed. "A piece of machinery is much easier to control, far better than an animal with a mind of its own."

"A tractor?"

"Yes, a tractor. You know, one of those things with four wheels and a motor." Fergus joked until he glanced at Alice and saw the frown furrowing her forehead. "You've never ploughed with a tractor before?"

"No," Alice replied timidly.

"Have you ever driven a tractor?" Fergus leaned down close to Alice and murmured.

She clenched her hands together, squeezed her shoulders up around her ears and looked wide-eyed up at Fergus. "No," she squeaked. "Whipsnade's tractor had been requisitioned for the war effort."

Fergus rubbed his chin between thumb and forefinger, shook his head from side to side and tutted like a wise old man faced with a dilemma. Then slowly a smile crept over his face.

"Ferguson is her name. Just like me. I'm sure you'll get along with her just fine. Runs on petrol instead of hay, that's all."

They passed the dog kennels. Joe gave a friendly bark. Alice thought it would be preferable to spend the day with the dog than drive a tractor. Her palms were clammy by the time they reached the sheds. Fortunately, Rangi, Jack and Danny had gone off to attend to the tasks assigned to them. Lou had stayed back at the house with some urgent phone calls, so they were alone.

"There she is," Fergus announced. "Pretty simple really. Climb on board and I'll give you a quick lesson before we hook the plough on."

The top of the bonnet was level with Alice's head. Trying to stay positive, her first thought was that at least this beast was shorter than Trigger. She grabbed hold of the steering wheel, hoisted herself up and sat down on the seat moulded to fit a bottom much larger than hers. She couldn't reach the steering wheel and had to shimmy forward. The hard steel of the seat was cold and sent a chill through her overalls.

"Right, you just put your foot on the clutch ..." Fergus paused, waiting for Alice to follow his instruction. He glanced at her, saw the blank look, shook his head with amusement and continued. "That's this pedal down here on the left. It won't start unless you have your foot pressing it down."

Alice had to almost stand with her leg extended to push the clutch down, she grabbed both sides of the steering wheel to anchor herself.

"We might need some choke this early in the morning. Just pull that knob out. The one under the steering wheel on the right. You'll have to remember to push it back in when we get her going."

Briefly lifting one hand from the steering wheel, Alice reached down and pulled the choke. Fergus turned the key, reached between Alice's legs and shoved the gear stick into start. The engine coughed, sent a plume of smoke from its exhaust stack and shuddered into life.

"Give her a bit of throttle now," he instructed, momentarily forgetting Alice's lack of knowledge. "That chrome lever on the steering column, pull it down."

Alice pulled on the end of the throttle lever and the tractor's revs reverberated through the tin shed.

"Gently! Just a little bit while we are still in the shed." Fergus yelled over the din, he reached over and pushed the lever back. "Save the big revs for when you are ploughing. There, that's better." Fergus grinned at Alice. "See, nothing to it."

Alice couldn't smile back; she was terrified of the machine juddering beneath her. She'd only driven the truck at Whipsnade once, from the safety of the cab with Duncan beside her. Perhaps she should admit defeat and swap places with Grace. Life at the flax mill must surely be easier than this.

"Put her into gear. We need to hook the plough on." Again, Fergus hesitated as he remembered Alice really had no idea at all. "That stick between your legs, it's the gear stick." Alice nodded. "There is a diagram on the knob." Another nod. "S is for start, then there are three forward gears and R is for reverse. Now we need to back out of the shed so please put it into reverse. You'll have to put your foot on the clutch again whenever you change gears."

Alice did as she was instructed, she watched Fergus step out of the way and turned her head back so she could see where she was going. The tractor stayed where it was. Puzzled, Alice thought it must need throttle, so she pulled gently on the lever. The tractor revved loudly but still stayed where it was. Bewildered, Alice shrugged her shoulders and looked wide-eyed at Fergus.

"You'll need some accelerator. The pedal on the other side. Release the clutch and apply the accelerator. Just like driving a car," Fergus explained. "Well, if you knew how to drive a car, it would be the same." He laughed. "By the look on your face, you haven't done that either. Where have you been living, Miss Alice?"

Applying the same pressure to the accelerator as Alice had done to the clutch, the tractor hurtled out of the shed.

"Gently!" Fergus yelled again. "Put the brakes on!" The tractor continued its trajectory. Fergus held his hands to his head and cringed. "Lift your foot off the accelerator. Hurry!"

The tractor came to an abrupt halt in the middle of the yard. Alice sat, eyes bulging, mouth agape. Indecipherable high-pitched squeals escaped her mouth.

"Sorry, forgot to tell you," Fergus smiled apologetically and pointed to the brakes. "These pedals back here, they'll make you stop, or turn if you put your foot on one at a time."

Alice shook her head in disbelief. "Thanks," she squeaked.

"Do you want me to drive?" Fergus offered to take over.

For a split second, Alice was ready to admit defeat and dismount from the tractor but that would mean she'd be down the road. If she couldn't swap placements with Grace, she'd be homeless. The thought didn't appeal. Alice took a deep breath, squared her shoulders, and put the tractor in first gear.

"Where's the plough?" she asked Fergus.

Slowly, methodically, Alice lifted the clutch and gently applied pressure to the accelerator. The tractor did a little bunny hop to start but then slowly edged its way across the yard to the plough. Fergus hooked the plough on and showed Alice the lever to raise and lower it.

"Stay there while I put some weights on the front. We don't want her nose sniffing the air and you not getting anywhere."

Alice had no idea what Fergus meant, she just had to trust he knew what he was doing. Fergus added two heavy tractor weights to a tray at the front of the engine, then he grabbed hold of the steering wheel and hoisted himself up to stand beside Alice, wedged between the seat and the rear guard.

"Right then, all ready for the paddock," he said.

Alice smiled meekly; she was anything but ready. Fergus was close, so close that his body touched hers and if she dared turn her head, she looked directly at his crotch. She did, but only momentarily. She felt the heat rise up her body and knew her cheeks had coloured a deep crimson. A nervous cough escaped her throat, she suddenly felt parched.

"Into gear, off we go."

Carefully and methodically, Alice put the tractor into first gear. She didn't want to bunny hop again and end up with Fergus in her lap. The tractor slowly crawled across the yard.

"You'd better give it a bit more throttle," Fergus suggested. "We don't have all week to plough the paddock."

With eyes straight ahead Alice pressed her foot down on the accelerator, both hands clasped tightly onto the steering wheel. They left the metal track and headed down a rutted laneway, the tractor ambling its way over the humps and hollows. With each bump, the tractor seat and Alice bounced up and down. Her shoulder brushed against Fergus's body. She wasn't certain but it seemed that Fergus was leaning in closer to her. Deliberate or otherwise, Alice couldn't tell, and she was too nervous to look. The tractor hit a sharp rut, distracted, Alice lost her grip on the steering wheel and the vehicle veered towards the fence.

"Whoa!" Fergus leaned down and grabbed the steering wheel, pulling the vehicle back on track. "We're going to do ploughing not fencing," he joked.

He kept his hand on the steering wheel, less than an inch away from Alice's until they reached the paddock. By that stage, Alice's heart was pounding in her chest. She breathed deeply to try and calm herself but inhaled the aroma that was Fergus; a combination of man and earth.

"Perhaps I should do the outside row," Fergus suggested as he jumped down from the tractor. "Lou won't want any broken fences."

Alice looked around the paddock, pretending to size up the job, while she calmed herself. It was preferable to making eye contact with Fergus who clearly was not as affected as she.

"No." Alice sat up straight in the tractor seat, squared her shoulders and tried to look as determined as she wanted to feel. "The job was assigned to me. I need to prove that I am just as capable as you."

"Very well then." Fergus stood back to clear the way. "Once right around the outside and then in rows up and down after that. I'll just stay long enough to see that you've got the hang of it."

It was just like Alice had done with Jess the horse. "Come on, Ferguson, off we go," she whispered. "Help me out old girl or I'll be down the road."

The pair edged their way along the fence line. Alice didn't look back to see if Fergus was keeping an eye on them, she couldn't risk the tractor veering into the fence. As the corner approached, she formulated her plan to turn the tractor and plough. Just as she'd done with Jess, she stopped and lifted the plough from the ground, grateful that the tractor had a lever to do this for her. Turning took more effort as she wrenched down one side of the steering wheel and manoeuvred the metal beast around a ninety-degree turn. She stopped, lowered the plough, and set off again. There was a triangle of earth, where the two fences met, that remained defiantly grassy. Alice hoped she wouldn't get fired because of it.

CHAPTER

5

"Right," Fergus said as Alice finished ploughing the outside furrow. "Now just up and back in nice straight rows. Well, as straight as you can get them."

If Fergus could see the perspiration beading Alice's forehead, he didn't acknowledge it. She was grateful for that. She didn't want to show any sign of the strain that ploughing was for her.

"You don't need to keep an eye on me," she said. "You can go and do your other jobs."

"Okay, if you're sure you'll be all right. I do have to service the seeder, get it ready to get the wheat planted."

Alice wasn't sure of anything but the need to prove she was capable of everything the men could do. She nodded, lowered the plough, and set off again.

By late morning, she sat with her hands scrunched around the steering wheel, unsure whether her fingers would unfurl after gripping the hard wheel for so long. Her shoulders ached, feeling as if they had been permanently wrenched from their sockets. She'd felt every bounce of the seat, either compacting her spine or stretching her beyond her body's normal capacity. But the worst pain emanated from her behind. The steel seat was moulded but it wasn't a shape that fit Alice's petite figure. Every time she bounced up, she landed with a thud. Bones, usually protected by flesh, seemed to connect directly with steel. Alice dreaded to imagine what colour her bottom would be in the morning.

Despite her pain, Alice took a moment to sit back on the tractor to admire her work. The furrows she'd created were relatively straight. There was just the odd kink where the plough had got stuck and she'd stalled the tractor. Working through the process Fergus had explained to her, step-by-step she'd managed to restart the engine, lift the plough, and reposition it past whatever hidden obstacle had ground her to a halt. She hoped that Lou would appreciate her efforts. She needed him to think she'd done at least a satisfactory job.

A hint of self-confidence straightened her spine and brought a smile to her face. Alice decided to push on and get the last rows done before lunch. She'd show these men she was just as good as them. She lowered the plough and pulled on the lever to increase the revs. Instead of surging, the engine sputtered and went quiet. What had she done wrong? Had she not followed Fergus's instructions?

"Come on, girl," she said, stroking the steering wheel as if it was an animal she could coax back into life. "We can do it. Just a few more rows, then we can rest."

Alice sat back on the seat, took a deep breath, and started the process again, one step at a time to ensure she didn't miss anything. Arrrh arrrh! The engine whined and went silent.

"Come on," she begged, turning the key again.

Arrh arrh! Silence.

"Third time lucky, pleeeease!"

The tractor groaned like it was taking its last breath and then went silent.

Alice thumped her hand on the steering wheel and cursed. "Blast!"

She climbed down and walked around the tractor looking for some clue that would solve her problem.

"If only you were a horse." Alice shook her head. "Not a collection of nuts, bolts and hoses; then I'd know what to do."

Any effort to fix the tractor was futile, she had no knowledge of how it worked. Alice had no choice. She'd have to do the very thing she wanted to avoid. She'd have to ask a man for help.

❦

Alice heard Fergus's cheerful whistle before she saw him in the back of the implement shed bent over the seeder, an oilcan in his hand. She glanced around, there was no sign of the others. Hopefully with Fergus's help the ploughing would get finished and no one else would know.

An invisible boundary, Alice couldn't bring herself to cross, kept her at the door of the shed.

"Hello ... hello ... Fergus," she called out, each holler louder than before until Fergus's head of brown spiky hair lifted.

"Miss Alice." Fergus smiled. "Have you finished already? That's good. Lou will be pleased." Fergus came to the front of the shed, wiping his hands on a rag. "Have you put the tractor away already? We'll need to take the plough off."

"Fergus." Alice raised her hand, palm facing out, a signal for Fergus to stop.

"What? What's wrong? What have you done?"

"I haven't done anything," Alice said indignantly. When would men ever stop blaming her when things went wrong? "It's the tractor, it just stopped, I didn't do anything."

"Oh, I'd better take a look. Lou won't be happy if you've wrecked it."

Alice stood, hands on hips, her anger at being blamed, rose like the heat of a furnace.

"I did everything you told me."

Fergus strode off towards the paddock. Alice willed her aching limbs to keep up, but Fergus was already seated on the tractor and trying the key by the time she made it to the paddock.

"I did that." Alice arrived at the tractor panting. "See, nothing."

"Mmmm. She turns over so we've got spark. Sounds like the fuel's not getting through. Did you check the petrol?"

"Did I ....?" Alice scowled. She didn't even know where the petrol cap was. "Did *you* check the petrol?"

Fergus jumped down off the tractor, reached over to the centre of the bonnet and unscrewed the petrol cap. The chain attached to the cap served as a measure; it was dry.

"You've run out of gas, Miss Alice," Fergus said. "First lesson in driving, always make sure you've got enough petrol."

Alice resisted the urge to snap at Fergus, she kept her voice calm and deliberate as she delivered her retort.

"First lesson in teaching someone how to drive is to show them where the petrol goes."

Fergus stopped. He turned to look at Alice as if seeing her for the first time. A smile slowly crept up his face.

"Point taken, Miss Alice, point taken."

"And while we are at it." Alice was fired up now. "Stop calling me Miss. Stop pointing out that I'm a female at every opportunity like it makes a difference to my ability to do the job."

It was Fergus who raised his palms, in defence, as he stepped back from the petite woman who was letting him know where he stood.

"Okay." He nodded. "Alice. Or maybe you'd prefer Al? That sounds like a bloke's name."

"I don't want to be a bloke. I just don't want you to highlight that I'm not a bloke."

"Okay."

Fergus was nodding his head as if he understood but the blank look on his face, told Alice she could have been speaking a foreign language.

"Where's the petrol?" she asked to bring the conversation back to the issue more urgent than her name.

"There's a five-gallon container back at the shed. We'll have to get that."

Fergus turned and was gone. His loping strides made Alice run to keep up again.

Despite Alice's protests that she could manage, Fergus insisted on carrying the petrol container back over the paddock and filling the tractor. She clenched her hands behind her back, tempering her frustration at having to accept his help. Was he just being a gentleman, or did he think she was incapable?

"Thank you, Fergus," she said with as much graciousness as she could muster. "I'll be right to get the ploughing finished now."

She waited until he stepped away before starting the tractor, lowering the plough, and setting off to complete the last few rows, every ache in her body punctuated by every bump she drove over.

"Don't you do that again," she muttered to the tractor. "Us girls have got to stick together."

Alice sighed with relief at the end of the final row. She'd done it, the paddock was ploughed. She'd done what was asked of her. She would have a bed to sleep in tonight.

Feeling she could do no more, Alice returned to the yards and backed the tractor up to put the plough down where it had been.

"Let me help you with that," Fergus offered.

Alice jumped. She hadn't seen him approach. How he managed to always appear where she was, she couldn't fathom. A voice in her head told Alice to refuse the offer of help but her body was exhausted and sore.

"Thanks, Fergus," she replied.

"Was Ferguson good for you?" he asked, unhitching the plough. "After we sorted the petrol problem."

"Yes, I think so." Alice compared ploughing with a horse to the tractor. It was certainly a lot quicker, but her body was just as sore.

"Take her over to the petrol tank. We'll leave her full so she's ready to go tomorrow."

The snarly response that formed, never made it out of Alice's mouth. She had no energy left.

By the time she positioned the tractor next to the petrol tank, Fergus had the hose in his hand ready to do the job for her. Alice smiled, he really was very kind and seemed to want nothing in return. Perhaps that was what big brothers were like. Alice had never had one to compare.

She drove the tractor to its shed and without thinking, went to climb down. Her back muscles protested, a painful spasm arced down her lower back, and she howled in agony.

"What is it? What's wrong?" Fergus stood in front of her, his concern etched in a frown.

"Just my back," Alice whimpered. "It's a little sore."

"Here." Fergus moved closer; his arms outstretched. "I'll carry you."

Alice froze. Images of a man's arms around her filled her with fear. But this was Fergus who'd been nothing but helpful all day, and it was broad daylight, out in the open, not closed away in a changing room. Perhaps she could trust him, just this once.

"Okay," Alice conceded. "Just lift me down. I'll be alright then."

Fergus wrapped his large hands around Alice's waist and foisted her clear of the mudguard. Before she knew it, he hooked one arm under her legs and the other around her back and started across the yards.

"Fergus! Fergus! Fergus!" Alice wanted to say that she was alright, that Fergus could put her back on the ground and she would walk back to the house under her own steam

54

but all that would come from her mouth was his name. Exhaustion stole everything else.

Cradled against his chest she felt safe and protected. As she relaxed the spasms in her back abated. Her body's reactions were incongruous with her experience. Being this close to a man had never been safe before, how could it feel that way now? And with a man she barely knew? She wanted to feel anger, anger at men for doing to her what they had done, anger at herself for not adhering to the rules she'd self-imposed for her own protection. Alice replayed her short time at Orari Estate over in her head, examining the footage for any clues where she might have been remiss, may have inadvertently indicated she was available as anything other than a work colleague. She told herself, it was because she was tired, her body was telling her to rest.

"Here we are," Fergus announced as they reached the house. "Brownie will take care of you now."

"No, I'll be fine," Alice said in a panic, she couldn't let anyone else see her being carried. "I am fine. Please put me down."

Fergus did as he was asked but he saw Alice wince with pain as she stood on the back doorsteps.

"I just need some water." Alice felt her cheeks were glowing. She told herself it was from the ploughing, that she just needed some sustenance. She couldn't admit defeat; she'd be out of a job for certain.

When Alice came downstairs for dinner, the space between Rangi and Fergus, that seemed to have become hers, sat waiting. She needed to climb between the two men and sit on the wooden bench seat without revealing any of her injuries to Lou who sat opposite. She took a deep breath, lowered her head to hide any facial expressions that might give her away and gingerly lifted one leg then the other.

"Hello, Alice," Fergus said. "How are you feeling now?"

"Fine!" Alice replied more curtly than Fergus deserved but she didn't want him giving her away. She inhaled sharply as she sat, her bruised behind unappreciative of the hard wood. Alice glanced around the others at the table and was glad to see they were more intent on dinner than her.

"I've inspected the ploughing," Lou announced looking directly at Alice.

She swallowed. Dread filled her on two counts – firstly whether her ploughing was up to Lou's standard and secondly, whether Lou had seen Fergus carrying her. She hoped for a positive on the first and a negative on the second.

"Not bad for a beginner," he continued.

Alice took that as a positive and breathed a sigh of relief.

"At least we've found something you can do without mucking it up. There's another paddock, I've decided we'll put into crop. It's almost too late in the season but we should get away with it if the weather holds. You can plough that paddock too."

Alice nodded slowly. Every muscle in her body ached at the thought of another day in the tractor seat but at least Lou didn't appear to know about Fergus carrying her. She took a mouthful of the stew that had been dished up by Brownie.

"Do you think you'll be able to manage by yourself tomorrow?" Lou asked.

It was a question that needed an answer. Alice couldn't reply. Her throat constricted, her cheeks coloured, the mouthful of food she was struggling to swallow threatened to expel itself in a very unladylike manner. She nodded again. More vigorously this time, hoping that Lou would take her response as enthusiasm and not nerves or guilt. Of course, she could manage without Fergus.

When Lou turned his attention to his meal, Alice dared to glance sideways. Fergus's dimple teased her with its presence. She would be able to get the ploughing done without Fergus's help, but she conceded, his assistance had been welcome.

Alice retired early to her attic bedroom. She needed a good night's sleep if she was to manage another day of ploughing. A long soak in a hot bath would have been lovely but she hadn't been at Orari Estate long enough to justify that. It wasn't Sunday and she didn't want anyone to think she was just a frivolous female. She filled an empty beer bottle with hot water and enclosed it in a sock, hoped that hugging it into her body would help ease her muscles.

Her head had barely hit the pillow when the day's efforts took her into a deep sleep. She didn't know when or how but Fergus made his way into her thoughts. He had his arms around her again and she felt that sense of contentment, protection, strength and caring that she had felt for real during the day. This time though, when she looked up to smile at Fergus, his sparkling eyes looked back. Alice had never noticed a man's eyes sparkling before. The only ones that she had seen up close had been threatening and horrible and she'd closed her eyes to block them out. She wondered what made eyes sparkle, it wasn't daylight, there was no sunshine to make the iris glisten. It was as if a light was shining from within, a signal that the person was good, radiating all the way from their heart. When Fergus winked at her, she felt a little giggle escape. He'd done it the first time she'd met him and numerous times since.

Then Alice found it wasn't Fergus's eyes that held her focus, it was his lips. They were full and inviting, surrounded by a black stubble that seemed to be his normal. She tried to imagine him cleanshaven, but the image wouldn't materialise. When Fergus's eyes closed and his lips came closer, so close that all she wanted to do was taste him, Alice gave into the urge. She felt his lips on hers. The stubble was bristly; when she was expecting it to irritate, she found that it tickled. She hadn't known how he would taste; she'd never kissed a man before. A little boy had given her a peck on the cheek once, by the rope swing that hung from the walnut tree at her grandfather's house. He might have been her cousin; she couldn't remember but he certainly wasn't a man like Fergus. There was no taste on Fergus's lips. Alice explained that away by assuming he would have had a wash before bed. Then his lips parted and encouraged hers to do the same. The tips of their tongues tantalised one another, tempting the other to explore. From the faint aroma of beef stew Alice realised that, of course, a man would taste of what had last been in his mouth. Her mind wandered. There were images that didn't seem possible, or right or proper but still her mind seemed to conjure them. It was like one of her mother's Mills and Boon books that Alice used to read snippets of when her mother had drunk too much and fallen asleep. Alice was lost in the moment and forgot to breathe.

She awoke gasping for air, flushed and with an unfamiliar feeling of heat emanating from deep within. She felt wet between her legs and hoped she hadn't been so tired she'd had an accident. Alice could hear her heart thumping in her chest. She considered casting off her bedding to cool down in the night air, but her arms were already cold. She reached down to move the hot water bottle, thinking that it had been on her belly for too long, but it was already down at her feet. When Alice eventually realised that everything was as it was supposed to be, she felt relief, almost delight that dreams of Fergus could make her feel so good.

CHAPTER

6

A short, sharp scraping noise pierced the quiet. All thoughts of Fergus were gone, and Alice sat up rigid in her bed. The noise seemed to come from the bottom of the stairs. Alice strained to hear, to work out if someone was outside her door. She sat in the silence, counted the seconds, wanting to hear the noise again so she could determine what it was and reassure herself she was safe.

There was no more scraping but there was a creak. One, then another and another. Floorboards creaking under the weight of someone, and they were getting closer. Alice pulled her bedding up under her chin and clenched her teeth to stop her jaw from chattering.

"Alice?" A barely audible whisper came from the stairwell. "Alice, are you alright?"

"Fergus?" Alice pinched her cheek, to check she was awake.

"Yes. I was just passing your door and heard a noise. I thought I'd better check you were okay."

Alice didn't reply. She sat pondering why Fergus was passing her door in the middle of the night. Had she made a noise? She thought the only noise she'd heard came from outside her room, not from her.

Another creak of the floorboards, made Alice back up against the headboard, drawing her knees up as a protective shield. Should she stay in the dark, use it to her advantage to avoid a would-be attacker? Fergus, an attacker? Not the Fergus of her dream, the one with light radiating from a good heart, the one with very kissable lips? The alternative was to leap out of bed and grab the cord, to flood the room with light so that she could see Fergus.

"I'm fine," she replied as she slid off the end of the bed and crept toward the pull cord. "Is it morning time?"

"Morning time?" Fergus laughed. "No, I'm just going to bed."

Alice felt like she had been asleep forever. She couldn't comprehend why Fergus might have stayed up so late, but it did explain why he was outside her door, if she believed him, if she trusted him. There was only one way to find out. Alice pulled the cord and illuminated the room. She blinked several times to adjust to the brightness and found herself face to face with Fergus. He was still partway down the stairs but with his height it meant they were now level-headed. He was almost as close as he had been in her dream. She noticed his eyes were sparkling and his lips were parted.

"What are you doing going to bed at this time?" Alice needed to distract herself from her thoughts.

"I've been working on Victor," Fergus replied.

Alice had no idea who Victor was, and she was too tired to ask.

"As you can see, I am perfectly fine," she said with a hint of indignation she didn't really feel.

"I can see." Fergus smiled and his dimple smiled too. "You are perfect."

Alice blushed from head to toe. She felt that funny feeling inside, almost welcomed it until reality dawned on her. It was the middle of the night. She was in her nightie. A man was in her bedroom. If somebody else should discover this situation, she would be sent away, fired on the spot and it would be nothing to do with her inadequate farming skills.

And Fergus must surely be lying to her, for she was anything but perfect. She could never be perfect, not after what had happened.

There was an awkward silence where they stared at one another. In the end it was Fergus that spoke.

"Right, if you're certain you are alright then ...." He hesitated. "Then I'd better get to bed."

"Yes," Alice replied, nervously wringing her hands. "Yes, you'd better."

"Perhaps ..." Fergus paused, ran his hands through his hair.

"Perhaps what?"

"Perhaps, a goodnight kiss? I'd sleep much better with a goodnight kiss."

If it was possible, Alice blushed again, pink upon pink, she felt certain her face must be a scarlet beacon. Memories of her dream, the feel and taste of Fergus's kiss made her want to experience it for real. She didn't want to lead him on though, to have him think that a kiss would entitle him to other liberties. She didn't want to appear naïve either, to make a big thing about a mere kiss.

"Just one," Fergus implored like a child asking for a lollipop.

Alice closed her eyes. She felt his lips. They gently touched her cheek. It was a peck, much like the boy by the swing.

"Good night, Alice. Sleep tight." Fergus took the stairs two at a time, closed the door and left Alice standing bewildered on her own.

The only good thing about another day of ploughing was when it was finally over. Every limb, muscle and sinew in Alice's body cried out for a long soak in a hot bath as she tiptoed back from the tractor shed to the house.

She hadn't seen Fergus all day, well not in person but he was in her thoughts. He must have realised that she was tainted. One kiss on the cheek was enough to make him stay away from her. It was better that way, then she wouldn't have to reveal the true depth of her imperfection. Alice and men, they didn't have a place together in her life except as her boss or work colleague. When the steel seat jarred her, Alice dared to imagine that if she were boss one day, she would order others to drive the tractor. She would assign the jobs according to physical capabilities not the need to prove oneself.

She didn't notice Brownie standing at the back door until he spoke.

"Here's some Epsom salts, lass." He handed Alice a small glass jar, half full of clear crystals. "Looks like you could do with a soak. You'd best get up there before the others get home."

"Thank you, Brownie, you must have read my mind."

"And there is a letter for you too, lass." Brownie retrieved an envelope from the sideboard. "News from home? Or do you have a sweetheart?"

The way Alice's cheeks coloured a bright red, you would have thought she had a million sweethearts, and no one would have believed any denial she voiced so she stayed silent and left the room. The envelope's postmark was local and the writing a delicate scrawl, the letter wasn't from Alice's mother. She hadn't expected it would be. Alice had no delusions about receiving anything from the woman who'd borne her. She had lost her battle with the bottle about the time the last of a long line of men walked out on her.

Another reason to stifle the thoughts about Fergus. Men weren't to be trusted with your heart. Her mother's had been trampled on so many times, the bottle was the only thing that offered solace.

An address in Geraldine told Alice the letter was likely from Grace. She propped it up beside the foot of the bath and turned the taps on. After sprinkling the Epsom salts under the running water, Alice left the bath taps on and went to her room to get her dressing gown, shampoo and a towel and flannel.

Steam was rising from the bath by the time she returned. She shut the door and slid the lock across before she undressed and dipped her toe to test the water. It was hot, almost too hot to get into. A few splashes of cold water lowered the temperature enough for Alice to climb in.

The relief was instant. As her body sunk down into the water, the aches lifted away. Alice reached over the side of the bath and retrieved the letter.

'Dear Alice, I don't think you would like the linen flax mill. It's back-breaking work ...'

"Well, so is farming, Grace," Alice muttered as she read. "It was your decision to swap, not mine."

'And, if you thought the pig sties stunk, the retting room is even worse. The putrid smell of rotting flax almost made me choke. I spend all day standing on concrete twisting flax fibres into 40-pound hanks. I can hardly feel my fingers when five o'clock rolls around.'

Alice sighed. Lying in the bath with the Epsom salts working their magic to relieve her muscles, she almost felt grateful to be at Orari Estate.

'I hope you have found the animals that you adore at Orari Estate. There is a cat at the boarding house that I'm staying at in Geraldine but nothing at the factory.'

Images of Joe the dog and the horses, Barnaby, Trigger and Misty came and went. Yes, there were animals at Orari Estate but the only one Alice was being allowed close to, was the damn sheep that jumped the railing and trampled her. She looked down at her bruises, a hint of yellow tingeing the edges as they slowly healed.

'There are some men here. Mr Cresswell you met and a couple of others, but we don't see much of them. Miss McPherson seems a good boss, she doesn't appear to know that I am not you. I work with Moo, Chook, Ronnie and Nonie. Yes, everyone has a nickname, although they haven't come up with one for me, yet.'

Male voices echoed up the staircase, reminding Alice that she was surrounded by men at Orari Estate. Lou, the one in charge of her fate, wouldn't take kindly to hear she was soaking in a hot tub, and it was still daylight. Nor did she want to be caught by Fergus in her dressing gown. She'd better finish the letter and get on with her bath.

'I hope you are doing alright. I look forward to seeing you at the races. Take Care, Grace.'

"I'm trying to take care, Grace. I'm trying."

Not even a world war could stop the races going ahead at the Orari Racecourse. There weren't as many horses as a lot had been requisitioned for the mounted troops, shipped off overseas, unlikely to return, but jockeys there were a few more of. They were fortunate to be of a stature that meant they didn't meet the criteria for enlisting.

The racecourse was a collage of colours and a clamorous chorus of chatter. Women took advantage of the opportunity to wear their best dresses in a combination of florals and checks, many with hats to match. The jockeys wore their racing silks to designate, for those in the know, the stable of the horse's trainer. Large floral wreaths adorned the winner's circle.

The first race was scheduled for 11.30 a.m., still half an hour away but already the crowds were gathering. It was an outing for the entire district, where everyone came together for a catch up and a flutter on the horses. The weather was playing its part, the sun shone and the wind that yesterday had been from the south had turned northerly overnight and brought with it, warmer temperatures. As warm as you could expect this time of the year in the South Island.

Alice found the other land girls at a picnic table off to the side of the grandstand and joined them to catch up on everyone's news. They'd become good friends in the short time they were together at Whipsnade. Alice sat quietly, admiring Grace's beauty, her blonde hair blowing in the breeze, her blue eyes animated as she led the conversation.

"It's lovely to see you all," Grace said. "Betsy, what are the new trainees like? Do they know what they are doing? How are Duncan and Nel?"

"One question at a time." Betsy held up her hands to slow Grace's barrage of questions. "They all knew each other in Christchurch so I feel a little excluded. It's okay though, I don't mind the time to myself. There they are over there." Betsy pointed to a group of women laughing and flirting with one of the few young men at the race meeting.

"That's Jake, from the dairy factory," Moira said.

"Have you heard from Roland?" Grace asked Betsy.

"No."

The sun glistened on Betsy's ring as she twirled it around her finger. What should have been a happy symbol was bringing tears to her eyes. At least she had experienced love, thought Alice.

"William?" Grace held Betsy's hand across the table.

"No, not directly. Duncan got a telegram though."

"A telegram. Oh no, was it bad news?"

"Yes, but we're not sure how bad," Betsy replied. "William's been injured and is being shipped home."

"You'll be able to take care of him," Moira said. "I wouldn't be any good at it, but you will."

Alice quietly chuckled. Moira hadn't changed; she was as wild as her red hair and more interested in herself than anyone else.

"I just wish we knew the extent of his injuries," Betsy said. "There are more questions than answers. When will he arrive? Will he be okay after a recuperation period? Is it a permanent injury that we'll have to adapt to?"

"It will be alright, Betsy," Grace said.

That's what Grace had said to Alice before she'd swapped placements with her. Three weeks later Alice still wasn't sure anything was alright.

"And now my sister, Irene, has gone and joined the Tuis," Betsy continued.

As far as Alice knew, Tuis were native birds, but Betsy's concerned look didn't indicate Irene was having anything to do with the vocal birds.

"What are Tuis?" Alice asked.

"They're supposed to provide the home touch for the soldiers," Betsy replied.

"Nothing wrong with that." Moira laughed. "I wouldn't mind doing that myself."

"Moira!" Betsy growled. "It's just preparing and serving meals, visiting soldiers in hospital, and doing their shopping."

"Oh," Moira replied looking disappointed. "What's the problem then?"

"She's shipped out," Betsy said. "They're based in Cairo."

"The soldiers will look after her," Grace said. "She'll be alright."

Betsy shook her head. Alice couldn't tell if it was a no of denial or to shake negative thoughts away.

"What about you?" Betsy asked Grace. "Have you heard from Ben?"

"I was going to ask you, if anything else had turned up at the farm?"

"No, but I'll keep an eye out and let you know."

"Moira, how is Bill?" Grace asked. "I see him over by the fence talking to Duncan."

"Well, it would be nice to say that we're enjoying an intimate relationship but I'm not certain that is the case."

"What?" Betsy's eyes went wide. "Surely, either you are, or you aren't."

"We are sleeping in the same bed." Moira smiled. "But I don't have any memory that we've actually had sex."

Alice blushed. She didn't know if she'd ever get used to Moira's brazen talk.

"Oh, you'd know that, if it had happened." Betsy's mouth fell open as she realised what she'd said. "Well, I did with Roland, I mean, on our honeymoon."

Moira laughed. "It's okay, Betsy. You don't have to still be a virgin at your age. And I'd have thought so too," Moira continued. "Except when I've had too much to drink, but that hasn't been the case with Bill. More like too much work. I'm exhausted. I wake up in his bed, uncertain how I get there and even less certain about what's gone on during the night. And now, he seems to be happier spending time with Duncan or Fred or anyone else other than me."

Alice squirmed. The wooden boards of the seat bit into her bruised behind and she sucked in a breath. The other land girls were so worldly compared to her. She felt inadequate beside them.

"I think we're making Alice uncomfortable," Grace said. "What about you, Alice? Is everything going alright at Orari Estate? I've worried every day about you, hoping that I'd done the right thing in swapping places."

Alice recalled her short time at Orari Estate and decided, on balance, she could report that everything was going alright.

"I've been doing some more ploughing." She sat on her hands to ease the discomfort. "On a tractor this time."

"Alice, driving a tractor." Moira wolf whistled. "Next you'll be cruising the main street of Geraldine on a Friday night."

"No, I won't."

"She's just teasing you, Alice," Grace said. "What else have you been doing?"

Alice spied Fergus over by the betting booths. Their eyes met and he winked which made her smile. She contemplated whether she should mention him. He'd continued to be a presence. He wasn't overbearing, he didn't ask anything of her - apart from the good night kiss - and he just seemed to be always there in the background, like a sturdy post you could lean on when you needed.

"Who's caught your eye?" Moira asked. She swivelled around and saw the source of Alice's delight. Moira turned back to the women and wolf whistled again. "Come on, tell us everything."

Alice blushed and the fact that she was blushing made her feel even more embarrassed.

"Well, well, the love bug has bitten Alice," Moira teased.

"Love! It's not love," Alice said in denial. *It was only a kiss on the cheek.*

"Well, you've gone as red as a beetroot, over a handsome young man who appears as equally enamoured with you, so in my books that usually means one thing," Moira said. "So, what is his name?"

"Fergus," Alice answered.

"I assume Fergus works at Orari Estate," Grace said.

"Yes, but he's not the only one," Alice replied.

Moira sat forward on the seat. "Not the only what?"

"Not the only man." Alice's voice was a high-pitched squeak, aghast that defending herself from the unthinkable was necessary.

"How many men are there?" Moira asked.

Alice counted them off on her fingers. "Fergus, Rangi, Lou – he's the foreman, Danny, Jack and Brownie. You met him Moira – he does all the cooking."

"Well, you have got your hands full." Moira joked. "Go Alice."

"Oh, are you leaving already, Alice?" Fergus had approached the group and overheard Moira's comment. "I was hoping you'd come and watch the first race with me. I've put some money on Little Flyer and I think you'll be my good luck charm to make sure she wins."

Everyone turned to look at Fergus, eyed him from head to toe and turned back to Alice, who had, once again, coloured the brightest shade of pink.

"The only place she is going," Moira replied on Alice's behalf, "is to watch the race with you. As long as you are a gentleman and take her hand to look after her." Moira nudged Alice under the table with her foot and smiled knowingly.

Alice had no choice but to stand. Fergus held his arm out, waited for Alice to hook her arm through and when she lay her hand on his forearm, he covered it with his. Off they walked with the eyes of Grace, Betsy and Moira watching their every movement.

CHAPTER

7

The commentator announced over the loudspeaker that there were two minutes until the start of race one, that on-track betting would stop in a minute and the horses were making their way to the start gate. There was a late scratching; Inquisitor was without its jockey. After an extra-long stop in Ashburton for refreshments, the train bringing passengers to the races was delayed with one of the jockeys on board. They'd only just arrived, too late for him to get weighed in.

Fergus made sure he and Alice were right by the finish line. He held the betting slip between thumb and forefinger and kissed it for good luck.

"You kiss it too, Alice. If the horse wins, I promise to take you out."

Alice kissed the piece of paper and as it happened, Fergus's thumb nail as well.

"Which horse is it, so I know who to yell for?"

"Number five, it's called Little Flyer. It's drawn wide so it'll have to work hard but according to the bookie it won at its last start and so is in with a chance. The odds were good so here's hoping." Fergus lifted Alice's hand up to his mouth and kissed that too. "For good luck," he said with a wink.

Fergus seemed to know all about horse racing and like she had with everything else, Alice just had to believe him. She was too short to see the horses start from the other side of the track and by the time they made it onto the home straight she was too short to see around all the crowd that were jumping and yelling with excitement. Alice heard them though, the thundering of hooves as they galloped down the track pounded in her ears, and she felt the reverberations through the earth. She hoped she wasn't standing too close to the action.

"And it's Little Flyer by a nose. Queen Sweep is pushing him to the end. Little Flyer for the win, second place to Queen Sweep and third place to Kelso." The commentator's announcement was barely audible over Fergus's yelling.

"We won. We won, Alice," he called out. He released her hand to grab her around the waist and lift her into his arms then he spun around and around in a celebratory twirl.

"Fergus!" Alice squealed.

He put her back down, made sure her feet were on the ground before he released her waist, moved his hands from there to her cheeks which he squeezed while he planted a kiss on her lips.

The kiss was over before Alice had time to realise it was happening, to respond in the way she thought she'd want to, but it was a kiss on the lips. Did that mean that Moira was right, and Fergus loved her?

"Alice, you are my good luck charm," Fergus held her hand as they walked away from the track. "I'll go and collect the winnings and we'll work out which horse to pick for the next race."

Alice's insides were conflicted, she needed to sit down, to have some time to try and decipher the butterflies in her stomach, the heat on her hand where Fergus had held it in his, the tenderness on her lips, the dread, and the anticipation.

"I'll catch up with the girls and wait for you there," she said, breaking away from his hand.

Fergus leaned in and gave Alice a peck on the cheek. "Okay, then, I won't be long."

Grace was talking to an older gentleman when Alice returned to the picnic table.

"This is Mr Cresswell," Grace introduced the man to Alice. "The manager from the flax mill."

"Hello, I remember your face from when you dropped Grace off, but not your name, sorry." Mr Cresswell raised his hat in acknowledgement.

"Alice. Alice Clark," she replied.

"Your name sounds familiar. Are you from around here?"

"No, we all came over from Christchurch to train as land girls at Whipsnade."

"Mmm," Mr Cresswell rubbed his chin between thumb and forefinger, deep in thought. "I know your name from somewhere. Never mind," he shook his head. "It'll come to me. Right, I'd best get back to my wife, the children appear to be running amok. Enjoy your day." Mr Cresswell doffed his hat to the land girls and wandered off.

"Why did you tell him your full name?" Grace asked as soon as he was out of earshot.

"I wasn't thinking, sorry."

"No wonder you weren't thinking." Moira laughed. "You're all starry eyed about Fergus."

"No, I'm not," Alice said in denial, but she blushed again. She shrugged her shoulders in defeat, it seemed to be futile to deny what her body appeared intent on expressing.

"Well, I hope he doesn't remember or you two will be in trouble," Moira said. "I was only the driver. I didn't swap placements."

The thought of having to change places with Grace, to have to go to the flax mill didn't sit comfortably with Alice. She finally believed she'd managed to convince Lou that she could make a valuable contribution at Orari Estate and then, of course, there was Fergus.

Just as if Fergus had heard Alice's thoughts, he materialised back at her side.

"Alice are you coming to check out the horses for race two?" he asked.

Alice wanted to escape, to pretend that everything was all right. "Yes, please, that would be nice."

There was an area set aside where the horses could be warmed up before their race, the punters could get a closer look and the jockeys could mount their ride before heading to the start gate. Fergus and Alice stood behind the wooden barrier fence watching the procession.

"You know all about horses, don't you? Which one do you reckon, Alice?"

Alice's limited knowledge of horses didn't extend to racehorses, apart from their smell, that familiar horse smell that always conjured happy memories for her. She wasn't going to pretend she had experience she didn't.

"There's a pretty grey one," she offered with a giggle.

Fergus roared with laughter.

"Well, it just so happens that you're right but it's nothing to do with its colour. The trainer lives just down the road from my parents, and he reckons that it's in the best form it's ever been."

"What's it called?" Alice asked.

"Paper Money."

"That sounds lucky too."

Fergus chuckled again. "We'd best go and place the bet then. We won ten shillings on the first race, I say we should reinvest it; five shillings on the nose and five for a place. What do you reckon, Alice?"

Alice had to work for two days to earn that sum of money. It seemed frivolous to gamble it away, but Alice felt she had no right to tell Fergus what to do so she just smiled and nodded.

With the betting slip safely stowed in Fergus's jacket pocket, they opted to watch the race from the grandstand so that Alice could see better. There were some spare seats in the very back row which provided a view out over the gathering. As the horses went into the start gates on the far side of the track the commentator ran through their names, their numbers and the gates they were starting from. Several people in the grandstand had the benefit of binoculars but Alice and Fergus had to rely on the commentator to know that Paper Money had drawn the inside gate which boded well for a good finish.

Fergus clasped Alice's hand, he gave it another good luck kiss and rested it on his thigh which jiggled with excitement. He looked down at her and winked. She giggled shyly.

"They're off," announced the commentator. "Magic Wonder is first out of the gate, Gallante close behind. Paper Money has made a slow start, Splendour and Nightglass are following in fourth and fifth. Last Effort is tale end."

Alice was focused on the race; she could see the grey of Paper Money leading the field as they came onto the home straight. What she didn't see, was Mr Cresswell approaching her.

"I've worked it out," he said. "I've worked out where I've seen your name."

Alice gulped, forgot all about the horses and stared at Mr Cresswell like a possum caught in car headlights. Life as she knew it was about to change again.

"You were assigned to the flax mill. Your name was on the letter I received from the Women's Auxiliary Placement Officer. It was your name, not Grace's. I just hadn't been able to locate the letter the day you arrived."

It was all true. Alice couldn't deny it. She looked up at Fergus, hoping he would be able to help her, but he'd stood up, was yelling, and jumping on the spot, cheering Paper Money, spurring the horse on to win. He was oblivious to her dilemma.

Alice shrugged her shoulders and splayed her hands out, palms up. She'd have to take whatever action Mr Cresswell decided on.

"Well, I can see why you would do it," Mr Cresswell said.

Alice cringed. He couldn't possibly know why Grace had swapped places with her. Grace was the only person Alice had told of her past and surely, she wouldn't have told the flax mill manager.

"I can't say that I approve." Mr Cresswell tutted. "Do your parents know of the situation?"

"No," Alice replied. Explaining to a stranger that she didn't know her father, and her mother was an alcoholic was the last thing she wanted to do.

"Young man," Mr Cresswell tried to catch Fergus's attention.

"Yes!" Fergus yelled and clapped his hands at the victory. "We've won. We've won."

Mr Cresswell tugged on Fergus's sleeve. "Young man," he repeated.

"Bloody hell, Alice, you really are lucky." Fergus was grinning from ear to ear, until he finally turned to look at Alice, saw her forlorn look and the stern-looking face of the man staring at him. "Oh, sorry about my language, I got caught up in the moment."

"Young man, it appears you have been caught up in a great number of moments."

"Pardon?" Fergus looked blankly at Mr Cresswell.

"I trust you will be doing the honourable thing by this young lady."

"The honourable thing?" Fergus looked at Alice, his eyes wide.

"It is apparent she is lacking parental guidance so I would be negligent if I didn't offer my opinion."

"I have no idea what you are talking about. Alice and I work together, we are just enjoying a day at the races."

"Yes, but she is supposed to be working at the flax mill. She's obviously swapped places to be closer to you. While I've not been disadvantaged, Grace is a good worker, I should rightly report them to the authorities."

Alice wanted to stand and protest, to state her case. The truth needed to be told. Mr Cresswell had it wrong and now Fergus would think the worst of her too. Alice wanted to yell out to Grace, to demand she come and fix the mess she had made.

"Well, I don't know about Alice being at the flax mill," Fergus said, "but I can assure you there is nothing untoward going on between us. We've only just met."

"That is certainly not how it appears," Mr Cresswell continued. "This may be war time, but etiquette must be observed. Alice has a reputation to protect. If I become aware of any shenanigans, I will be obliged to make a report to the Women's Auxiliary Placement Officer."

Fergus waited until Mr Cresswell was out of earshot before he turned to Alice.

"Hell, Alice, I'd better take you back to the others. I don't want any trouble."

"What about Paper Money? Didn't it win?"

"Yeah, it did. I'll take you back and go and collect the winnings. Maybe we can celebrate when there are no nosey parkers around."

"Sorry, Fergus. It was Grace's idea not mine."

❧

"Alice, what on earth did you do?" Moira asked. "All I can see is a handsome young man walking away without so much as a second glance at you. Do I have to give you some lessons on dating?"

80

"I didn't do anything." Alice sniffled; her tears threatened to overflow. "It was Grace."

"What was me?" Grace joined the conversation. "What did I do?"

"You swapped places with me."

"I knew this would come to no good," Betsy added.

"I thought it was for the best," Grace said. "You seemed very happy to be at Orari Estate with Fergus."

"I was," Alice replied, "But ..."

"But what?" Grace wrapped an arm around Alice's shoulder. "What's happened?"

"Mr Cresswell," was all Alice said in response.

"Oh." Grace gulped.

"What's Mr Cresswell got to do with Fergus?"

"He's the manager of the flax mill," Grace explained to Betsy. "The man that was here before."

"And he thinks that I swapped places just to be close to Fergus." Alice was incredulous that everything had gotten so messy so fast. "And demanded that Fergus do the honourable thing, or he would report us."

Moira howled with laughter. "Love and marriage all in one day. Well done, Alice. I don't need to give you lessons at all. In fact, perhaps you'd better give me lessons."

"It's not funny, Moira." Alice's stomach churned. She looked around for Fergus but couldn't see him anywhere.

"No, Moira, it's not funny," Grace repeated.

"Well, it was your idea, Grace." Moira stood, hands on her hips. "What are you going to do about it?"

"Perhaps, Alice wants to marry Fergus," Grace suggested.

Alice's head jerked back. She broke away from Grace, away from any suggestion that she wanted to marry Fergus or any man. She held her hands over her ears to block out any more outlandish suggestions.

"I think that's a no," Moira said. "Don't know why though. Alice can't see a good opportunity when it's right in front of her."

"He's just a work colleague." Alice defended herself. "We haven't even been courting. Now he's gone off and won't even talk to me."

"Come and sit down." Grace guided Alice back to the picnic table.

Alice was still sitting at the picnic table, shoulders slumped, and a glum look on her face as the last race of the day was announced.

"Come on, Alice." Grace tried to coerce her into a better mood. "It's the last race. Let's go and watch the horses."

Fergus hadn't come anywhere near Alice after Mr Cresswell's talk. She needed the opportunity to explain to him she wanted nothing from him, certainly not marriage. If the worst came to the worst, she would have to apply for a transfer. Like every bad situation she'd encountered so far in her short life, moving on was always an option, one that she was getting tired of but if she had to then she would.

"At least I know where I am with the horses," she said as she stood and followed the other land girls.

An unruly brawl had erupted and stopped them in their path. A dozen young men, half-drunk beer bottles in their hands, jostled for position as they encircled two fighters, and yelled and cheered.

"You bloody bastard."

"Get him, Ferg. Get him."

"Ouch! That's gotta hurt."

Punches flew. Fists connected with flesh. Inebriated men stumbled back as the impact of a punch sent its recipient lurching towards the ground. The circle was broken, and all Alice could see was that it was Fergus who had thrown the offending punch.

"It's Fergus," Moira nudged Alice with her elbow. "You really got him all riled up, Alice."

"No," Alice yelled. Whether it was a 'no' of denial, that she hadn't made Fergus do this, it wasn't her fault, or whether it was a 'no' of anguish as she saw blood run from Fergus's nose and his eye swell shut, Alice couldn't decide. Either way, she didn't feel good, her stomach churned. The sausage she'd eaten for lunch threatened to rise.

"Come on, Alice." Grace put her arms about Alice's shoulders and guided her away from the fracas. "We'll leave them to sort out their differences and go and watch the horses."

Alice let herself be led away but she couldn't help but glance back. Fergus had his fists raised in front of his face, he stepped side to side, light on his feet like a professional boxer, waiting for his opponent to re-join the battle. She could see the fire in his eyes, determination and anger mixed in an explosive brew. Alice hoped she hadn't been the cause of it.

"It'll be alright," Betsy said. "The police are coming. They'll stop them."

Alice shuddered. What if Fergus was doing this because of her and he got arrested? He might lose his job and it would be her fault. Alice knew she should have kept her distance. Men were trouble.

"Come on you lot, break it up." Two uniformed officers, hands on their batons, strode up to the brawl. "That's enough. Those just looking, be on your way. Those fighting, stay right where you are."

Alice's final glance was of a punch aimed at Fergus. He side-stepped and the fist, hit the chin of a course official, whose hat flew skyward as his suited body crumpled to the ground.

"You've done it now, lad." Both officers grabbed the punch thrower, pulled his hands behind his back, and shoved him face down to the ground, kneeling on his back until handcuffs were secured.

"What horse do you want, Alice?" Grace asked when they reached the rail.

"What?" Alice shook her head.

"We'll pick a horse each and see which one wins."

"I can't see them." The horses were lined up on the other side of the track, Alice couldn't see them, or Fergus as other spectators gathered behind the girls at the rail.

"Pick a number then," Grace said. "What's your favourite number?"

Alice let herself be distracted by Grace. "Seven."

"Number seven in race seven, sounds lucky to me, I'll have number five."

"I'll have number one," Moira said. "It's destined to be first."

"Number two for me then," Betsy added.

The commentator called the horses by their name so it wasn't until the field was abreast of where they were

84

standing, that Alice could see the grey horse several lengths ahead of the field, its silver tail flying in the wind, was number seven.

"I'm winning! I'm winning!" she squealed with excitement.

CHAPTER

8

Picnic hampers were packed up, farewells were said, and the crowd started to disperse after the final race ribbon presentation. There was no sign of Fergus nor any of the other young men who'd been cheering him on.

"Well, I biked here," Grace said. "So, I'll be off now. How are you getting home, Alice?"

"Oh!" Alice swallowed loudly as her predicament dawned on her. "Fergus gave me a lift, but I don't see him anywhere. Do you think he might have been arrested?"

"Probably just sleeping it off in the truck," Moira suggested. "Come on, we'll head to the carpark. Hopefully Bill is there too."

The neighbour's paddock, adjacent to the racetrack had been commandeered as a carpark. Brown grass sat in the gap where Fergus had earlier parked the Orari Estate truck.

"It's not here." Panicked, Alice spun around on the spot. "How am I going to get home?"

"I could double you," Grace offered. "It won't be very comfortable on my carrier though."

"And you're going in the opposite direction." Betsy pointed out the obvious.

"Are you ready to go, Moira?" Bill approached the land girls, oblivious to Alice's dilemma. "We'd best get home so I can check on the animals."

"We can give Alice a ride, can't we?" Moira asked. "She seems to have been abandoned."

"Sure." Bill opened the passenger door of his truck. "Hop on in."

Alice stepped forward to take the middle seat, which as the smallest, always seemed to be her allotted spot. Moira feigned a cough, loud enough to get Alice's attention and allow Moira to slip past her and slide into the middle seat. Of course, thought Alice, Moira wouldn't let anyone close to her man.

"See you again soon." Grace called as she pushed her bicycle to the road. "Send me a letter, let me know how you're getting on."

Bill started the truck and waited for a gap in the queue of vehicles leaving the racetrack.

"I've got a cow looking close to calving that I need to check on," he said. "Would you like to visit with Moira for a while and I'll drop you home afterwards?"

Alice was glad she was facing the window and Moira wouldn't see the look of shock on her face. Visiting Moira isn't something that she'd imagined herself doing but the alternative was having to deal with Fergus if he was even at home and not stuck in a police cell somewhere. Spending time with Moira was the easier option.

"That would be fine, thank you," she replied.

Bill disappeared into the bedroom when they arrived home to re-emerge a few minutes later back in his farm clothes.

"There, that feels better," he said pulling the elastic of his braces up onto his shoulders. "I'll leave you girls to have a natter."

As soon as he was gone, Moira started.

"I really don't know what to do about that man," she said. "He's so lovely when we're alone but it's like he's afraid to be seen with me in public."

"A bit like Fergus, scared of having to get married."

"He's already been married." Moira pointed to the photo on the sideboard. "I'm haunted by the ghost of his wife."

"Oh, she is pretty."

"You're not helping, Alice," Moira groaned.

"Sorry." Feeling uncomfortable, Alice turned away from the photo, pulled out a chair and sat down at the dining room table. "You're pretty too, Moira."

Alice stared out the window and her thoughts raced as fast as the darkening clouds scuttled across the sky. Moira was pretty; not plain like her. Moira could relate to men so easily; she was comfortable in their presence; she knew the right words to say and when; she shared her body freely. Would Alice ever be able to do this? Would she ever be free from the fear that gripped her when she was alone with a man? She couldn't imagine how it was going to happen.

Alice bit her lip at the sight of the farm truck parked outside the Orari Estate house. It signalled Fergus was home and that meant she would have to deal with him – it was an opportunity to explain herself but a likelihood that the one ally that she seemed to have made at Orari Estate would now want nothing to do with her. Her struggle to assimilate herself into this world of farming would take another step backwards.

"Thanks for the ride," she said to Bill and Moira. She wanted to ask if she could stay at their house for the night, to delay the inevitable, but Moira leaned over her and opened the passenger door.

"Bye, Alice," Moira said.

The green door to the kitchen opened and Brownie poked his head out.

"I wondered where you were," he said, waving to Bill as he drove off. "When you didn't arrive home with the others, I thought there was more trouble that we don't need."

"Trouble?" Alice fished for information.

"Never mind, you'd best get inside, supper is nearly ready."

Alice scooted through the door to find the table set but no-one else in sight.

"Where is everyone?" she asked.

"Getting cleaned up."

If Brownie said any more Alice didn't hear it over the bang and clatter of pots and plates as he busied himself at the bench. She disappeared up to her bedroom to change out of the skirt and blouse she had worn to the races. The hum of male voices resonated from behind closed bedroom doors. She didn't know which room was Fergus's and couldn't discern his voice amongst the mumbling.

When she was back in her overalls, Alice sat on the side of her bed, closed her eyes, and took a calming breath. The moment she needed to face Fergus had come and it couldn't be avoided any longer. Alice took the steps out of her attic room slowly, tip toeing, listening for the men. She heard nothing until she reached the top of the staircase. It wasn't the usual laughter and bravado that echoed from the kitchen but a subdued murmur. Alice gulped, whatever awaited her wasn't good. Frozen, halfway down the staircase, Alice looked up at the stern faces of the portraits hung on the wall; she felt their judgement as they stared down at her. She wanted to cry out that it wasn't her fault. Instead, she did what her grandfather always used to do in times of doubt. He would put his hand on his chest and say 'all you ever need is in here, lass'. Alice tried it, she put her hand on her chest and whispered the words. All she felt was emptiness.

"There you are." Brownie opened the kitchen door and spied her. "Come on, you know this lot, they'll eat your portion too if you don't hurry."

Alice jumped, involuntarily bit her lip until the pain was worse than the relief she sought. She cleared her throat, pulled her shoulders back and straightened her spine to walk like a soldier into battle.

She'd only eaten one barbecued sausage all day and the smell of Brownie's stew filled the room. Her stomach rumbled in anticipation before she dared to raise her eyes and look about the kitchen. The space where she normally sat on the wooden bench seat was empty but so was Fergus's space. He wasn't here. Where was he? Alice shifted nervously as she swallowed. Her parched mouth had no saliva but still she swallowed. Fergus must be in prison, and it was all her fault. She expected the men to look at her, accusation in their eyes but they continued to eat. Steam rose from her plate of stew, wafting toward the ceiling in a carefree design. Alice wished she too could float away so blithely.

"Looks like there is a storm brewing," Lou said. "Hopefully it will hold off until tomorrow so we can move the stock away from the river paddocks."

Alice felt the storm looming, not on the horizon but inside her own head.

"Don't you want your stew, Alice?" Rangi leant over towards her plate with his fork suspended.

"No … I mean yes, I want it." Alice sat down and tucked into the food, not daring to look at anyone at the table. There was no mention of Fergus, and she wasn't brave enough to ask. She'd pull Rangi aside later and quiz him. Hopefully he'd be able to provide the answers she desperately needed.

"Now that we're all here, well those that can be, I want to say I'm disappointed." Lou looked around the table. "The actions of some of you today have not reflected well on Orari Estate."

Alice tucked her elbows into her sides, she tried to make herself as small as possible, but she felt the heat rise, her cheeks become the scarlet beacons that so frustratingly gave her away time after time. She didn't look up at Lou but felt his words hit the top of her head like cracks of a whip. It was the punishment she deserved. She should never have swapped places with Grace.

"We all know Fergus's reason for defending himself," Lou continued.

Alice's head jerked up. No, we don't, she wanted to yell. Instead, she forced a fork full of stew into her mouth to act as a muzzle.

"A night in the cells will sober him up. Truth be told, you should all have spent a night there. Well, except for you Alice." Lou looked directly at her. "I don't imagine you've been drinking, have you?"

Alice had chewed all the moisture out of the stew, and it sat in her mouth reluctant to be swallowed. She nodded 'no' and instead digested the news that Fergus was in prison.

"Good, at least there is one among you that behaves as expected. I'm yet to think up a suitable punishment for the rest of you. Having to be out in this storm, might be enough of a lashing."

The stew that Alice managed to swallow sat heavy in her stomach. She couldn't look the others in the eye. If Fergus had told them her lie, if that was the source of his anger and they were punished because of it, then her guilt would increase tenfold. Lou's comment that the men already knew Fergus's reasoning never registered with Alice. She, as always, held herself responsible.

The meal was finished in silence. One-by-one the men excused themselves from the table and left the kitchen. Alice had to hurry to catch up to Rangi at the bottom of the stairs.

"Rangi." She tapped him on the back. "Will Fergus be back tomorrow?"

"Suppose so." Rangi continued up the stairs. "He wasn't charged, it wasn't his punch that connected with the course official."

"Why were they fighting?" Alice tried to sound casual, as if she was just making conversation.

Rangi stopped, rested his hand on the balustrade and turned to look back at Alice. His height towered over her when they were on level ground and now with several steps between them, he was a monolith capable of crushing her.

"Rob called him a white feather."

"A white feather?"

"Yeah, you know, a yellow-bellied chicken for not having signed up."

"Oh!" Alice remembered back to the first time she'd met all the men at Orari Estate. They all had valid reasons for remaining at the farm, all except Fergus. He'd winked at her, and she'd never thought to question further. "Is he?"

"He's a pacifist," Rangi replied, continuing up the stairs. "But the outcome is the same, in the eyes of those that think everyone should give their lives for King and country."

"Oh."

"Good night, Alice." Rangi turned at the first of the bedroom doors. "You'd better get a good night's sleep if we've got to contend with a grumpy Lou and a storm in the same day. It'll be a toss-up which will be worse."

"Good night, Rangi."

Alice hurried up to her bedroom and grabbed her toiletries to use the bathroom. In her rush, she didn't consider that the open bathroom door would mean anything other than it was free. She walked straight into the sight of Jack bent over the basin, clad only in long johns that looked as if they'd missed laundry day.

"Oops, sorry." She backed up to exit the room.

"No need to leave, lass." Jack grabbed a towel and turned to wipe his face. "I was just going."

Jack in long johns was even less pleasant front on. His belly spilled out over the top of the elastic waist band and the stitched groin flap gaped to reveal a sight that Alice would have rather not seen. He came towards the door and Alice backed into the corner. She clutched her towel and toothbrush to her chest, as if they were weapons. She would not allow herself to be a victim again. Seconds ticked by as she formulated her plan of attack, she turned, her shoulder became a shield ready to protect her torso, her leg was poised ready to fire her knee into Jack's groin. In the confined space of the bathroom, she could smell alcohol and a sweet sugary scent that Jack always carried. Her senses were on high alert. Her pulse beat out a Morse code alarm at her temples. The smell. She recognised the smell. It was Brylcreem. Her boss at the department store had worn it. He had the same slicked back hair as Jack. She hadn't seen Jack as a threat before but had that just been her innocence, her blindness in not seeing the bad in people. His toothless grin which had appeared friendly, now became an evil sneer as he walked past.

"Goodnight, lass."

Alice's body gave way to trembling. Had she just imagined what had happened? It had been an eventful day but was she now conceiving threats where there were none? Alice closed the bathroom door and pushed the latch across to ensure it was her space and hers alone. She leaned back on the door and took several deep calming breaths.

The only noise Alice heard when she crept back along the passage was the rumble of men's snoring. Perhaps she should have drunk some beer as well if it meant sleeping so deeply. But then she didn't want to sleep if Jack was the threat, she thought him to be. She left the light on until her bedroom door was safely closed behind her. If only it had a lock, then she could sleep soundly.

Thoughts of Fergus and Jack jostled for position as they raced about her head. She crawled between the sheets and wished Fergus was home to keep her safe. She'd never seen inside a police cell but imagined it would have none of the comforts that she was enjoying.

Alice was still awake, staring into the darkness of her room, when the patter of rain drops on the roof signalled the storm had arrived. The spits were faint and sporadic at first but quickly grew in intensity until it seemed all the clouds must be directly overhead her bedroom and releasing their bounty simultaneously. The thundering beat on the iron roof reminded her of the horse hooves as they raced along the home straight – the source of her anguish. If only, she had stayed with the land girls and not gone off with Fergus, Mr Cresswell would not have interfered, Fergus wouldn't have got drunk and wouldn't have over-reacted to the taunt he must have heard many times before.

She wondered what made him a pacifist. In her eyes, that only made him more attractive. It signalled he was kind and gentle; that perhaps she was safe with him. If he couldn't kill another man, then surely, he would never hurt a woman. It was all irrelevant anyway; Fergus was unlikely to ever look at or speak to her again.

Alice's eyelids eventually grew heavy, and she drifted off under their weight. From the safety of a deep sleep, she heard a scraping. She imagined it was Fergus coming to say goodnight to her again, to ask for a kiss. She would make sure it was on the lips this time, she would make sure everything between them was alright. She wanted to stay in the dream, where she was in-charge of the outcome.

Brylcreem. Alice was jolted out of her stupor by its sickly odour. She sat bolt upright, sucked in a breath, and held it so she had no need to inhale again while the smell was so close. Jack. He was in her room. How was she going to escape? How was she going to protect herself?

Thump. Crash. "Bugger."

Alice opened her mouth to scream. Images of all the men coming, ensured no sound escaped. It would just be like before; Jack had been at Orari Estate much longer than her. He was older than her. Who would they listen to? Not her. If Alice spoke up, when nothing had happened, then she would be homeless again.

She listened but heard nothing. Silence brought more questions. What had happened to Jack? Where was he now? Alice crept out of bed and stood at the top of the stairwell to her room. She heard Rangi's voice and dared not venture further.

"What are you doing, Jack?" Rangi asked. "Are you sleepwalking again? Come on, back to bed with you."

All the air went out of Alice, and she flopped down onto the top stair. Jack was just sleepwalking. The comfort that the explanation brought was short-lived. People could achieve all sorts of feats when they were sleepwalking. Lack of conscious thought didn't make the acts right. Alice knew

96

then that restful sleep would elude her until she felt safe behind a locked door.

CHAPTER

9

"Come on you lot," Lou yelled as he walked down the passage banging on bedroom doors. "Word's come through; the river has broken its banks. The Orari bridge has been washed out again. We've got to move the sheep to safety. Hurry up!"

Alice heard the yelling and was already out of bed before a knock resounded on her bedroom door. She was surprised to be moving so quickly given her lack of sleep. Adrenaline kicked in. Today needed to be better than yesterday and following Lou's orders would be part of that.

They all assembled in the kitchen in varying states of dishevelment. Alice caught a glimpse of Jack out of the corner of her eye; the same dirty long johns were visible under his unbuttoned shirt. She shivered involuntarily.

"Right," Lou said, making sure he had their attention. "We'd best take the horses in this weather; they'll be able to wade through any flooding. Damn! Fergus is still missing just when I need him."

Lou rubbed his stubbled chin while he thought of a plan. The scowl that drew his ragged eyebrows into one, signalled whatever he was thinking wasn't good.

"Lass!" he finally said, louder than was necessary.

Alice's head jerked up and she sucked in a breath.

"Brownie said you could ride. Is that true?"

"Yes, sir," Alice uttered before she considered whether her riding ability would be up to Lou's expectations.

"Right then, without Fergus I have no choice. Rangi, you, and the lass take two of the horses and head out to the river flats to round up the sheep. I'll take the other and open all the gates through to the paddocks over by the macrocarpas. That'll give them some shelter until this storm passes over. Jack and Dan, we'll need to feed out some hay. You load up the wagon and meet us over by the trees. Everyone know what they're doing?" Lou scanned the group and satisfied with the nods said. "Right, get your wet weather gear on and get to it then. And … be careful … we want everyone back here safe."

Alice felt as keen to head out alone with Rangi as Lou was to have her riding a horse. There had always been others around. It was never just her and the Maori. She hoped it didn't mean trouble. Her second problem was she didn't have wet weather gear. That hadn't been part of the land girls' allocation. There was one coat left on a hook in the porch. It was Fergus's so would be way too big for her. Lou and the other men left before she had time to ask. Alice had no choice but to run after Rangi. It was only water, she had her woollen jumper, she'd just change when they got back.

The raindrops were heavy, and they were falling with a fury Alice had not been out in before. Each drop hit her skin with a whack and left a red splotch in its wake. Her thick hair was drenched before they reached the horses and tendrils clung to her face.

"Bloody hell, Alice," Rangi said. "Where's your raincoat? You'll freeze."

"I don't have one," Alice replied. "I'll be fine."

"You should take mine."

"Thank you, Rangi." The kind gesture was unexpected. "But it'll be too big. Come on, we'd better get going."

There was a brief respite in the shelter of the tack shed while they fit Barnaby and Misty with their bridles and saddles.

"Here," Rangi said. "Tie this rope to your saddle, in case we have to lasso any animals."

Alice's skill set didn't include lassoing, but there was no time to worry about that now as they saddled up and headed out into the storm. Rangi led the horses quietly over the farm, allowing them to find their footing in the sodden paddocks.

"Easy girl." Alice spoke quietly to the horse, hoping her voice sounded calmer than she felt. She was glad to be atop Misty and stroked the horse's neck. Like the lucky grey horses at the races, Alice wanted her and Misty to still be there at the finish line.

"Nearly there," Rangi yelled, but the wind whipped away his words and Alice only knew he had spoken, not what he'd said.

The closer they got to the river, the larger the puddles were. Rain and river water combined to cover the earth. Alice couldn't believe the river was the same one she had bathed in. The torrent of muddy water raced over the rocks with a deafening rumble, carrying branches and unidentifiable debris in its wake. The willow trees that grew on the riverbank were now waist-deep in water, their branches plunging into the river as if trying to anchor themselves to safety.

The sheep's paddock could no longer provide any sustenance. Any grasses that had survived into the winter were beneath water. At the side of the paddock furthest from the river, sheep wedged themselves against the fence, like prisoners at the security gate, desperate to escape. The huddled mob lent all their weight and Alice felt for the sheep pegged against the barbed wire.

Out in the paddock, small mounds of earth and tussock had become refuges for other sheep huddled together. Their harrowed bleating added to the tumult of the storm. Alice was glad she had at least put her woollen jersey on; she had some of the protection afforded to the sheep by the lanolin of their pelts. The rest of her was drenched. Her wet hair sent trickles of water down her back. Her overalls were no longer the light brown of their issue. The splotches of rain that landed on her front and legs joined together to paint the fabric a darker shade.

"You go and open the gate." Rangi came up beside Alice and pointed to a gate in the far corner. "We'll let those buggers escape and I'll start rounding up these stranded ones who hopefully will have the sense to join them."

Alice nodded and turned Misty to head for the gate. She let the horse find her way, each fall of her hoof splashing water skyward.

"Come on girl." Alice patted Misty's neck in encouragement. "We can do this."

The horse neighed. When they reached the gate, Alice could see fear in the whites of the sheep's eyes and almost hear their cries for help as they bleated in unison.

"Don't worry," she said. "We'll soon have you to safety."

Alice had to dismount to unlatch the gate. Water splashed up her gumboots. Fortunately, it didn't reach the top. She tied Misty's reins loosely to the top wire of the fence and waded over to unhook the gate. Mud and silt had collected in the gateway, and it took some effort to push it open. She didn't have to muster the flock through, they were eager to escape and almost pranced with delight when they reached the higher ground in the next paddock.

Rangi headed over with another mob he'd encouraged off a mound.

"Just a couple of stubborn buggers back down by the river," he said. "You wait here, keep an eye on the gate and I'll go back and get them."

"They're probably too scared to move," Alice said. "I'll come help."

Rangi was gone before Alice remounted Misty. She couldn't see any need for her to guard the gate; after spending the night without feed, the sheep already in the next paddock were busy eating any grass they could find. The sooner they got the last of the sheep out of this paddock, the sooner they could get out of the storm. Alice turned Misty to head towards the river.

She saw Rangi beside the biggest of the willow trees, its branches thrashing about in the winds. He appeared to be facing off with two sheep stranded on rocks and surrounded by water. They stared straight at him, unresponsive to his coaxing, either stubbornly or stupidly refusing to move.

Rangi unhooked the rope he'd brought and swung the loop around above his head before casting the lasso towards the sheep. His first attempt fell short, and the sheep continued to stare blankly. He hauled the rope back and rewound it as he moved Barnaby carefully, deeper into the water.

His second throw was successful, and he pulled the noose tight around one of the sheep's necks.

Thwack! A limb of the willow split from the trunk and crashed into the raging current.

"Rangi!" Alice's warning fell on deaf ears. She sat stunned as disaster unfolded before her.

Barnaby, startled by the noise, reared, and stumbled unsteadily on the rocky riverbed. Rangi too, was caught by surprise. He lost his grip on the reins and fell backwards into the river. Alice squeezed her eyes shut, praying that when she opened them again, everything would be alright. It wasn't. She lost sight of Rangi but saw the fallen willow branch swept up in the current and thundering to where he had been.

It was only seconds, but it seemed like a slow movie, without a happy ending, was screening before her. Alice looked around; she was the only one here. What she did now would determine the outcome for Rangi, the sheep and for her. She had to act, and she had to act now. It was as if something clicked inside her, somebody took over and gave her a strength she never dreamed she had. Alice took off towards the river, pulled her own rope free and although she'd never used a lasso before, wound it above her head, spinning it around as if it was an extension of her arm.

"Whoa, girl." Alice pulled Misty up at the water's edge and scanned the muddy river. "Rangi! Rangi!"

Alice's nostrils flared as she gasped for air, sitting rigid in the saddle, she caught glimpses of debris in the water and imagined they were Rangi. It didn't matter that he was Maori. He was in trouble, and she needed to help him.

"Rangi!" she yelled again but her words were lost in the fury of the storm.

She moved down the riverbank, the wind whipped the raindrops onto her face. Each landed like a slap, a wake-up call—as if she needed one—that this man's life depended on her. Alice didn't know where her strength came from, but still she continued to spin the lasso, scared that the moment she let it fall would be the moment she needed to cast it out to Rangi.

There he was. She blinked quickly. He was still there. Clinging to the broken willow branch, now wedged on some rocks in the middle of the river. Muddy water rushed around and over him.

"Hang on Rangi," she yelled. He didn't answer but appeared to lift his head in acknowledgement.

Alice played through scenarios in her mind. Could she throw that far? Did she have the strength to haul Rangi to safety? What would happen if she was washed in too?

"You'll have to help me, Misty." Alice lowered the rope and led the horse over to another stand of willows where she dismounted. She tied one end of the rope to the saddle and

104

faced Misty away from the river and clear of the trees. The middle of the rope she looped around the willow with the thickest trunk, trusting it to be strong enough to hold its ground. Then she waded as far as felt safe into the river. Alice wedged her feet behind some rocks and steadied herself as water rushed around and over her boots.

"Rangi!" Alice spun what was left of the lasso above her head. "Grab hold of this."

Even though Alice believed she'd thrown with all the gusto she had, her first throw fell dismally short. The river grabbed hold of the rope and carried it down stream.

"Oh no, you don't." Alice grabbed at the rope; grateful she'd had the sense to secure the other end. She hauled the wet lasso back and wound it up and above her head to try again. Her arms ached. She didn't know how much longer she could keep her raised arms working. The wet rope was heavy, it made it harder to cast, but perhaps the weight would carry it further. Alice hoped so. It had to work.

"Rangi!" Alice yelled to get his attention as she threw the lasso again.

It didn't reach Rangi, but it did hook over a limb at the end of the branch he was clinging to. Alice pulled the rope tight.

"Can you move along the branch?"

"My leg." Rangi began to inch his way along the branch. "I think it's broken."

Where the branch dipped into the water, Rangi dipped too. He came up gasping for air, coughing up the muddy waters. His harried, wild appearance scared Alice but she couldn't abandon him now. The man was clearly in pain, and she was his lifeline.

When Rangi finally reached the lasso, it felt like Alice had been standing in the cold water for hours, her body trembled, her throat was raspy, and her chest ached.

"Can you hook your arm through the rope?" Alice eased her grasp on the rope so Rangi could get his hand through the noose. "Great! Pull it up over your head. Don't let it go!"

Alice bit into her lip. She wanted to scream. Tears mixed with rain and ran down her face. Pull yourself together she muttered. Don't act like a girl. You're stronger than that. He's in more pain than you.

She could see Rangi's pain. She imagined his broken limb submerged in the murky water, battered against the rocks every time his face winced, and he clenched his jaw. Pulling him to shore would exasperate that but they had no choice. If they didn't get him out of the water, he would most certainly drown.

"I've got it." Rangi yelled before he slumped back down on the branch, the effort having sapped his strength.

"Hang on, we'll haul you in." Alice turned to the horse. "Walk, Misty, giddy-up girl. That's a girl. Slow and easy."

With the rope under one armpit and across his chest, Rangi let go of the branch and rolled over onto his back. He disappeared under the water again and came up sputtering.

"Pull," Rangi yelled before he submerged again.

There was no being gentle to protect Rangi's injured leg; if they didn't hurry, he'd drown before he reached the riverbank. Alice wrapped the rope around her hands and pulled. She ignored the pain as the fibres cut into her skin. She backed herself out of the water. With each step Rangi came closer to the shore.

"Pull, Misty." Alice repeated the desperate plea.

When they had dragged Rangi to the shallow water, Alice pulled on the rope to stop Misty. There were too many rocks to drag him further. Alice had to help him get the rest of the way. She crouched down beside Rangi, loosened the lasso, and lifted it off over his head.

"I'll help you up," Alice said.

"My leg." Rangi's breathing was ragged. "I won't be able to stand on it."

Rangi's boot was missing, blood stained his torn trouser leg, and his shin was bent at an unnatural angle. The sight of a protruding bone churned Alice's stomach. She had to swallow hard.

"I'll make a splint." Alice ducked back to the willow trees. The lowest branches were too spindly to serve as a brace. She managed to get a foothold and climb onto a thick branch with several limbs that looked perfect. Her attempts to snap them off were futile. The branches were too green and sprung back into place when she let them go.

Alice glanced back at Rangi. He hadn't moved but the flood waters about him appeared to be rising. She needed to hurry. The flood brought the solution to Alice. Two broken fence posts washed up at the foot of the willows. She jumped down and grabbed them before they were swept away.

"Hang in there, Rangi." Alice crouched down beside him. "I've got some splints. We just need something to tie them with."

Rangi didn't offer any suggestions. His eyes had closed, and his head hung awkwardly as if he no longer had the strength to hold it upright. Alice imagined the leg wound would likely get infected; it needed rinsing with clean water, but all of that would be irrelevant if she couldn't move Rangi. Another rush of water cascaded over them. When the deluge subsided Alice saw his sock half off his foot. The sodden woollen sock became the first of the required ties and Alice knotted it around the bottom of the splints at Rangi's ankle. With time against her, she felt desperate. Another tie was needed and needed now. It was right in front of her. Rangi's trousers were held up with a baling twine belt. She just had to remove it. She glanced at his face. His eyes were closed, he was of no use, nor would he know if her hands were at his waist. There was no chance he would get the wrong message. She pulled at the loose end of twine, begged it to come free.

"Yes!" she yelled as she pulled it through the belt loops. The wind caught the loose end and tried to steal it away. Alice grabbed it. "Oh no you don't."

She threaded the twine under Rangi's leg and wrapped it twice around the splints before knotting it off.

"Rangi! Rangi, wake up!" Alice tried to stir him. "I've splinted your leg; we have to try and get you up."

Rangi groaned. Alice moved around behind him and hooked her arms under his armpits. She heaved but his bulk went nowhere. She knew it was a David and Goliath battle for her to move him alone.

"Rangi, you have to help me." Alice crouched down beside him, she wedged her shoulder into his armpit and wrapped his arm across her shoulders. Her tiny hand was too small to clasp his wrist, so she gripped his thumb in her fingers. She nudged Rangi in the ribs until he was coherent. "On the count of three, come on, you can do it. We'll just get you onto drier ground and then I can go for help."

Together they moved. Rangi howled in pain, but they managed to get him upright. Slowly, Alice walked around, turning Rangi so they were facing the paddock. She braced herself and pushed against him as he used her as a crutch to take a small step. She wrapped her other arm around his waist. There was no time for thoughts to wander, no time to consider that she vowed she'd never get this close to a man under any circumstance, no time to consider what danger she might be in.

CHAPTER

10

They inched their way across the rocks. Alice felt Rangi's body stiffen with each step, as if he anticipated the ensuing pain. It seemed to take forever but eventually they got beyond the rocks and up onto what, without the storm, would have been paddock.

"I'll sit down here," Rangi muttered through his clenched jaw.

Alice moved from Rangi's side to behind him, her back to his. She dug her heels into the muddy earth and slowly they lowered to the ground.

"What the hell!" Lou yelled as he came upon the scene. "What the hell have you done woman? This is no time to be sitting down on the job."

Alice's nostrils flared. Partly to suck in the oxygen needed to repower her lungs after the marathon effort to rescue Rangi but mainly with the anger that seethed through her. Lou's assumption that it was her that had caused their predication was like a kick in the guts. She wanted to swear, to curse the man that was looking at her with contempt. She affixed him with a cold, hard stare.

She wanted to say *if you had half a brain, you would see* but she just said, "Rangi has broken his leg."

Rangi couldn't confirm this. His face had turned an ugly shade of grey and the whites of his eyes rolled back in his head.

Lou's eyebrows drew into the single line that indicated he was thinking. "I'll go and get the others and the wagon," he said. "We'll lift him onto that to get him out of this weather and back to the house. Do you think you can stay with him until then?"

Alice was dumbfounded. How could this man be so oblivious to how patronising he sounded? She muffled the sarcastic reply that was threatening to explode.

"I think I can manage that," she said, glaring at Lou.

"Right then, I'd better hurry." Lou turned Trigger and rode off across the paddock without a second glance to Alice's welfare.

She knelt behind Rangi and rested his head on her knees, holding it gently while she talked to him.

"Rangi, try to stay awake, help is on its way. You've done the hard bit. You'll be right as rain before you know it."

An indiscernible grumble was Rangi's only response but at least it was something. Alice dared to look down at his injury. Blood seeped through the ripped pants leg. Despite the fence post splints holding the leg straight, Rangi's shin still had an unnatural bend in it. The muddy river waters that had spilled out into the paddock lapped against them, not dangerously but enough to rob them of their body heat.

111

Alice sat there waiting, unable to move for fear of causing Rangi more pain. She lost feeling in her own legs as Rangi's weight and the cool of the water numbed them.

Her back provided some protection for Rangi as it bore the brunt of the wind's force whipping down the river. She was drenched, her sodden clothes clung to her body like an ice blanket. Shivers started in her teeth, they chattered uncontrollably. Then her head and shoulders trembled. The shudders must have roused Rangi, he lifted his hand and laid it over top of Alice's.

"Okay," was the only word Alice could discern Rangi mouthing as his eyes fluttered open. She didn't know if it was a statement or a question but his large hand atop hers was somehow comforting, a signal that they were in this together and they would get out of their predicament.

Alice looked out at the river and blinked. As her adrenaline ebbed, replaced by the realisation of the danger of the situation, tears threatened. Don't you dare be a girl and cry she growled to herself, but they weren't to be stopped. Her tears fell freely, blended with the rain, and ran down her cheeks.

Men's voices brought her attention back. She rubbed her eyes with the back of her hand and sniffed loudly before the cart pulled up beside them and Lou arrived back on Trigger.

"You're going to have to help us, girl," Lou said. "We'll need all four of us to lift him. You take his good leg. I'll take the splinted one. No second thoughts, Dan you'd better take his injured leg, I'll be able to clamber up onto the wagon easier than you."

As Alice eased her way out from under Rangi and tried to stand, she felt her legs were as wooden as Danny's prosthetic. She rubbed her thighs to encourage the blood flow. The legs of her overalls were stained with blood and Alice realised Rangi must have a head injury as well.

"Don't muck around girl, we'd better hurry," Lou said. "When we get him onboard, I'll ride ahead and phone for the doctor."

Alice shook her head. Lou seemed determined to place no value in her abilities. She felt like an inconvenience, someone to be tolerated out of necessity and certainly not appreciated for all she had done.

"Rangi," Lou yelled over the noise of the storm. "This might hurt a bit. Just hang in there and we'll get you out of this storm as quick as we can."

They positioned themselves, Alice and Dan at Rangi's legs and Lou and Jack at his shoulders.

"On the count of three." Lou eyed each of them in turn. "One … two … three, heave."

Rangi howled. He sounded like a wolf separated from its pack, baying to the full moon. When they released his limbs onto the hay, his head rolled to one side and his eyes closed.

"You climb on with him, girl," Lou said.

"What about Misty and Barnaby?" Misty was still tethered to the tree by the lasso rope and after galloping about the paddock in fright, Barnaby had now calmed and joined the mare.

Lou noticed the horses and changed his instructions. "Jack, help the girl grab the horses. Tie them to the back of the wagon and then climb on board." Lou turned to leave but hesitated. "Is that blood on you, yours, or Rangi's?"

Alice was stunned, did Lou care about her wellbeing? "Rangi's," she replied. "I think he hit his head on the rocks."

"We'd better hurry then." Lou shook his head. "Those sheep will just have to save themselves. Where the hell is your raincoat? You'll probably catch pneumonia out in this weather dressed like a townie."

Alice looked back towards the river at the sheep who remained stranded like a sacrificial lamb on a platter. She felt as valued as them.

❤

Doctor Green arrived at the farmhouse at the same time as the wagon. He had been on his way home for breakfast after an early morning call out to a woman who was in the early stages of labour. With Brownie's help they lifted Rangi from the wagon and carried him in onto the dining table. Brownie seemed unperturbed by the mud and water the men traipsed inside and Rangi's wet and bloody body on his table.

Rangi barely groaned. His condition was deteriorating, and Doctor Green got straight to work. He put his medical bag on the bench seat, withdrew a stethoscope and listened to Rangi's heart and lungs.

"He's still alive, isn't he?" Alice panicked that her efforts hadn't been enough.

"Just checking for water on his lungs. I'm assuming from the look of him he's been in the river. I don't know how long."

While it seemed like an eternity at the time, everything had happened so fast, Alice couldn't be sure how long Rangi had been under water, so she stayed quiet.

Next the doctor shone a light in each of Rangi's eyes and he groaned. "Good he's still conscious and responsive. Rangi, let me know where it hurts."

The doctor turned Rangi's head so he could inspect the gash.

"Can you get me some hot water in a bowl Brownie. I think it's just a surface wound, but we'll need to clean it up and stitch it."

As Brownie turned to the bench, the back door opened, and Fergus walked in.

"Phew!" Fergus said. "That's one hell of a storm out there. Shit, there's a storm in here too. What's happened?"

Alice watched as Fergus scanned the room, taking in the scene. Their eyes met briefly but she was unable to gauge whether his look was one of concern or contempt. His dimple never moved to wink at her and give the reassurance she wanted.

"Rangi." Fergus moved to stand beside the table. "What have you done?"

Rangi groaned. "Alice," he mumbled. "Save."

Fergus looked from Rangi to Alice and back again. He angled his body, tilted his head, and narrowed his eyes as if mentally weighing the situation. With his arms folded across his chest, it looked as if any trust that had existed was a distant memory.

"It's alright son, don't try to talk, Alice is safe." Doctor Green moved his hands down the length of Rangi's body, but he got no further reaction from him.

"Who did these splints?" Doctor Green asked.

"Me." Alice's timid reply was little more than a squeak.

"Well done." The doctor commended her as he cut through the ties and removed the fence posts.

Alice looked across at Lou to see if he noticed someone appreciated her efforts.

"You'd best get yourself upstairs," he said. "Get out of those wet clothes. Brownie, next time you're in town get this girl a raincoat will you. She'll die of pneumonia out in this weather."

"Yes, your lips have turned purple, I suggest a hot bath, and fresh dry clothes." The doctor glanced up at Alice before refocusing his attention on Rangi. "This might hurt a bit son, the fracture in your tibia needs to be realigned."

Rangi's howl sent a chill down her spine, but Alice left the room smiling. Her lips might be purple, but she was getting a raincoat. Lou wasn't going to fire her. She didn't glance back at Fergus. He would just have to make up his own mind.

❧

It wasn't until Alice made it to the bathroom and saw herself in the mirror that she realised the danger she had been in. She looked like she'd been in the eye of the storm. Her hair was knotted with twigs, mud caked strands of hair together, much like the dags of a sheep. Her cheeks were smeared a dirty brown and as the doctor had pointed out her trembling lips were purple. If she clenched her jaw, she could stop the movement, but she couldn't stifle the blubbering that seemed to start in her belly. A tightness in her chest forced the tears upwards. The eyes that looked back at her were already red from crying but without energy to battle they surrendered, and Alice cried and cried until she had nothing left. The mirror didn't lie, Alice was a mess and no use to anyone in her current state.

She ran the bath and stripped out of her wet clothes. She dipped her fingers into the water, her frozen fingertips gave a false reading of its temperature and Alice added more cold water to be safe. Hanging onto the side of the bath she gingerly stepped one foot into the water, gasping as the heat bit into her skin.

"You can do it," she told herself. "You're only wet and dirty. It's Rangi with the broken leg."

Slowly, she added the other foot then lowered herself down. As her body temperature rose, Alice reclined further into the bath until only her face remained above the water. She closed her eyes and said a silent thank you to whatever force had kept her safe today.

The water turned a muddy brown as the debris from the storm washed free. Alice scrubbed her face and rinsed her hair several times until it felt clean. Feeling clean and warm, Alice stood and pulled the plug. Her relaxed state was gone in an instant when she heard voices outside the bathroom door. She was terrified that in her exhaustion she'd forgotten to lock the door. Her heart thumped until her eyes riveted on the door latch, saw it was pushed hard into the lock, and she was safe.

Over the gurgling of the water spiralling down the plug hole, Alice couldn't be certain whose voice it was. Fergus? Her heartbeat quickened; it would be nice if Fergus was outside the bathroom, but that would mean she'd have to have a conversation she wasn't yet prepared for.

The voices disappeared as quick as they came leaving the exhausted Alice, uncertain whether they were real at all.

❦

When Alice returned to the kitchen, Brownie was scrubbing the table clean. There was no sign of Rangi or Fergus.

"Where's Rangi?" She sucked in a breath, worried that something drastic had happened. "Did the doctor take him to hospital?"

"No, it's only a broken leg, we'll have to nurse him here, I'm afraid." Brownie abandoned the rag to grab the mop and clean the floor. "We've set up a stretcher in the sitting room. Doc will be back tomorrow to change the poultice on his leg. We've got to check his temperature regular and monitor the injuries for infection."

"So, he's not out of the woods yet?"

"No, but apparently you did a very good job of getting him out of the river."

"What? Who? Me?"

"Well, you were the only one there, weren't you?"

"Umm … yes." Alice's cheeks reddened. Now that she was getting credit for her actions, she didn't want to accept it.

"Well, Rangi is very grateful for your efforts."

"He said that?"

"Yes," Brownie replied. "Go on, go and see him."

Alice hesitated. It was one thing to be out in the open with Rangi but another entirely to be alone in a closed room with him.

"What are you waiting for?" Brownie asked. "I'm sure he'd like to tell you himself. He might be a bit groggy though. Doc gave him something for the pain."

Surely Rangi couldn't be trouble if he was injured and groggy. The sitting room door was closed, Alice knocked lightly and pushed it open. The velvet drapes had been drawn but she could still make out the elegance of the furnishings. No wonder none of the farm workers had been allowed in here, it was too fancy for them.

Rangi was on a cot in front of the unlit fire. A grey woollen blanket covered his legs, but Alice could see the broken limb was held rigid and straight, just as she had tried to do. She felt proud that she had done the right thing.

As Alice approached the cot, she saw Rangi's eyes were closed. She heard a light rumble, he was snoring, and she turned to leave him to rest and recuperate.

"Alice," he mumbled and reached up a hand. "Stay. Sit."

Although she had clean overalls, Alice daren't sit on the brocade upholstered settee. She crouched down beside the cot.

"I need to thank you." Rangi tried to raise himself up on his elbows and groaned in pain, before slumping back down, his face contorted in agony. He closed his eyes and took several deep breaths before he was able to speak again. "Hero. You're my hero."

"No … no I'm not," Alice protested.

"Sorry. Heroine. You're my heroine."

Alice giggled. The female equivalent didn't sit any more comfortably with her.

"No, Rangi," Alice said. "I'm not that either. I just did what anyone would do."

"But …" Rangi appeared to struggle for words. He closed his eyes again and breathed deeply. He didn't get to finish his sentence. Painkillers or exhaustion took over and his eyes remained closed.

Alice waited, willed his eyes to open again, she wanted to ask about Fergus, but Rangi started snoring and the opportunity was lost. She doubted she'd be able to believe anything he said. Rangi was clearly groggy from the accident and the painkillers the doctor had prescribed.

CHAPTER

11

The rain persisted long after the sun had gone down. Everybody seemed subdued after the day's events and the effort they had all put in to get the sheep to safety. Brownie had made a shepherd's pie for dinner. Its breadcrumb topping was nicely browned, and it tasted as good as it smelled. Alice was grateful for Rangi's absence from the table. It gave her space to sit on the bench seat beside Fergus but not wedged into his side. She could have been a million miles away for all the attention he gave her. There was no conversation, not even an acknowledgement.

"I heard old Fred wasn't as lucky as Rangi," Lou said.

"Why was Rangi lucky?" The question slipped from Alice before her brain registered that she should have been more concerned about Fred, whoever he was.

"He had you to save him. Fred got washed down river. They found his body at Whipsnade."

Alice gasped. Fred? Whipsnade? Was that the Fred that had kindly helped her down off the haystack? Who found him? Could it have been Betsy?

"Fred who?" she asked.

"Fred Belcher." Brownie joined the conversation. "Do you know him? He's married to Joan."

It was Fred from the haystack. Alice remembered the dance at Orari Hall where Joan and Fred had danced together almost as much as Moira and Bill.

"Yes, I met him at Whipsnade," she replied.

Alice felt the impact of the day's events like a tidal wave washing over her, its retreat sucked all the air from her lungs, and she retired early, grateful for the solitude of her bedroom, to contemplate just how much danger she had been in. It could just as easy been her or Rangi that they were talking about, washed away to their death. Her first thought was Maori were trouble; beyond anything she had ever contemplated. But then logic edged its sensible way in, and Alice realised what happened didn't occur because of the colour of Rangi's skin. Anyone, including Fred, could be in the wrong place at the wrong time.

The comforting noise of the raindrops on the iron roof allowed Alice's mind to quieten, to stop playing through what-if scenarios, none of which had happy endings, and fall to sleep.

Alice woke to a rumbling noise that sounded like Rangi's snoring. She was immediately alert, fearing Rangi or Jack had snuck into her room while she was asleep. The silence of her awakening and the dryness of her throat brought the realisation that it had been her snoring. Her nose was blocked, and her throat felt raspy. It appeared Alice had done what Rangi and Lou had predicted; she'd succumbed to a cold.

A sudden change in body temperature as her warm bare feet touched the cold floor brought on a sneeze which without a handkerchief, Alice had to catch in her hands. Glad that she had stowed her hankies on an open shelf she reached over and grabbed one to wipe her hands and catch the volley of sneezes that followed. The sudden movements jarred her head and now she had a headache to add to her symptoms.

Alice sat on the side of the bed, disappointed that her good work in proving herself worthy, would be undone when she went downstairs with a cold. She didn't have any option, she couldn't spend the day in her room, she had to soldier on. She blew her nose before changing into farm clothes ready for the day, stuffing a handkerchief in each of her overall's pockets.

In the bathroom Alice splashed her face with cold water. It did little to dull the redness around her nose or clear the shadows under her eyes. She hoped the men wouldn't notice, she didn't want Lou's disdain but neither did she want or deserve their pity.

When she entered the kitchen, Jack, Lou, and Danny were being dished up a bowl of porridge by Brownie. There was an empty bowl where Fergus would normally sit indicating he'd already eaten. Alice wondered where he had gone; perhaps he was still being punished by Lou and had been sent out in the rain to work. That didn't seem fair but at least it meant she didn't have him to deal with.

"Sit down, lass," Brownie said as he filled her bowl. "Eat up while it's still hot."

Alice poured cold milk over the oaten mixture to quell the steam rising from the plate and added a spoonful of honey to sweeten it. She stayed focused on the plate hoping everyone would leave her alone. It wasn't to be.

"Fred's funeral is at the end of the week," Brownie said. "I will be going if you want a lift."

"Thank you, Brownie. Could I borrow the telephone and call Betsy? Just to make sure they're all okay at Whipsnade."

"Just a short call," Brownie said. "The phone has been going crazy through the storm."

"Is everyone else, okay?" Alice asked. "Fergus?"

"He's helping out the Works Department," Lou said. "The powers-that-be think the Kurow flood damage is more important than the Orari bridge washout. They clearly don't live around here. It'll be another month before the Works bulldozer is back on site, so Fergus has taken the tractor over to help with the repairs."

Through the kitchen window Alice saw that rain was still steadily falling.

"I hope he'll be careful. It's still raining."

"Yes," Lou said, looking directly at Alice. "Which means you, without a raincoat, who now looks and sounds like she has a cold, will be staying inside today."

"Oh, I'm okay."

"Clearly, you are not, and I won't be held responsible for you getting pneumonia."

Alice knew from Lou's tone, that there was no point arguing. She slowly nodded her head.

"We need someone to care for Rangi," Lou continued. "And you are it, nurse Alice. Keep him entertained, will you? He'll likely get a bit cranky being couped up."

Relegation from farm worker to nurse didn't sit well with Alice. She shook her head in denial and silently cursed herself for catching a cold. Another sneeze was her undoing. There was no denying she was unwell but being made responsible for Rangi, caring for a Maori, entertaining a Maori, Alice wasn't sure she knew how to do that.

"How long for?" she dared to ask.

"As long as it takes to sort out some other accommodation for Rangi," Lou replied. "A fractured tibia apparently takes months to heal. He'll be no use around here for some time."

Alice swallowed. She'd never voice it aloud, but she hoped that it didn't take long to find alternative lodgings for Rangi. Perhaps there was a marae close by that he could go to.

"You can start by taking him in a plate of porridge," Brownie said.

♡

Rangi wriggled his way up to the top of the cot and sat propped up with pillows at his back. He licked his lips as Alice placed the tray with the plate of porridge on his lap.

"Aren't you going to feed me?" he teased.

"It's your leg that's broken, not your hand," Alice replied. "And I've got a cold which you won't want to catch and add to your worries."

"True. *Tena Koe*, Alice."

"*Tena Koe*?" Alice repeated. "I haven't heard you speak Maori before. What does that mean?"

"So used to being rapped over the knuckles for it at school, I forget my *te reo*." Rangi blew on a spoonful of porridge. "It means thank you."

Alice left Rangi to eat his porridge and wandered about the room. She pulled the drapes and welcomed what light there was from the grey sky. Either side of the fireplace were built-in wooden shelves. One side held a collection of expensive-looking vases that Alice daren't touch. The other side, held a library of books that rose from the floor to the ceiling, arranged according to size with their spines all neatly facing out. Whoever the collection belonged to must have been an avid reader. The higher shelves held older leather-bound books with titles Alice didn't recognise. At eye level was a shelf where the paper jackets of the more modern books captured her attention. There were none of the Mills and Boons titles Alice's mother would have read.

"Are you going to read to me?" Rangi asked.

Thinking it was unlikely that she and Rangi would have the same tastes in reading material, she suggested that he read one for himself.

"Can't," he replied.

"I can get it off the shelf for you, but I repeat, it's your leg that's broken, not your eyes."

"Can't read," Rangi said.

"But you just told me you went to school." Each time Alice and her mother had moved she'd had to start at a new school, it was hard trying to make friends, so she focused on her learning and reading was her favourite subject.

"Not much." Rangi licked his spoon clean with a satisfied slurp. "It wasn't a good place for us to be."

"Us?" Alice encouraged Rangi to continue.

126

"Maori. School was set up by you Pakeha, run by Pakeha and served Pakeha. We had to conform or be punished. I didn't like being punished. Besides, my koro taught me all the important stuff."

"Your koro?"

"My grandfather. He taught the stories that his father had been taught by his father and his father before that."

Alice glanced back at the library of books and wondered how Maori stories differed from those printed and bound.

"But how did you relay your Koro's stories if you couldn't read?" She seemed to be asking question after question, but Rangi appeared happy to answer. If this was all it took to entertain him, then her job would be easy.

Rangi tapped the side of his head with his forefinger. "All in here," he said with a chuckle.

"You can tell me a story then," Alice suggested. "What were they about?"

"The moon and the stars, how they guide you when to plant and fish, how you can find your way home when you've had a few too many." Rangi chuckled. "Legends of our great warriors, their strength and courage to stand up for the truth. But I know them in *te reo* and you won't understand that."

Alice scanned the titles on the shelf. *As I Lay Dying* by William Faulkner didn't seem at all appropriate for a man stuck in bed, *Cold Comfort Farm* by Stella Gibbons sounded equally unappealing. The cover of the next book Alice pulled from the shelf looked as if it could have been set in Orari, a big red full moon rose above mountain ranges. It was called *The Hobbit* and Alice considered reading it to Rangi, until she saw it was three hundred and ten pages long; she didn't want to be stuck in the sitting room reading for ever. She'd come here to be a farmer.

Gone with the Wind sat beside *The Hobbit.* Alice remembered the kissing scenes in the movie they'd all gone to watch a few weeks back. She didn't want to read that to Rangi, who knows what ideas he might get? Alice glanced at the sitting room door to check it was still wide open, she felt safer that way. The next book sounded ideal, Agatha Christie's *Murder on the Orient Express.* If Rangi proved to be too much trouble, Alice might get an idea of how to dispose of him. She giggled to herself.

"What's so funny?" Rangi asked.

"Nothing." Alice coloured, feeling guilty for her thoughts. "I think this looks good."

After returning the empty porridge plate to the kitchen, Alice took a seat on the chair closest to Rangi and started reading.

The body of Ratchett had just been discovered with twelve stab wounds when Doctor Green arrived to check on Rangi. Alice was so absorbed by the story, where the elegance of the train stranded in a snowstorm seemed much like her own predicament, that she jumped when the doctor knocked on the door.

"Sounds like a good story," he said.

"It is." Rangi's eyes were wide with delight, and he grinned from ear to ear.

He had the straightest and whitest teeth Alice had ever seen. It was as if she was noticing them for the first time. Alice shook her head and moved out of the way for the doctor.

"I need to check the wound." The doctor lifted the blanket away. "Make sure the poultice is doing its job."

"What's in it?" Rangi asked.

The doctor pulled a new packet from his bag. "I think it's got bran and mustard. I'm not sure though, the label doesn't say the ingredients. They generally work well."

"We should get my *kuia* to make something up," Rangi said. "She knows all the old ways of fighting infection."

"I believe the Maori make a very effective antiseptic paste out of Kawakawa leaves," Doctor Green said.

Alice did a double take; the doctor was praising Maori medicine. She figured if he was a doctor, he'd have to be intelligent and if he'd reached that conclusion then perhaps, she'd better rethink her views on everything Maori. She sat back on the settee and thought through all her interactions with Rangi. Apart from the river incident, which wasn't his fault, she conceded he'd been nothing but polite. Her mind replaced Rangi in the cot with an image of Jack in his dirty long johns and Alice nearly gagged. As she didn't know why her grandfather had said Maori were trouble, she decided it would do her better if she adhered to one of her grandfather's other sayings: treat people the way they treat you. While Rangi continued to be polite and friendly, Alice would return the sentiment.

"The wound is looking good," Doctor Green said as he replaced the bandage. "We won't be needing your *kuia* this time."

"So, I'll be up and out of here soon then?" Rangi asked.

"Well, not too soon, I want to hear who committed murder on the Orient Express."

Alice smiled. It was nice to know Rangi was enjoying the story as much as her.

"Ummm." Doctor Green rubbed his chin between thumb and forefinger. "Alice had better read slowly; tibias can take some time to heal."

"A week?" Rangi screwed up his face.

Doctor Green shook his head.

"A month?"

Alice watched Rangi's shoulders slump as Doctor Green kept shaking his head.

"Hell," Rangi swore. "Alice will have time to teach me to read the book myself."

"You're fit and healthy Rangi," Doctor Green said. "So, it might only be two or three months. For some people it can take up to six months. You've just got to stay off it."

"Holy hell!" Rangi screwed his eyes shut tight.

Alice didn't react to Rangi's swearing. She was too busy absorbing the time she might be expected to look after him. Surely, she would be needed on the farm more than here, surely Lou and Brownie couldn't ask her to be a nurse any longer than her cold kept her inside.

"Doctor Green," she said. "Do you have any Vicks VapoRub in your bag?"

"It just so happens I do," he replied. "I noticed you'd caught a cold. I thought you might. Here you go, put some around your nose and on the soles of your feet when you go to bed at night. You should be right as rain in no time."

"Lucky Alice," Rangi groaned.

❦

Voices from the kitchen told Alice and Rangi it must be lunchtime. Alice daren't do as she would normally do, and fold down the corner of a page, so she found a piece of paper to act as a bookmark.

"I'll go and see what's for lunch," she said to Rangi.

Rangi squirmed awkwardly as if he was embarrassed. One advantage of being dark-skinned, she thought, nobody could see when you blushed.

"What's wrong?" Alice asked.

"Umm … I need to go to the toilet."

"Oh." Alice coloured from head to toe. Did her nursing duties extend to helping Rangi toilet? She hoped not. "You can't walk there, can you?"

"Better not, not after what the doc said." Rangi scratched his head. "I don't want to be stuck here any longer than I have to. I just need the bedpan."

Getting a bedpan would be easy, Alice could do that, but helping Rangi to use one and disposing of its contents afterwards, she couldn't face that.

"I'll get Brownie," she said and hurried from the room.

Much to Alice's relief, while she ate bacon and egg pie, Brownie dealt with the bedpan. Fergus was still nowhere to be seen and Alice thought he'd likely end up with a cold too, the longer he was out in the pouring rain.

She managed to put a call through to Whipsnade Farm, but Betsy was still over the paddock checking the sheep for unmothered lambs. Thoughts of the lambs Alice had fed flooded back and Nel must have heard the concern in her voice.

"Don't worry, dear," Nel said. "The new trainees are taking very good care of all the unmothered lambs, including the two you started to feed."

"That's wonderful," Alice replied. "I just wanted to check everyone was okay. I heard that Fred was found at Whipsnade. That must have been horrible."

"Yes, poor dear Fred. Joan is beside herself. Inconsolable."

Alice couldn't imagine what it would be like to lose your husband. She'd never been close enough to anyone to miss them when they died. Well, maybe her grandfather, but he was old, sick and in lots of pain before he passed away. So as her mother and everyone else at his funeral kept repeating, it was a blessing.

"I was going to go to the funeral on Friday." Alice thought she'd have to pluck up courage by then to say something appropriate to Joan. "Are you, Duncan and Betsy going?"

"Yes, dear, we'll be there." Nel tutted. "I imagine all of the district, will be there, if this storm breaks by then."

"I'll see you there," Alice said. "I'd better go now. Say hi to Betsy from me."

"I will, Alice. Best you look after yourself and get over your cold."

Alice hadn't mentioned her cold, but of course, Nel could tell from her nasal tone.

CHAPTER

12

Friday's sky was painted with doomfully grey clouds, fitting for the melancholy mood of Fred's funeral. With the Orari Bridge still undergoing repairs, everyone attending the service, had to drive the long way around into Geraldine. It explained why Alice still hadn't seen Fergus, just his empty plate at the breakfast table.

The church was overflowing with people. Alice and Betsy stood back on the lawn outside so that others who knew Fred better than them, could find a pew. Moira joined them as Bill, who was holding a bunch of pink carnations, disappeared around the side of the church.

"Where's he going?" Alice thought it was a nice gesture to bring Joan flowers. "Joan is in the church."

"The flowers aren't for Joan," Moira replied with a tone that warned Alice she'd best not ask too many questions. "They're for his darling wife."

"Is she buried here?" Betsy asked, saving Alice the trouble.

"Yes," Moira snarled. "Apparently the whole district turned out for that funeral too. I guess that's what small town people do when there isn't much else going on."

"Is your placement with Bill not working out?" Betsy continued. She looked unperturbed by Moira's demeanour.

There was a glimpse of a smile from Moira, but it disappeared as fast as it arrived and was replaced with a scowl.

"When we are at home on the farm, just the two of us, he is the most attentive man I have ever known, but." Moira sucked in a breath and put her hands on her hips. "But when we have to be around other people it's almost as if I don't exist."

"That's no good," Betsy said. "Have you talked to him about it?"

"Fat lot of good that would do."

"Well, you don't know unless you try," Betsy replied. "Bill seems like a reasonable man."

Moira looked everywhere but at Betsy and Alice. She was clearly uncomfortable with the conversation and Alice wasn't brave enough to say anything.

The murmurings inside the church hushed and the service began so the women stood quietly together. Although the words of the minister's sermon resounded around the church, Alice didn't catch what he said nor the readings given by the family but like everyone, she was familiar with the words and music of *Amazing Grace* and was able to join in. The hymn was followed by *The Lord's Prayer,* and they bowed their heads and recited this.

After whispering amen, Alice opened her eyes to see Grace cycling down the street towards them.

"Who's died?" Grace whispered as she pulled up beside them and climbed off her bicycle.

"Fred Belcher," Betsy replied in a hushed voice.

"How?" Grace was wide eyed.

"Drowned," Alice said.

"How?" Grace repeated. "In the storm?"

"Trying to rescue sheep," Betsy explained. "Duncan found him."

Alice gulped and wrapped her arms around herself. She and Rangi were so lucky it wasn't them.

"Was he at Whipsnade?" Grace asked.

"No. He must have hit his head and been washed down river."

"Oh, how horrible. At least at the flax mill we don't have to be out in that weather."

Alice's nose chose that moment to run, and she had to use her handkerchief. Grace put a hand on her shoulder.

"Sorry Alice," she apologised. "I guess you've been out in the weather too and caught a cold."

Alice nodded as she blew her nose.

"At least Alice won't be able to smell you." Moira squeezed her nostrils shut. "Grace, to be blunt, you stink."

Grace lifted her hands to her nose. "It's the rhetting of the flax. It gets into your pores, and I can't get it out. You get used to it."

"Just as well Ben is away in the detention camp," Moira said. "He mightn't want to get used to it."

They had to step aside as the pall bearers carried the coffin out and over to the pre-dug grave. Joan followed the coffin supported by what must have been her adult children. She looked like she was struggling to walk. Alice decided

135

there and then that Joan didn't need Alice's cold to add to her worries. She'd best stay away from the poor woman.

The mourners gathered around as the minister recited the committal and the coffin was lowered into the grave. The land girls moved to stand on the outskirts of the group, ending up between the other graves.

Alice was careful where she stood, particularly when the headstone beside her looked relatively new. She read the inscription and stepped back in fright as she realised it must be Bill's wife. The bunch of flowers he had carried were sitting in a glass jar, inset into the concrete, their colour and softness a stark contrast to the severity of the gravesite.

"Ouch." Moira elbowed Alice in the back. "Watch where you're stepping."

The people standing in front of them turned and glared.

Alice mouthed a 'sorry' to them and whispered to Grace.

"It's Bill's wife," she said as she pointed to the grave.

Moira moved so she could read the headstone.

"Past tense Alice, past tense." She looked away from the grave and straightened her spine. "She was Bill's wife."

Alice read the inscription. *Miriam, dearly Beloved Wife and Soulmate of Bill.* Miriam might be dead and no longer Bill's wife but as far as Alice knew, from the Mills and Boon books she'd read, soulmates were forever. Alice doubted she'd ever have a soulmate; she couldn't imagine even wanting one, but she wasn't brave enough to point any of this out to Moira.

As was custom, those gathered selected a small flower from the basket held by the funeral director and filed past the grave to cast their flower onto the coffin, a final gesture of farewell. Alice reluctantly joined the other land girls and the rest of the procession. After all the rain the freshly dug grave held its own earthy aroma, the musky scent combined with the perfume of the flowers made Alice feel queasy. She stepped uneasily past the grave, afraid to look into the deep, damp hole.

❦

Afternoon tea and a chance for everyone to gather and reminisce was offered in the church hall. A collection of coats amassed in the foyer as everyone stripped off the extra layers, they had worn to ward off the chill of the weather. At least the funeral hadn't been dampened by the rain which had eased off yesterday evening.

"Have you heard anything more about Ben?" Betsy asked Grace.

"Not directly," Grace answered. "But I've been told that all of the conchies are being sent to detention camps, the closest is in Christchurch at Balmoral."

"Conchies?" Alice asked.

"Conscientious objectors," Grace explained. "Ben isn't exactly one of them, because he had signed up but they're being treated the same after a stint in prison. They're not allowed visitors, even family. Family is allowed to write but their letters get censored."

Alice sucked in a breath, Fergus was being labelled a conscientious objector, that's why he got in the fight. What if they sent him away? She shuffled backward to be out of earshot, as if that would make a difference to the truth.

"You won't be able to get in contact with him then," Moira said.

Grace tapped the side of her nose, leaned into the group, and lowered her voice.

"One of the girls at the factory has a brother whose been sent there. She is going to write and ask if he knows Ben. If he does, I can sneak a letter in with hers."

"Surely the censors will see you're not family and destroy it," Betsy said.

Grace smiled and tapped the side of her nose again. "I'm not going to write a separate letter to Ben, just include what I want to say in her letter. They have a special code."

"A code?" Alice was intrigued.

Grace glanced around, checked no-one was party to their conversation and lowered her voice to a whisper as an added precaution.

"Using little pencil dots under letters until they make words and sentences."

"I guess he'll have nothing else to do but decipher it," Moira said.

"Apparently, they work them hard, clearing scrub all day every day, no matter what the weather. He'll be catching a cold like you Alice."

"I got mine rescuing Rangi," Alice said.

"Rangi? Whose Rangi?" Moira glanced around the room. "What happened to Fergus? Where is Fergus? I thought he would be here today."

"Fergus is fixing the Orari Bridge." Alice balanced the cup, saucer, and plate she was holding in one hand to free up the other to take a bite of scone. The cream and blackcurrant jam topping tasted delicious. "At least I think he is."

Alice thought of Fergus being dragged off to the detention centre. She hadn't seen him for days, only a dirty breakfast plate she was assuming was his.

"That explains why he isn't here," Moira said. "But why are you talking about Rangi and not Fergus? Have you not sorted things out after race day, Alice? You really do need some lessons with men don't you."

"Moira!" Grace intervened. "More important, given why we're here today, is why Alice had to rescue Rangi, she might have been in danger herself."

Alice finished her mouthful before she spoke.

"It was pretty scary, the river flooded."

"Well, we know that." Moira huffed, making it obvious she didn't like being shut down by Grace.

"We had to rescue the sheep. Rangi was on the horse in the water when it was spooked by a branch and threw him off. He broke his leg and I had to use my horse to pull him out of the river."

"You did that." Grace rested her hand on Alice's shoulder. "That's so courageous of you, Alice. Well done. I hope Rangi appreciated your efforts."

Even at Grace's praise, Alice blushed. She wished she could control whatever made her cheeks colour. She thought about Rangi, despite him being a Maori, they were getting on quite well. He could be funny at times and often made her laugh.

"With a name like that he must be Maori," Moira said. "How come he got to stay behind? Weren't they all recruited into the Maori Battalion?"

"Yes, he's Maori, but there's nothing wrong with that." Alice heard herself defending Rangi and wondered what her grandfather would think. "He's colour blind."

Moira laughed. "Everything is black and white to him, is it?"

Grace must have seen Alice's discomfort and changed the subject. "How did you get here then?"

"Brownie brought me." Alice searched the hall until she saw Brownie, it wasn't difficult, he was several inches taller than the men he was standing with. They all seemed to be enjoying a glass of beer instead of a cup of tea. She hoped he didn't drink too much and be incapable of driving home.

"Betsy, have you heard anything more about Roland or William?" Grace asked.

"Nothing from Roland, I've almost given up hope of ever hearing from him." Betsy closed her eyes and sighed. After a moment of silence, as if she was saying a prayer, she opened her eyes and continued. "William is apparently on a ship due to arrive in Wellington within the month. They'll keep him in a hospital there until he is well enough to be sent home."

"Do you know what injuries he has?" Grace asked.

"No," Betsy replied. "But he's requested that only Duncan collect him from the train when he does come so I'm guessing it's serious. So serious, that he doesn't want his mother to see him."

"Oh, Betsy, that's so sad." Grace said what Alice was thinking.

"At least he's alive." Betsy sniffed back tears as her eyes glassed over. "At least he is alive."

By the time everyone was leaving, Brownie and the group of men he was with, had imbibed several more beers and were talking and laughing at a decibel louder than everyone else.

"I do hope he's going to be alright to drive," Alice said to Grace.

"Oh, don't be a worry wort." Moira looked over at Bill. "Bill's had a couple too. He'll be fine to drive. Brownie will have more capacity for drinking than a lightweight like you."

Alice couldn't deny that everybody probably had more capacity than her. Watching the result of her mother's addictive habits had scared Alice from ever touching a drop.

"Hello ladies." Nel joined the land girls. "Are you ready to go, Betsy? Duncan wants to get back and make sure the new trainees haven't mucked up the jobs he gave them."

"Nothing has changed then," Moira muttered.

"When are we going to meet up next?" Betsy asked the others.

"I've been playing cribbage," Grace said. "They have cribbage nights once a week."

"In Geraldine?" Betsy asked. "I won't be able to come in here every week."

"They have a club that meets at the Orari Hall," Nel explained. "And then monthly there's an interclub night where the clubs play against one another."

"I don't even know how to play cribbage," Alice said.

"They explain all the rules to beginners and team you up with someone until you've got the gist of it," Grace explained.

"Sounds pretty boring." Moira looked as interested as she sounded. "But I guess there isn't anything else to do around this place."

"Right, we'll see you at cribbage then." Betsy gave each of them a hug and headed off with Nel towards Duncan who was restlessly pacing by the door.

The crowd had thinned considerably by the time Brownie came over to Alice, who sat alone on a seat at the side of the hall, Grace and Moira having also left.

"You right there, girlie?" he asked. "We'd best be on the road. Those boys at home will still want dinner."

A man Alice didn't know gave Brownie a friendly slap on the back as they exited the hall. Brownie turned to see who it was, missed the step and stumbled onto the footpath.

"Hey, you cheeky bugger, you nearly made me fall over."

The man laughed. "You silly old fool, Brownie. It was that fifth beer that made you stumble not me. Best you let the lass drive you home."

When Brownie finally got his balance and stood upright, he stopped and looked at Alice as if sizing her up, just like he had on the first day. She didn't know what to think, should she offer to drive? She'd only driven the once at Whipsnade and that was over the paddocks not out on the road with other cars around. She felt the hairs on the back of her neck prickle. Could her driving be any worse than a drunk man? She needed to keep herself safe. If Brownie deemed himself unsafe to drive, then she would have no option. She looked at him and awaited the outcome.

"Ummm, he may just be right," Brownie said. "What you reckon girlie, are you up to driving me home?"

"I suppose so," Alice replied in little more than a mousey squeak.

Brownie fumbled in his pocket for the keys, leaned over to give them to her and burped loudly in her face. She got more than the keys as she inhaled a great whiff of Brownie's beer breath. Sickened by the odour and the thought of the trip home, Alice turned and hurried to the vehicle eager to get it over and done with.

Sitting on the edge of the seat, Alice could just reach the pedals. She tried to remember driving Duncan's truck and what each of the pedals were for, not wanting to confuse them with the Ferguson tractor. She rolled her coat up and stuck it behind her back for support and then put the key in the ignition. Alice closed her eyes as she turned the key and said a tiny 'please get me home safe' prayer. The engine cranked into life and the vehicle lurched forward.

She screamed with fright, rousing Brownie from his drunken slouch.

"What? What the hell?" he yelled.

Luckily there was a spare carpark in front of them and no damage was done to the vehicle.

"Nothing," Alice replied. "I just didn't realise the car was in gear."

"You can drive, can't you, lassie?" Brownie burped again and the car interior filled with the smell of beer.

"Yes," Alice lied. Lies were okay, she told herself, when the truth would only make her predicament worse. She moved the gearstick into neutral, at least the position of the gears seemed to be uniform in all vehicles and turned the key again.

Brownie leaned over and his large hand landed with a thump on her thigh.

"That's the girl, that's the way."

It may have meant to be an encouraging pat, but it felt like an intrusive grope. Alice froze, every muscle in her body tensed and she was right back in the changing room at the department store. A confined space. A male, much larger and stronger than her. With his hand on her, when it had no right to be, regardless of Brownie's intentions. Alice wanted to yell at him, but the words stuck in her throat.

What seemed like minutes passed in the space of a few seconds. Before Alice could react with anything more than a whimper the hand was gone, and Brownie was back on the passenger side of the bench seat.

"Off we go then," he said.

The trip home passed in a blur. Alice was conscious of everything and nothing at the same time. She had to make sure she remembered how to drive. She had to make sure she remembered the way home. But most of all she had to keep herself safe from Brownie. All the blood drained from her hands, her white knuckles clenched the steering wheel and her stomach churned as she strained to manoeuvre the vehicle around the country roads. She felt like vomiting, and it wasn't carsickness.

"Whoa back, lassie." Brownie sat up and braced himself on the door. "You'll miss the driveway if you don't slow down."

Alice's foot jumped off the accelerator and onto the brake. She wished the car had been more like a horse, at least it would have known the way home. By the time the heavy beast had slowed enough to turn, she'd overshot the driveway and had to find reverse and back up. She yanked on the steering wheel and pulled the vehicle off the tar seal into the track that led to Orari Estate. It wasn't until the car was safely parked outside the house that her legs stopped trembling.

CHAPTER

13

Anxious to get to the safety of her room, Alice abandoned Brownie to make his own way inside. She hurried through the empty kitchen but came to an abrupt halt in the passage when she heard her name. Voices were coming from the sitting room. Rangi had company. She couldn't discern all that was being said but knew she was the topic of their conversation. She'd hurried too much to be able to stop the kitchen door slamming shut and announcing her presence. The sitting room went silent. The quiet confirmed it was a conversation that wasn't meant to be overheard.

Alice took a deep breath to calm herself and smoothed down her skirt, an attempt to look casual and relaxed before she passed the open door. As she expected Rangi was sitting up in the cot, pillows behind his back. What she didn't expect was the animated grin on his face. He smiled like that when she'd read something humorous in the book. Was he now laughing at her? And who was he laughing with? It

145

was Fergus. Fergus was back but he looked angry. His legs were planted wide, his arms folded across his chest, and his eyes pierced into Alice's with a stare that was cold, hard, and flinty.

Alice couldn't stay, she didn't have the energy or the courage to confront either of them. Her legs threatened to collapse from beneath her. She rushed to the staircase, held tight onto the balustrade, and climbed the stairs two at a time.

"Alice!"

She heard Rangi's call but ignored it. If they wanted to talk and laugh about her, then let them. She didn't need them. She didn't need any man.

Alice didn't stop until she reached the safety of her bedroom. Leaning back against the closed door she finally breathed again, deep, and long and slow until her heart stopped thundering in her chest. She couldn't stop the tears, she tried but once they started, they kept flowing until her eyes were red, her cheeks were ruddy, and her nose dripped. Eventually, with blurred vision, she made her way to her bed and curled up, hugging her knees into her chest.

It was dark when she awoke still lying in the same position but cold and stiff. Anger festering deep inside her stirred her blood and heated her cheeks. How could men keep treating her like that? Were they all predators? Did she look like a victim? How could she keep herself safe? Alice had more questions than she had answers.

She managed to stand, get undressed, pull her nightie on, and slide back between the sheets. Alice had no idea of the time but even if Brownie had been capable of cooking dinner for everyone, she wanted none of it. She didn't want to go anywhere near him until she had her wits about her. It was yet another reminder that men were not always what they seemed. She recalled her first day at Orari Estate when Brownie had drunk tea from a china cup. That Brownie would never have touched her, would never have laid a hand on her, let alone her thigh.

Alice tossed and turned until sleep eventually claimed her again. It was short-lived. Terrifying images played like a horror movie inside her head. Brownie, Jack, Rangi, Fergus, and worst of all her old boss all loomed larger-than-life in front of her, bloated faces and bulging eyes, gargantuan hands poring at her with twisted fingers and gnarly knuckles. She tried to run away but dare not turn her back on her attackers. She had to stay strong, she had to confront them, not hide. She was not a victim. She could and would take care of herself.

"Just try it," she dared them. "Come on, you'll never beat me!"

The sound of her yelling, echoed in her ears. It was real. Was everything real? Alice dug deep and found the courage she needed to open her eyes. Her room was still clothed in darkness. She waited for her vision to adjust and slowed her breathing. If there were men in her room, she would be able to see them any second now. She balled her fists under the blankets, ready, and primed to ward off any offender.

The seconds ticked by. Alice could make out the top of the stairs and see the end of her bed. She was alone in the room. It had just been another nightmare. She was safe. She'd be safer if she locked the door. Alice climbed out of bed and tiptoed quietly to the bottom of the attic stairs. The cold wooden floorboards sent a chill through her bare feet and a shiver up her spine. The realisation that there was no lock on this door hit the bottom of her stomach with a thud. She wasn't safe.

❧

"What would you like me to do today?" Alice asked Lou at the breakfast table the next morning.

Lou's eyes narrowed as he looked askance at her and rubbed his chin.

"I'm feeling much better," she said. "I think I'm fit and able to do some farm work."

She tried to look as energetic and enthusiastic as possible. The thought of another day stuck in the house with Brownie and Rangi filled her with dread.

"What do you reckon, Brownie?" Lou asked the one person Alice didn't want to pay her any attention.

Brownie coughed. "You're looking a bit tired, lassie, big black bags under your eyes, like you've had a hard night or something."

Alice's eyes bulged and her nostrils flared like a raging bull ready to charge. How dare Brownie accuse her of the very thing he had done? Why didn't he have black bags under his eyes?

"I .... am .... fine!" She sat with her hands on her hips and looked Lou straight in the eye.

"Mmm, one more day I think," Lou said. "Rangi still needs a nursemaid. He's off home tomorrow. It's best you stay with him today."

"But ...."

"No buts, I'm in charge around here. The decision is made. Final." Lou stood and left the room before Alice could protest further.

"Take this through to Rangi, please." Brownie put a plate with toast, scrambled eggs, and a rasher of bacon on the table beside Alice. "Before it gets cold would be good."

Alice looked up to glare at Brownie, but he had already turned back towards the sink full of dirty dishes and was oblivious to her anger. She finished the last few mouthfuls of her own breakfast and left the dirty plate sitting on the table as a final token act of revenge.

"Oh, I thought I could smell bacon." Rangi had already wriggled his way up to a seated position and licked his lips in anticipation. "Thank you, Alice. How are you today? You're not looking so good."

"Not you too!" Alice growled. "I am fine."

"Sorry, I just thought you looked a little tired."

"Well, I had a nightmare, so my sleep wasn't so good."

"What about?" Rangi asked before eating a mouthful of eggs and toast.

Alice considered whether she should relay the gist of the nightmare to Rangi. It would mean revealing things about herself she wasn't prepared to do. Although Rangi's actions over the past week had been nothing but friendly, brotherly even, that could just be because he needed Alice while he was stuck in bed. If she couldn't trust him, who could she trust? The realisation that the answer to that question was herself, and no-one else, felt very lonely. Deciding that attack was the best means of defence, Alice's demeanour and tone of voice changed.

"It's all your fault anyway!"

Rangi gulped down his mouthful and looked wide eyed at Alice.

"What?" he asked, a confused look on his face. "What's all my fault?"

"You, you and Fergus, talking about me when you had no right to."

"No, we weren't."

"Yes, you were." Alice's fists thumped into her hips. "I heard you."

Rangi's shoulders raised up towards his ears and he looked sheepish.

"Okay, you got me, but they were only nice things."

"Huh! You just lied to me. Why should I believe anything you say now?"

"Because …" Rangi smiled as if his being cheery would cheer Alice too. "Because Fergus was just saying how much he likes you."

Alice shook her head in denial and looked everywhere but at Rangi while she considered what he'd just told her. Was he lying again? Trying to placate her with empty compliments. Of course, he was. Fergus had glared at her with such animosity; that wasn't how you looked at someone you liked. And besides, why would he like her anyway? She was nothing to look at, her mother should have called her Jane, plain Jane. And even if he wasn't shallow and got past her looks, he would surely know she was damaged. Nobody wanted damaged goods, least of all a handsome young man like Fergus.

"I don't believe you," she said. "Besides, you're leaving tomorrow. If you want to hear the end of the story, we'd best get onto it."

"You can change the subject all you like, Alice," Rangi said. "It doesn't change the truth."

"Then why doesn't Fergus tell me himself?" Alice huffed. "I'll tell you why, because it isn't true."

"He's busy working on the bridge repairs."

"It's Saturday, he wouldn't be working there today."

"He's working every day until the bridge is repaired," Rangi continued. "As we, of all people, know, it was a big storm, and it did a lot of damage."

Alice grabbed *Murder on the Orient Express* and opened the book where they had left off.

"Alice!"

She shook her head again. "If you keep on about it, there will be a murder at Orari Estate, in this very room, and I won't be the victim."

Rangi raised his palms in front of his chest. "Okay, I won't say another word."

It was late in the afternoon when Alice finally put the closed book back in the bookcase. She yawned, stretched her arms, and arched her spine to get the blood flowing again.

"Cassetti deserved to die," Rangi said.

"Of course, he did." Alice sounded indignant. "He kidnapped an innocent child and murdered her."

"His death was a bit brutal though," Rangi continued. "If only he'd locked his cabin door, Poirot might have discovered his true identity and got him arrested."

Alice's focus drifted away, as thoughts of attackers and locks, justice and punishment raced through her head.

"I'd like to be able to lock my door," she mumbled.

"What?" Rangi asked. "I didn't catch that."

Alice shook her head and looked at Rangi. "Nothing."

"It wasn't nothing." Rangi's dark eyebrows drew together like storm clouds. "Why do you want to lock your door, Alice?"

"You said you didn't hear me." She attempted to distract Rangi. "You lied again."

"Don't change the subject, Alice." Rangi shook his finger at her. "Has something happened? Was it more than just a nightmare that kept you awake last night? Are you lying to me?"

Alice wished she'd kept her mouth shut. Rangi didn't need to know about her problems. He wasn't any use to her, stuck in the cot with a broken leg. He was leaving tomorrow anyway. But …. it was nice that he seemed concerned about her welfare. She was holding herself together until he showed he cared. Now, her eyes welled up, her bottom lip trembled, and she had to turn away and look out the window to stifle the tears that threatened.

Rangi reached his hand out to grab hers, but she flinched, desperate to avoid his touch, desperate to avoid the touch of any man.

"There's a lock on the door to the whare," Rangi changed tack and suggested.

"How do you know?" Alice snapped. "When have you been in there?"

"I used to sleep there." Rangi spoke calmly despite Alice's accusatory tone.

"Why?" Alice demanded.

Rangi laughed. "You've spent too much time with me, Alice. You've forgotten I'm Maori."

"You've got a room in the house," Alice said. "You're not treated any different than the others."

"Not now," Rangi said. "But I had to prove myself. When I first arrived …."

Rangi shook his head and left the sentence hanging.

At that moment, Alice felt more akin with Rangi than with any of the others. They were different, but they were being treated the same, being made to prove themselves worthy of being at Orari Estate.

"I'd help you move your stuff." Rangi smiled. "But as you know, I'm not much use to anyone at the moment."

Alice blushed. It was like Rangi had read her thoughts.

"You've been a great help. Thank you, Rangi." Alice felt like a weight had been lifted off her shoulders. "I might go and move my stuff now, that is, if you don't need me anymore."

"Don't let me stand in your way."

Rangi and Alice both laughed at the irony of those words.

This time when Alice took the stairs two at a time, it was with energy and excitement for her move into the whare. She grabbed her bag and stuffed all her clothes and toiletries untidily into it. She untucked the bedclothes and rolled them up. With the bag hooked over one shoulder and the bedroll tucked under the other arm, Alice went back downstairs.

"Bye," she called out as she passed the sitting room door.

Rangi's cheerful laugh echoed down the passage after her.

Brownie was in his usual position at the kitchen bench. It seemed a never-ending task to keep so many fed, but Alice was glad he was pre-occupied as she tried to sneak past.

"Where are you off to?" Brownie turned and wiped his hands on the tea towel slung over his shoulder.

"Blast," Alice grumbled. Brownie must have eyes in the back of his head. "I'm moving out to the whare. I'm going to sleep out there from now on."

"You do realise there is no power out there."

"Yes," she replied. *But there's a lock to keep you and everyone else out.*

Brownie must have seen the determined look on Alice's face and opened the door for her.

"Would you like a hand with that?" he offered.

"No." Her reply came swift and sharp. "Thank you," she added, remembering her manners, and not wanting Brownie to pry any further.

"Okay then, I'll carry on preparing dinner," Brownie said as he closed the door behind her.

Walking into the whare was like lying back in a warm bath, all the tension drained from Alice's shoulders. She put the bedding and her bag down on the cot and returned to test the lock. It slid into place with a reassuring thud. Her deep, gratifying sigh was the only sound in the whare as she leaned back against the door and eyed her new room.

It was a small building with its roof slung low to the ground but still plenty big enough for Alice. It felt solid, the thick walls, plastered in a biscuity colour, appeared to have been there forever. Wooden rafters supported an iron roof Alice imagined would shelter her, while raindrops beat a rhythm on winter nights. She was happy to share the space with the Daddy Longlegs that had made a home in the corner.

"You keep the other spiders at bay," she said to the insect. "And we'll get along just fine."

154

A hint of mustiness indicated Rangi had probably neglected to clean the whare. She'd borrow a dusting cloth and the broom from inside and give it the once over. Alice pictured the bric-a-brac store in Geraldine, its window frontage a muddled glimpse of the treasure held inside. She planned to visit when she next got to go to town, to shop for an old painting to brighten up the walls, maybe a dog or some kittens so if she couldn't cuddle the real thing at least she could look at them. A rag rug for the floor, like the one she had at Whipsnade, would be good on cold nights. If she couldn't find one, perhaps she could buy a bag of rags and make one herself. And a pretty vase to replace the glass jar she'd been using. Some perfumed roses or some lavender from the garden would take away any remaining odours. Alice clapped her hands as she surveyed the room and smiled as if it was already finished.

She jumped at a knock at the door, her smile disappearing in an instant.

"Who is it?" she asked, glad that she had the power to decide who entered her space.

"Brownie."

Alice flinched. He was the last person she wanted knocking on the door.

"What do you want?"

"I've got your raincoat."

A raincoat. Her raincoat. The proof that she was worthy of being at the farm was on the other side of the whare door. She had no choice, she had to open it, to allow Brownie into her space. Alice slid the lock back and inched the door open.

"Sorry," Brownie said as he handed her the folded oilskin. It felt like a peace offering, an unspoken apology for

Brownie's actions, his drunkenness, his trespassing hand. "I forgot to give it to you."

"Thank you," Alice said as she lifted the raincoat to her face and inhaled its protective newness.

CHAPTER

14

A rejuvenating sleep in the comfort and safety of the whare had Alice leaving with a skip in her step and a smile that came from her heart and beamed from ear to ear. The noise of a vehicle stopped her on the back step of the house. An old jalopy came into view, slowly chugging its way up the driveway. Whether the speed of the vehicle could be attributed to a safe driver, or a decrepit vehicle was debatable. Alice assumed it was the latter when she saw the truck, it was red, rust red, probably more rust than its faded red paint job. A headlight hung precariously, saved only by the connecting wires, the glass cracked and half missing. One side of the tray had no sideboard, the other was fractured and incapable of protecting a load.

The morning sun reflected on the windscreen; Alice could only see the silhouettes of two people, until the vehicle pulled up in front of her. She saw their dark skin before discerning their facial features. Rangi's parents. The woman in the passenger seat had Rangi's smile, at least the teeth were the same, her lips were etched in dark ink. An elaborate tattoo flowed from her bottom lip, covering her chin like the fresh tendrils of a vine unfurling. Alice was captivated. Although she knew it wasn't polite to do so, she stood staring at the couple.

The man climbed out of the truck first. His head of greying wiry hair nodded a silent greeting before he ambled, with the aid of an ornately carved walking stick, around to the passenger door to open it for his wife. The act earned Alice's respect, watching the gentleman reminded her of her grandfather. He too would have opened the door for her grandmother, but he wouldn't be standing here waiting to welcome the Maori couple.

Alice cleared her throat and looked at the closed door behind her. Perhaps she should just go inside and let Brownie deal with the visitors, but Alice wasn't her grandfather, she didn't have to treat these people differently because they were Maori. If her week with Rangi had showed her anything it was that she should keep an open mind, not be judgemental, and get to know the person beneath the skin. That was where the true value of friendship lay. If she desired others to do that for her, then she had to be prepared to return the kindness. Anyway, it was too late, when Alice turned back around the couple were standing in front of her.

"Ah, *wahine toa.*" The man grinned a toothless grin, stepped forward and extended his hand. "*Kia ora*, Alice."

He knew her name. Rangi must have talked about her to his parents. Would his words have been complimentary?

Alice wished she taken time over the past week to learn some more Maori. Now the opportunity was ending, and she'd never know what *wahine toa* meant.

Grateful that Rangi had taught her *kia ora,* Alice replied with her Pakeha pronunciation marring the words. Her eyes went wide, and she sucked in a breath as the man clasped her hand and leaned forward. His breath touched her skin before his broad nose pressed into hers and their foreheads brushed together. Terrified of having a stranger invade her space, Alice stayed alert to whatever she may have to rescue herself from. As the seconds ticked by, a calmness seemed to flow from the man to Alice; she saw that his eyes were closed, so she shut hers too.

"I'll go and tell Rangi you're here," she said nervously when he finally pulled away.

Alice turned to open the door, only to find it already unlatched and Fergus barricading the entrance in that same stance he had the other night, legs spread, arms folded across his chest and a scowl on his face. Alice hadn't a clue what she'd done to deserve it.

At times she was grateful for her tiny stature, and this was one such time. She ducked and darted between Fergus and the doorframe before he had time to react. She skipped through the kitchen, calling out to Brownie and Rangi as she went.

"Rangi's *koro and kuia* are here. Rangi, your *koro and kuia* are here."

"My grandparents?" Rangi asked when Alice reached the sitting room. "How did they get here?"

"In a truck."

"That'll be my Papa and Whaea, my father and mother, not my grandparents." Rangi laughed. "Wait until I tell them what you said."

"Oh, no, don't do that." Alice coloured with guilt. "You've already been talking to them. What did you say? And don't lie. They said *wahine toa*, what does that mean?"

"When you pronounce it properly, waa-hee-nee toe-ah, means warrior woman." Rangi swung his legs around over the side of the cot ready to stand.

"Why would they say that to me?" Alice asked.

"Because Alice - get my crutches for me please—because you saved my life. You had the strength of a warrior and pulled me from the river."

"The horse did." Alice grabbed the crutches. "Not me."

"You can deny it all you like but I know I would not be here if it wasn't for you. End of story." Rangi hooked a crutch under each of his arms and left the room. "Can you bring my bag please."

Someone had packed Rangi's things into a canvas satchel and left it on the settee. Alice hoisted its strap over her shoulder and followed Rangi.

"You sure don't travel light, do you?" Alice slumped the bag down on the kitchen floor expecting to see Rangi's parents sitting at the table.

"See you in a few months, Brownie." Rangi passed through the kitchen and manoeuvred himself awkwardly down the back stairs.

There wasn't going to be any grand farewell, nor was there a welcome for Rangi's parents. It was as if that barrier called racism was all but invisible. Alice swallowed hard, feeling embarrassed and ashamed that she was a part of it.

She picked the satchel up and lugged it outside to the back of the truck. If she was a warrior woman, then she should be able to lift it onto the tray. She heaved and got it halfway but didn't have the strength to stop it from falling to the ground again.

Confirmation thought Alice. Confirmation Rangi and his parents had it wrong.

Fergus appeared at her side, and without acknowledging her presence, grabbed the handle of the bag in one hand and swung it up onto the tray.

"I'll put it behind the cab, Rangi," he said. "You can use it as a bolster."

Alice stood back and watched Fergus help Rangi onto the back of the truck. Warmth filled her, Fergus too, saw beyond the colour of Rangi's skin. He treated him the same as any other man.

"Come visit," Rangi said as he slid his way to the front of the tray. "When you get a day off."

"Yeah." Fergus looked tired. "Whenever that is. I'd better get to work now. See you, Rangi."

Fergus glanced at Alice before he headed down the driveway to the ride that awaited him. Again, she couldn't decipher any meaning from his look, other than there was no dimple winking at her. Whatever friendship they'd had, seemed to be lost forever.

"*Kia ora*, Alice," Rangi yelled over the rumble of the truck engine.

"*Kia ora*, Rangi," Alice echoed back to him before confusion furrowed her brow. Why had she said hello to Rangi when he was leaving? She wished she'd taken the opportunity to learn more about the Maori ways over the past week. Now, that too, seemed to be lost forever.

She waved as the jalopy ambled its way back down the driveway. The lack of speed now a necessity with Rangi wincing at every bump. Again, Alice wished she'd done more. She turned and headed back inside. At least now, Lou would have no excuse but to let her do farm work.

"Right, lass," Lou said. "Get your breakfast into you. There is work to be done."

Jack, Danny, Lou, and Brownie were already tucking into steaming plates of porridge and another plate sat awaiting at her usual seat. Alice was back among the fold; pride, determination and a sense of belonging swelled her chest and made her feel six feet tall.

"What job would you like me to do today?" Square-shouldered she looked directly at Lou.

"We've been working on the fences, repairing those damaged in the storm. There's just the one paddock left, the one where you and Rangi were."

Alice swallowed. She pretended it was just a mouthful of porridge, not the sense of dread she felt.

"The water has finally drained away," Lou continued. "It's just a mud hole now, with debris everywhere. Can't tell the extent of the damage to the fences until we pull the rubbish off them so that's today's job."

It seemed a job that would allow Alice to show her worth. She ate quickly.

"We'd better get going then," she said running her spoon around her plate to get the last of the porridge.

"You and Jack can make a start. Danny and I will feed out and check on the sheep. Then the wagon will be free to load the rubbish on. When it dries out, it can be burnt."

Alice had stood, ready to take her plate to the bench. Jack's name sat her back down. She glanced across at him, his hair slicked back with Brylcreem. He was smiling but all Alice saw was an evil sneer.

A shiver ran down her spine. She closed her eyes, inhaled deeply, and stood. Once again, she had to draw on her inner strength to keep her safe. She really hoped she was a *wahine toa*.

Only pockets of the paddock resembled something that could sustain an animal, the rest was covered in a layer of silt. It was as if the river had swallowed the land and regurgitated the waste. Alice surveyed the area and knew at once this job wasn't going to be finished any time soon.

She stood behind Jack and shut out the image of his unlaundered long johns, grateful that his dirty, baggy overalls hid any reminder that he was a man.

"You start here, and I'll start at the other end of the fence." Alice moved away before Jack had time to suggest another option that would have them working together.

The humps and hollows of the paddock sat hidden beneath the silt. Alice lost her footing when her gumboot sank into a hole. The mud slurped, reluctant to release its catch, as she pulled her booted foot free.

With ominous grey clouds lingering over the mountain ranges, Alice had worn her new raincoat as a precaution. The rain stayed at bay and the warmth of the raincoat had her glowing by the time she reached the other side of the paddock. Wearing the coat while she cleared the fence line wasn't practicable but tainting its newness with the mud that caked the fence didn't sit comfortably.

Alice set to work pulling the reeds, grass, and willow branches from the fence. Caked mud served as an adhesive to bind them to the wires and a wedge of mud accumulated under her fingernails by the time, she had freed sufficient fence to create a hanger for her raincoat. She imagined Moira's reaction if she'd been assigned the same task and had a little chuckle.

It was much easier to work without the constraints of the coat but every so often Alice glanced back to check it remained safely where she'd put it. The river water was still a muddy brown, but the ferocity of the storm had settled to a steady flow that encouraged Alice to do the same. She worked methodically, clearing each segment of the fence between the battens, before moving onto the next, adding to the pile of debris building behind her.

Danny and Lou arrived with the wagon hitched to Trigger and Barnaby. Trigger stood calmly but Barnaby's ears were forward, and his nostrils flared, returning to the riverside had him on high alert. Alice rested her forehead on his neck and rubbed the underside.

"It's alright, Barnaby, you're safe," she whispered to the horse. She smiled at the irony, her the smallest one here trying to convince the biggest one that he was safe.

"Good work, Alice." Lou began forking the pile onto the wagon. "You keep going and we'll load the wagon."

Alice's cheeks, already red from exertion, coloured a deeper shade on hearing Lou's gratitude. It was the first time the man had offered praise. She looked back over the paddock to compare Jack's efforts and shone with pride seeing she had cleared twice as much fence as him.

It seemed pointless for Alice to create more work by adding to the pile, so she carried loads of debris direct to the wagon. The front of her overalls was covered in mud, but it would wash out, just like the mud that she'd dragged through her hair as she pushed it off her face. If they didn't get this job finished today, she'd remember to tie her hair back tomorrow.

The wagon was full, and Danny and Lou were ready to go and dump the load.

"I'll grab your raincoat for you, Alice," Danny offered.

Alice gasped. Surprise at Danny's offer, turned to anger at herself for forgetting her new raincoat and then flowed into gratitude that someone else was thinking about her.

"Thank you," she said, her eyes glowing.

She watched as Danny grabbed the coat and headed back to the wagon. His wooden leg found one of the muddy hollows and sent him sideways. He splayed his arms to break his fall. Alice's coat hit the earth first, Danny landed solidly on it.

Alice froze. 'My raincoat' she wanted to scream.

Danny was uninjured and hauled himself up. He picked up the coat and shook it. Drips of mud plopped to the ground like the tears Alice itched to cry for her soiled coat. That she hadn't been concerned about Danny being hurt only occupied her thoughts for a split second.

"Sorry about that." Danny threw the coat behind the wagon seat. "I'll hose it off later."

"Right, we're off then." Lou climbed aboard the wagon. "Another pile like that for when we get back would be great."

Alice huffed. She'd never been on a roller coaster, only seen a picture of one on the front page of the newspaper when Playland had opened for the centenary celebrations in Auckland, but it felt like her life was one big roller coaster of ups and downs and twists and turns and you never knew what was coming next. Just when she thought things were going to plan and looking up, something beyond her control, would suck the air out of her lungs.

She gave herself a few seconds to sulk as the wagon crossed the paddock. Realising the futility of sulking, she went back to her job. Yanking at the reeds she tossed them away as if each handful was a frustration to be extracted and cast aside. As the second pile grew, her mood improved even to the point she started humming. It wasn't a tune that had a name that Alice knew, just a happy beat that lifted her spirits.

Her hands stopped in mid-air, and she drew a sharp, painful breath as the roller coaster ride took another rapid spiral that turned her stomach inside out. The hum caught in her throat and stopped her retching as a tiny carcass sat in the reeds in front of her. The river had dragged the lamb from safety, sucked the life from its lungs and discarded its broken frame to be strung on the wires of the fence. It was a burial of sorts but not one Alice was going to allow. When freed from the fence, the limp body sagged in her hands. She lay the dead lamb on the ground and stomped around until her feet found a hollow. Down on her knees she clawed at the earth until the hollow resembled a small grave.

"Goodbye, little lamb," she whispered as she lay the small stiff body in the grave and dragged the dirt back. "It's a cruel world isn't it. I'll keep battling on in your memory."

CHAPTER

15

Dirt was deeply embedded under Alice's nails. A quick scrub in the laundry tub failed to clean her nails or ease the redness of her fingers and hands. She dreamed of soaking in a hot bath, but that would have to wait until the job was finished.

Danny wasn't true to his word; her still muddy raincoat hung on a hook in the porch. Getting wet hands again was the last thing she wanted to do at the end of the day, but the coat deserved to be clean. She hosed it down and left it to drip dry before stowing it away in the whare. It wasn't as if anyone would steal her coat, it was far too small for any of the men, she just wanted to keep it nearby, like a symbol of her security, safe from the weather, safe in her job.

It took another two days before the fence line was cleared. Fortunately, the rain stayed away although the temperature dropped with a dumping of snow on the Southern Alps. The landscape was like a choice of icing for a cake, the whiteness on top of the Alps sat in contrast to the paddock that remained coated in chocolate. Alice would normally choose chocolate but after days of squelching through mud, its stale odour seeping into her pores, she longed for the cleansing purity of the snow.

"That's a big job done," Lou said as the last of the piles was loaded onto the wagon, Alice and Jack having met in the middle of the fence.

Well, Jack might say it was the middle, but Alice knew she'd done more than her fair share and it was more like a sixty-forty split in her favour. The only favour it gained her was a sense of pride which she carried with her head held high.

"We'll have to come back tomorrow and replace the broken battens," Lou said.

"The strainer closest to the river might need replacing too." Alice spoke as if she'd been fencing for decades but began to question herself when she saw the strange looks the others sent her way. "The river has gouged out the base, the silt mightn't be strong enough to hold it in place," she said justifying the temerity of her comment.

Lou cleared his throat. "We'll check it out tomorrow."

They arrived back at the sheds the same time as Fergus pulled in with the tractor and the sun dipped down behind the hills taking what little warmth there had been in the day with it.

"All finished?" Lou asked. "It'll be good to have the tractor to help with fencing. And to have the bridge fixed."

"It's still one lane," Fergus replied, "but it's drivable."

"Good," Lou said. "I've got a phone call to make before dinner. I'll see you all back at the house."

Danny and Jack left to take Trigger and Barnaby back to the paddock. Alice put the forks back where she'd found them and turned around to find herself alone with Fergus. There was an awkward silence where they looked at each other. Alice knew her face wouldn't give away her thoughts, because she herself didn't know what the jumble of emotions racing around her head meant.

"Hello, Alice." Fergus and his dimple smiled.

Alice sucked in a breath, surprised by his friendly tone. She'd missed his dimple winking at her. Hell, she'd missed Fergus, but she wasn't going to admit that aloud.

"Hello, Fergus."

They stood facing each other, seemingly afraid to move, least they destroy whatever was happening between them. Danny and Jack's approaching voices spoiled the moment.

"I'm starving." Fergus patted his stomach. "Shall we head over for dinner?"

A shaky laugh escaped Alice. She was unsure whether to be relieved that the moment was over or relaxed that the tension between them had eased. They turned and walked back to the house, Alice taking two steps to Fergus's one.

Dinner was sausages, mashed potatoes and silver beet, a plain and simple meal that did what it needed to do, filling the stomachs of the hungry workers.

"If you want a bath tonight, you'll have to share the water," Brownie announced as he brought an apple pie to the table for dessert.

"What?" Danny laughed. "All this water and not a drop to bath in."

"Too much water," Lou explained. "It's cracked the guttering and the weight pulled the spouting out, smashing it on the ground. I've phoned but they don't have any pipe in stock, it has to come over from Christchurch."

Alice closed her eyes and dropped her head; a bath was all she had dreamed of. Finally soaking in a hot bath after three days of slog. Finally getting the mud out from under her fingernails. Finally, being able to put clean sheets on her bed. Now, the water might be cold before her turn came around, it might be dirtied with the mud from other people's fingernails. Her anticipation was replaced with disappointment.

"Surely the tank is full though?" Danny asked.

"Only discovered the damage today," Brownie said. "It must have happened in the storm, so no water has been collected since then. We must conserve what is left."

"Alice." Lou's mention of her name filled Alice with dread, but it was unfounded. "You can go first."

She grinned and gulped down the last of her apple pie, ready to race from the kitchen before anyone protested.

"Only use as much water as you need. The others can add a little more as they go."

Lou's comment removed any delusions Alice may have had about getting the first bath because she was special. It was simply because she was the smallest. At least sometimes that worked in her favour.

✤

If Alice had been Maori, you would have thought the bath water had rinsed the pigment from her skin. She climbed out and towelled herself off. She'd never felt so grateful for being the smallest.

171

In her hurry, she'd neglected to think ahead and bring spare clothes. Putting her dirty overalls back on wasn't an option. Alice wrapped the towel around her torso, bundled her clothes up under her arm and tiptoed from the bathroom hoping she could make it out to the whare without being seen.

Sometimes, she was so naïve. Fergus was the first person who saw her, nearly all of her as the bundle of clothes escaped her grip and the towel threatened to follow.

"Hello, Alice." Again, his dimple winked at her. Fergus bent down and retrieved the clothes. "Here you are. Don't catch a chill."

"Thank you." Alice turned to head down the stairs.

"Where are you going?" Fergus's face screwed up in confusion. "Your bedroom is this way."

"I've moved. I'm sleeping in the whare."

"Oh." Fergus nodded his head as if he understood but when his dimple disappeared, and his scowl reappeared Alice knew that wasn't the case.

Should she explain? Did she want to? Did she owe Fergus an explanation? No, came the answer to all three questions. Besides it was cold standing in the passage.

"Excuse me," she said. "I need to get dressed."

"Yes, you do," Fergus said with a commanding tone that Alice didn't think she deserved.

She stomped away. She passed Danny on the stairs but didn't speak. The thump of his wooden leg on every step was like an exclamation mark reinforcing her annoyance. She went through the kitchen with a demeanour that threatened anyone who dared to speak to her. No-one did. Brownie opened the door so she could pass straight through.

"Aaargh!" Her yell of frustration resounded off the whare walls. Why did life require her to constantly be answerable to men?

The only light in the whare was that seeping through from the house. After her eyes adjusted to the darkness, she made her way to the bedside table to light the candle. She usually found the flame comforting but now the shadows it cast onto the wall seemed to be taunting her, dancing a spell-binding ritual with sinister intentions.

Alice pulled her nightie on, climbed between the sheets, and snuffed the candle out. She wasn't going to allow a mere candle to frighten her. Her thoughts took over that role. She was back on an imaginary roller coaster ride as the highs and lows of her time at Orari Estate replayed before her. She saw the faces of the men who now seemed to have control of her life, sometimes friendly, sometimes threatening, sometimes lecherous. Did she just imagine it all or were they truly those things? She'd misjudged Rangi; by the mere colour of his skin, she thought him to be trouble, until he showed he was anything but.

She'd thought Fergus to be friendly, even brotherly apart from the kiss, brothers didn't do that, but now he mostly just scowled at her. Perhaps that was how big brothers saw little sisters, annoying and only to be tolerated. Alice had no siblings, she didn't know.

Maybe Jack had been wrongly tarred with the brush of his Brylcreem. Just because the man who had violated her greased his hair with the oil, didn't mean all men who did the same were guilty. As for Brownie, Alice had trusted him, but he was the one who'd overstepped an unspoken boundary.

Maybe everything was simply her fault. She brought it on herself. Her lack of forethought tonight certainly bore that out. What kind of woman walks around in a house full of men, wrapped only in a towel? She could hear the high pitch of her mother's drunken voice.

"Behave like that and you'll get everything you deserve."

There wasn't much Alice believed her mother got right but these words rang true.

Rays of light were sneaking through the sacking at the window when Alice woke, unsure how much sleep she'd had. She remembered tossing and turning and the dishevelled blankets on the bed confirmed her restlessness. There was dampness in the air, and her nose, acting as a thermometer, told her the temperature had dropped. Alice listened for the familiar pitter-patter of rain, but the roof remained silent.

She would be fencing today, so with a view to acting responsibly and being prepared, Alice climbed out of bed to check the weather. The floor felt icy beneath her feet, and she put on clean socks before heading to the door.

Unlocked and unlatched the door fell inward with the weight of a dumping of snow. Alice was mesmerised by the blanket of white. She could count on one hand the number of times she'd seen real snow, been close enough to touch it, and smell its cleanliness. Still in her nightie the chill edged up her bare legs. She shivered.

"Silly girl," she growled to herself. "You'll get everything you deserve, and it will be a chill if you stand around in your nightie in the snow."

Alice removed her socks and kicked the snow back out the door with her bare feet. They were red, cold, and wet by the time she had the door closed so she scampered back to her bed, climbed beneath the blankets, and rubbed her toes until they warmed.

"Snow." Alice giggled with the excitement of a child. She wished she was back at Whipsnade with the other land girls. They could have had a snow fight, built a snowman and stolen a carrot from Nel's garden for its nose. Would men do that? She didn't imagine so. Their snow fights would be more like a competition or a battle to see who they could hit and how hard.

Alice dressed warmly, double layers of everything and her raincoat over the top. She hesitated at the door, reluctant to damage the purity of the white blanket covering the ground. She stepped lightly, each footprint leaving an imprint that she hoped the falling flakes would erase. Free of the eaves, she stopped and raised her face to the sky, letting the snowflakes land on her cheeks, powder her nose and moisten her tongue which she poked out like a naughty child. There was a wonderment to the snow, like stardust falling from the sky, so magical and lively but so serene. She could have stood in one spot forever, become her own snowman, but following last night's motherly advice, she knew if she did so, she'd get just what she deserved. Reluctantly she headed into the house for breakfast.

"Looks like we're in for a long cold winter," Lou grumbled. "First the flooding and now this. Someone's got it in for us this year."

"Morning, Alice." Brownie greeted her. "Cold in the whare, was it?"

Alice smiled. "Not when I was asleep."

"There's an extra blanket in the hallway cupboard if you need one."

Brownie's concern was appreciated. "Thank you," Alice said as she sat at the table, grateful for the steaming plate of porridge that he placed in front of her. "I'd like to get a rag rug for the floor when someone is next going to town. I'm sure there will be something at the bric-a-brac store."

"I usually head in on Fridays for supplies, you can get a ride in then if Lou doesn't need you on the farm." Brownie raised his eyebrows at Lou as he made the offer.

Alice swallowed, not a mouthful of porridge, but the dread that sat in her throat. Did she need the rug enough to risk another ride in a vehicle with Brownie? Surely, he wouldn't be drinking if he was going to get supplies? She'd like to believe that what happened was only because of the alcohol. That didn't excuse Brownie's actions, but it did make a trip to town possible. Alice waited for Lou's response.

"We'll have to wait and see," he said, rubbing his chin between thumb and forefinger. "If this snow continues and there are new lambs to be rescued, there won't be trips to town for anyone."

Alice's eyes sparkled. New-born lambs. She imagined their tiny pink noses poking out from the snow. Alice would happily forget her rug and rescue lambs. She could even keep those that needed feeding in the whare, no-one would complain, no-one need know. Duncan wasn't here to growl at her.

Fergus's spot was empty, and she wondered if he'd gone back to work at the bridge after all. The door opened behind her, and the question was resolved as he took his place at the table. A small child could have sat between them, but Alice still felt his closeness.

"Morning, everyone," he said, but his eyes met Alice's when they both turned, and she felt the greeting was hers and hers alone.

"Right." Lou garnered everyone's attention. "Now that everyone is here, we'd best decide the plan for the day."

Alice thought Lou would already have made all the important decisions and her assessment proved correct.

"The sheep are in two mobs. Jack and Danny, you take Barnaby and the wagon and feed out to the old ewes. None of them should have lambed yet but have a look just in case the ram jumped the fence. Fergus and Alice take the other horses and head out to the back paddocks. The hoggets should be okay but we'll need to bring them in closer so we can feed out. Put them in the rushes paddock, at least they'll have something to eat until we feed out and they can shelter under the macrocarpas."

Fergus was tucking into his breakfast when Alice looked his way. There was no confirmation that he shared her excitement at working together.

"Alice!" Lou's tone demanded her attention. "There should be sixty hoggets. Do you think you can count them?"

"Yes … yes, I can." She was being tested again. While her verbal response didn't sound at all certain, Alice was determined she wouldn't fail this time.

"Now everyone be careful. I think the snow's been falling most of the night so there will be a good covering. We don't want any more accidents, we're already a man down with Rangi gone."

CHAPTER

16

When they reached the horse paddock, Barnaby, Trigger and Misty were frolicking about like children playing a game of tag. They whinnied and snorted as they stomped their hooves and created mishmash trails of trampled snow.

"They're having fun." Alice watched her warm breath float away into the cool morning.

"The first snowfall is always fun." Danny caught up to the rest of them. Walking with a wooden leg in snow was more difficult and left a distinctive trail. Footprint, square, footprint, square. "Wait until you've been out in it for days. It's not fun when the cold has burrowed its way into your bones."

The rubber of Alice's gumboots already felt cold. She wondered whether rubber provided more insulation than wood. She'd never heard Danny complain. He just got on with life and didn't speak of whatever had caused his disability. Sometimes his eyes had a faraway look as if he'd transported himself to another time, another place. Then after moments of stillness, his whole body would shake and he'd be back, attentive to whatever was happening.

Watching Danny was a reminder to Alice that you never knew what made other people who they were. That you couldn't let whatever happened in your past colour your present, it did, but you didn't have to give into it. She wouldn't give in to hers. Alice was strong and she wouldn't be a victim again. She was lucky, at least she still had both legs.

Her thoughts turned to Fergus. What made him a white feather, a conscientious objector? If he hadn't got into the fight at the races, she would never have known. She'd like the opportunity to ask him, one day.

"Alice!" Fergus's call pulled her out of her reverie. He was holding the gate open. "Are you coming?"

They caught the horses, saddled them up and headed out. Alice listened for the crunch of snow with every footfall, watched as the snowflakes splotched her raincoat and disappeared, and inhaled the purity of the air, filling her lungs with what felt like a new beginning.

The reins sat loosely in her gloved hand as she let Fergus and Barnaby lead the way and Misty follow at a safe pace. They passed the paddock where the crop had been sown. It was simply a square of white, framed by a fence whose bottom wire was peeking out from the snow. Alice hoped the crop would survive being encased in ice or all her ploughing efforts would be in vain.

Further out, the ewes sat in mobs, a united façade so that each had a side protected from the elements. Alice interpreted their bleating as a cry for food.

"Your hay is coming," she called out.

Fergus chuckled. "Sheep don't have the biggest of brains, Alice. I don't think they speak English."

"Baa. Baa. Baa." Alice bought into Fergus's teasing.

By the time they reached the back paddocks the wind had joined the fray and flurries of snow whipped in from the south. Alice's raincoat protected her body but the gap between the hem of her coat and the rim of her gumboots was cold and wet.

Fergus stopped and they surveyed the paddock. It was difficult to discern where snow stopped, and sheep sat.

"I think we'll head to the trees, maybe the sheep will come to us," he suggested.

If what Fergus had said were true, Alice doubted the sheep were that intelligent but sheltering under the trees sounded good and she turned Misty towards the macrocarpas.

A dozen sheep huddled amongst the sprawling roots of each of the trees.

"The sensible ones," Alice said.

She dismounted and walked Misty to a space between the trees. The branches meshed overhead and provided an umbrella that the snow hadn't permeated. Misty nickered in appreciation and shook herself. Alice did the same.

"Phew! That's better." Fergus came to stand beside Alice. "We'll wait here until the wind drops, otherwise we're likely to leave half the mob behind."

Alice looked out from under the trees. She didn't know much about snow, but it didn't look like the wind was going to drop anytime soon. There were worse places to be stuck and worse people to be stuck with. The familiarity that Fergus and Alice had previously shared was missing and Alice struggled to think of anything to say. Silence engulfed the space, hung awkwardly like a noose, as if saying the wrong thing would mean the end of everything.

Alice couldn't handle the silence any more than she could handle the thought of saying the wrong thing.

"Did you enjoy fixing the bridge?" The question stumbled from her. It was a start, nothing that would cause any friction, good or bad.

Fergus paused, as if he was organising his thoughts. "It was dangerous. The river was still high. We had to secure the poles. We tied ropes to those who had to go in the water, to keep them safe. Much like you had to with Rangi."

Alice felt her body heat rise, her cheeks colour. Fergus had turned the conversation back to her and she felt uncomfortable.

"I did what I had to do," she replied with a shrug as if her efforts were unimportant.

"You did more than you had to do Alice." Fergus coughed and shifted from one foot to the other. "The question is why."

"Why?" Alice thought the why was obvious. You wouldn't leave someone to drown if you could rescue them.

"Why did you rescue Rangi? Why did you spend the week with him?"

Alice turned and looked at Fergus, tried to interpret his questions. Was Fergus racist? Did he think Rangi shouldn't have been saved because he was Maori? She'd believed Fergus and Rangi to be friends. Fergus's face gave nothing away, his eyes bored into hers with almost an accusation.

"Come on, Alice." Fergus placed his hand on Alice's arm. "Don't play dumb. I just want to know what Rangi is to you?"

"Dumb!" Alice choked on the insult as rage simmered in her belly. "I'm not dumb and I'm not playing."

"So, you admit it then." Fergus removed his hand and took on that stance that Alice had seen too often lately. "You like Rangi."

She mirrored Fergus's posture, her fists thumping into her hips, incredulous at his accusation, his assumption about her feelings for Rangi. If they hadn't been in the middle of nowhere in a snowstorm she would have stomped off.

"Are you jealous? Is that why you keep looking at me with disgust?"

"No." Fergus's eyes went wide.

"No what? No, you're not jealous or no you're not looking at me with disgust?" She couldn't believe anyone would be jealous of her but plenty of people, her own mother included, had looked at her with contempt, with looks that said she wasn't worthy of the air she breathed.

"No, I don't look at you with disgust. Why would I?"

"Because ..." Alice stopped herself before she disappeared down the deepest of rabbit holes. "Why wouldn't you?"

"Because you're amazing, Alice."

"Pfff. Now you're just telling lies to get yourself out of trouble."

"No, I'm not. You give anything a go. You drive tractors, plough paddocks, ride horses, rescue men from rivers. And ...."

Alice interrupted Fergus. "You're supposed to do all that stuff when you work on a farm."

"Yes, but you're a girl." Fergus stuttered over his choice of words. "I mean a woman."

Alice huffed. There it was again. Men always brought everything back to the fact that she was a female. It made her wish she been born the opposite sex; life would be so much easier.

The sheep under the trees stirred, they turned to face the pair as if the interaction was a show scheduled for their entertainment.

"And …" Fergus went to speak but he was met by Alice's hand, her palm inches from his face.

"Don't say it. Don't say anything." Alice emphasised the don't. "You're just making things worse."

Fergus grabbed Alice's hand, pulled her to him and leaned down until they were face to face.

"Shut up, Alice," he whispered before planting his lips on hers.

The kiss warmed her, from the tip of her head to the end of her toes. The heat came not only from his touch but from the knowledge that he wouldn't be kissing her if he was disgusted. She leaned into him, glad for once that she was a female, that being a woman allowed her to be exactly where she was.

Alice gasped as Fergus broke away, terrified that the moment was gone but he only left enough space between them to speak.

"You're beautiful," he said.

She stiffened in his arms.

"Tut, tut, tut. I'm talking. Stay quiet and listen or I'll have to kiss you again."

That was a challenge that tempted Alice to speak. She had an urge to touch Fergus's face, to feel his skin to confirm he was real, the situation was real, the kiss was real but just as

Danny had said, the cold had already started seeping into her bones. She could barely discern the tips of her fingers beneath the leather of her gloves, their numbness was a warning to go no further, so she stood quietly and absorbed the warmth of Fergus's embrace.

"I was not, and am not in any way disgusted by you," Fergus continued. "I was jealous of Rangi, the time you spent with him, the laughter I would hear coming from the sitting room. His parents greeted you as if you were someone important to them. I thought I'd come back from the bridge and find that you had gone too. Moved to the *marae* to keep nursing Rangi."

"I never wanted to be his nurse."

Fergus placed a silencing finger on Alice's lips. "Sssh! I haven't finished yet. I was afraid to give in to my feelings for you, I could lose my job and without that I'd be forced to enlist or be imprisoned as a conchie."

Alice froze. She didn't like to think of Fergus as a conchie, not because it meant he didn't want to fight but because of the risk he might be imprisoned for his beliefs. Fergus must have misinterpreted her silence and pulled away.

"You too," he growled.

"Me too what?" The space between them filled with the chill of the day and the iciness of Fergus's look.

"You think I'm a chicken, that I don't want to enlist because I'm weak and afraid."

Alice reached out for Fergus's hands. Her fingers, in the cumbersome gloves, failed to grab hold of him but she was determined not to let another misunderstanding come between them. It was Fergus's turn to listen. She reached

184

out again, caught, and clasped one of his hands between both of hers.

"Fergus. Fergus." She pulled on his hand and repeated his name until he looked at her. When she knew she had his full attention she continued, "I don't think you're a chicken. I admire you for not wanting to fight. It shows you have a kind heart."

Fergus pulled back. He and Alice weren't so different. Their bodies gave away their emotions.

"Don't deny it, Fergus, or I will have to kiss you," Alice teased. "I would never want you to be imprisoned."

"But I thought you hated me because of the fight. Thinking about you, and the danger of the river terrified the wits out of me. What if you had been washed away? Drowned? I would have felt responsible. The stupidity of the fight, the arrest dragging me away to prison when I should have been home helping rescue the sheep, keeping you safe."

A sheep bleated; the baa echoed through the trees. Others joined in the chorus. It was like a round of applause for Fergus and Alice overcoming their stupidity, for speaking thoughts instead of making assumptions.

"Can I speak again?" Alice asked when the noise abated. Fergus nodded and smiled. "Do you want another kiss?"

Alice closed her eyes, her lips parted in an invitation that Fergus accepted. There was a tenderness to the kiss that Alice allowed to envelop her. Whatever it was that she and Fergus had was going somewhere she had never been before.

"I am not your responsibility Fergus," Alice said as they gazed into each other's eyes. She'd never noticed the flecks of gold that radiated out from his pupils like beams of sunlight. She waited until he slowly nodded. "I may be a woman, but I can look after myself."

"But I can care about you." There was almost a pleading tone to his voice.

"Yes, just as I can care about you."

They sealed this pact with another kiss. One where Fergus's tongue dared to explore, dared to tempt the relationship to go further. It scared Alice, it was all new to her, everything was happening fast, sensations and feelings she wasn't sure she was ready for.

She broke away and gasped for air. "What are we going to do?"

"What do you mean? Now? With the sheep?" Fergus chuckled again and squeezed Alice into his chest.

She looked out from under the trees. She felt like the wind with the puff plucked from her sails, the snowflakes now falling gracefully to the ground.

"No," she said. "I mean about us."

"Alice, I'm just grateful there is an us. I can't think beyond that at the moment."

"But Mr Cresswell, and there will be others like him, with expectations."

Alice felt the change in Fergus as her words brought him back to reality.

"If Lou or Brownie find out, we'll be forced apart. Me to the other side of the world to fight in this stupid war or behind a prison wall. Either way I might as well be dead."

"Well, we'll just have to keep it secret, won't we?" Alice suggested.

"But I want to see you, spend time with you."

Fergus sounded like a child eager to open presents at Christmas time. Alice had no idea how they'd got from scowling indifference to this, but she was glad they had. She adopted the mature adult persona and suggested they think about the job assigned to them first. If they did that well then Lou may assign them more jobs together.

"One more kiss first." If it was a question, Fergus didn't wait for the answer. His lips brushed hers, invited her to taste him, to share a moment that said more than any words could.

The sheep were as reluctant as them, to leave the shelter of the trees. Fergus had to manhandle a couple to their feet but once he got them moving, the rest did what sheep do and followed. They herded them along the fence line, the snow seemed deeper there but at least the fence was a barrier to keep them on track.

Once the first lot were through the gate, Fergus and Alice turned back to round up those who had opted to brave the open paddock. A group of hoggets close all stood and shook the snow from their fleeces before heading in single file to the gateway. Alice checked the ground where they had been, but there was no abandoned lamb in need of her help.

Fergus and Alice crossed the paddock in a zigzag pattern, sending any sheep they found on their way towards the gate.

"We should have brought one of the dogs," Fergus said. "It would have been much quicker."

Alice smiled. She was glad there was no dog. She didn't want her time with Fergus to be hurried. They met at the gateway confident that they'd found all the sheep.

"Oh, shit." The words slipped from her lips before she realised, she'd uttered them out loud.

"What's wrong? What's happened?" Fergus was at her side in an instant. "What can I do?"

Alice knew then that Fergus still wanted to be her hero, fix her every problem not just care about her like she had asked, but Lou had assigned her the job of counting the hoggets and with all that had transpired she had forgotten. She was the one whose actions, or lack of, were going to separate them. Lou would think her useless and request a replacement land girl.

"Stupid me," she said. "I forgot to count the hoggets."

"I'll ride ahead and count them as they go through the next gateway," Fergus offered.

"No, you won't." She spoke slowly and deliberately, ensuring Fergus heard and understood her. "It's not your problem, it's mine. You stay here in case there are some still missing."

Alice rode off and didn't look back to see or hear Fergus's protestations. She reached the next gateway just as the first of the mob were passing through, pulled Misty up to the side of the gate and began her count. When she had to pause and wait for the next bunch she repeated the count in her head, over and over, cementing it in her memory.

"Fifty-nine, sixty." Alice sighed with relief as Fergus and the last of the sheep reached her.

"Everything good?" Fergus asked.

"Everything good." Alice smiled.

They herded the sheep into the rushes paddock, riding side by side in companionable silence. To any onlookers they would have resembled work colleagues and no more.

To them, the silence carried everything, understanding, anticipation and a warmth that even the snow couldn't chill.

CHAPTER

17

The snow continued to fall. As Danny had said, the cold burrowed its way into Alice's core. The whare may have had a lock, but it was freezing. Alice thought long and hard, as she curled up under her blankets, about abandoning her security for the warmth of the house. She went to bed fully clothed, another pair of socks, a hat on her head, yet still had to rub her fingers and toes to ensure blood continued to reach her extremities and didn't freeze in her veins. There was a dampness to the air, it settled like a heavy mantle, not allowing any fresh air to circulate. Thoughts of Fergus were all that kept her going. Sitting next to him at mealtimes, not touching, but close enough to not be obvious while absorbing each other's energy.

They got to work together, but not alone, Danny, Jack, and Lou, one or all were always present. There were surreptitious looks but neither dared risk anything more. Each morning there was hay to be fed out to the mobs of sheep. The swollen bellies of the pregnant ewes meant they were frequently cast in the snow and unable to right themselves. Gloves had to be removed to grab fistfuls of the wool and haul the disorientated ewes back onto their feet. Lambs had to be checked for mismatching or abandonment. Alice searched eagerly for orphaned lambs to adopt, but relief quickly replaced disappointment when none were found. It meant she didn't have to brave the cold of the night for four-hourly feeds.

Any thoughts Alice had, about building a snowman were left as wishful notions and not given voice. Conversation was limited to the essentials. Inhaling the cold air burnt a trail all the way to her lungs. The tip of her upturned nose coloured red and if she faced into the wind, her nose dripped. Her handkerchief remained folded in her pocket, replaced by the fingers of her gloves to wipe away the mucus.

When the morning rounds had been done, it was off to the riverside paddock to fix the fences. It was the clearest Alice had seen the river; snow having cleansed the water. It took three long days to fix or replace the battens damaged by the storm. It was near impossible to hammer in staples with gloves on so they took turns in removing their gloves and hammering as many as they could before the cold seeped in. Without feeling it became dangerous.

"Bugger!" Danny yelled as he missed the staple and slammed the hammer into his thumb.

"That'll get the blood flowing," Jack joked.

"Come on now, fellas. Concentrate." Lou's tone was serious. "The sooner we get the job done, the sooner we get out of this weather."

Each time they left the house, Brownie filled an old beer flagon with boiling water and wrapped it in a woollen jersey. A metal cup became a drinking vessel and heater in one. Fergus, having finished his drink, refilled the cup, and passed it to Alice, allowing a smile and a touch to pass between them. Alice wrapped her hands around the cup and drank slowly so the water could defrost her fingers at the same time as sending heat into her belly.

Thursday brought a northerly breeze and with it came warmer temperatures, much to everyone's relief. The snowfall retreated to the Alps and as the snow melted, patches of brown pasture re-emerged, helped along by the urine of the sheep. Where the sheep squatted to relieve themselves, steam rose from little pockets of melting snow like geysers. The fence lines became quagmires, a risk that you would lose your footing, where boots had mashed the melting snow and earth together.

Lou kept them on task until the bitter end. Alice thought if she never saw snow again it would be too soon.

Friday came and so did the mail.

"A letter for you," Brownie announced at the breakfast table, handing Fergus a brown envelope.

Alice sucked in a breath. At Whipsnade brown envelopes had never delivered anything good.

"From the Ministry of Works." Fergus noted the red M.o.W. stamped on the envelope. "Perhaps it's a letter of thanks." He laughed sarcastically before ripping the envelope open.

A cheque fell to the table as he unfolded the letter.

"They're paying you," Lou said. "And so, they should."

"It should be yours, go back in the farm kitty," Fergus offered. "It was the farm tractor they used."

Lou shook his head and picked up the cheque. "No, son, it's made out to you." He passed it back across the table. "Put it in the bank, save it for your own property, one day, one day you'll have a family and want to build a life of your own."

Alice felt a heat and a redness rise. She tried to stop it, to quelch the guilt she felt. Was Lou looking at her? Did he know about her and Fergus? She kept her head down, sure that if Lou didn't know, her body would certainly give their secret away.

"I was going to go into town today for supplies," Brownie said. "You could go instead, bank the cheque, and collect the supplies. I've got a list; I'll get it for you."

The list was placed beside the cheque. Fergus was getting to go to town. Alice pictured the rag rug she wanted for the floor of the whare. She pictured her and Fergus, alone and away from the farm, away from the threat of being discovered. How could she get to town with Fergus without appearing too eager?

It was Brownie that solved her dilemma as he so often seemed to do.

"Alice, you wanted to go to town too, didn't you?" Brownie asked. "Something about the bric-a-brac store."

Alice's yes came out like a mouse's squeak. She felt like she was caught in a trap. She looked across at Lou, whose gaze was focused on the window.

"The weather hasn't improved," he said. "I guess we can spare you both for a while."

A breath escaped Alice; one she didn't realise she'd been holding. She put her hands down on the bench seat either side of her. Fergus did the same and their little fingers touched, interlocked in a conspiratorial link that no-one else could see beneath the table.

Had Alice not shared the same excitement as Fergus, the speed with which he drove down the driveway would have scared her.

"Finally," he said. "Time to ourselves."

The words echoed Alice's feelings. "You can slow down now; we don't want it to go too fast."

Fergus took the hint and lifted his foot. The drive into town was filled with chatter about nothing and everything; all the experiences that they had wanted to relay at the time but couldn't, all the emotions they wished to express but hadn't dared to.

Fergus pulled off the road onto a gravel siding just before the bridge and turned the car down a track that led to the river. The broom either side of the track had been hacked back, broken branches shoved into the bushes. Alice figured it must have been cleared to gain access for the bridge repairs.

"Do you want to show me the work you did on the bridge?" she asked as Fergus pulled on the handbrake and turned off the key.

"No, I want to do this." He pulled her into his arms and kissed her.

Alice's senses were immediately transported back to the changing room, a confined space, a man grabbing her, she froze and Fergus sensing the change in her, broke away. He looked hurt, and guilt replaced her fear.

"Don't you want to kiss me? I thought …." He stumbled awkwardly, searching for the right words. "I thought you felt the same way I do."

Wrapping her tiny hands around Fergus's helped assuage Alice's guilt while she searched for the words to convey her emotions.

"I do feel the same way, Fergus." Alice rubbed her thumb across the back of his hand, felt its strength, its power. She knew Fergus wouldn't hurt her.

"But …." His brow lowered in a frown, and Alice felt him withdrawing.

"But nothing," she whispered as she leaned in and kissed him; she wasn't ready to reveal her past.

Fergus was slow to respond, and Alice imagined she'd done it wrong. Could one do a kiss incorrectly? She wished she wasn't so naïve and inexperienced.

As the seconds ticked by and each became sure of the other, the kiss deepened. They stayed in an embrace, their mouths meshed, their tongues entwined until the windows of the car started to steam up. The pent-up passion of the past week was held in that kiss until Alice registered the roughness of Fergus's unshaven state. His prickles scraped her face, created a tell-tale redness that hurt only a little but would hurt a lot if it remained as evidence of their tryst.

"Oh, Alice." Fergus gently stroked her cheek. "I'm so sorry. I've hurt you." He rubbed his chin. "I should have had a shave this morning. I will, every day, from now on, I promise."

Alice blushed. It was nice that Fergus cared but he was overreacting a little.

"It's okay, Fergus. As long as it disappears before I have to explain how I got it."

Alice watched Fergus's eyes go wide as the realisation sunk in.

"We'd better get going." He pulled away, straightened in the driver's seat, and started the car. "Do what we're supposed to do. I'm so stupid. I'm sorry I lost control."

Alice had experienced a man losing control, taking what wasn't his to take. There was no comparison to be made between that violation and this.

"It's okay, Fergus," she repeated.

The remainder of the journey into town passed in silence until Fergus pulled up outside the bric-a-brac store.

"Is this where you wanted to go?" he asked.

The colourful window display had changed since Alice had last seen it, but it still held an array of goods designed to tempt shoppers inside to explore.

"We should leave this until last," she suggested. "Get your cheque banked and Brownie's supplies first."

Fergus leaned over and placed his hand on her thigh. Alice was transported back to the last time she sat in this vehicle, on this street and Brownie had put his hand on her thigh. Again, there was no comparison. Fergus's hand felt comforting, as if it belonged. There was another feeling, further up, that stirred. Alice was aware of it but not yet willing to explore it. Fergus opened the door and was gone before Alice had time to acknowledge that the feeling deep in her belly was a need, that now discovered, would seek to be satisfied.

She followed Fergus into the shop, the doorbell jingle announced their arrival.

"Let me know if you need anything," came a call from the back of the shop.

Alice couldn't see the person who'd delivered it and only barely heard him over the unsynchronized ticking of a collection of clocks hanging on the wall adjacent to the door. It was as if the clocks were confused, their hands all at angles as different as their faces and unable to agree on the co-ordination of their time keeping.

Eager to explore, Alice entered the depths of the shop, in search of treasure. The inventory was stacked haphazardly in higgledy-piggledy aisles. Plates sat precariously on stacks of books that stood on three legged tables. Sideboards that should have held crockery were home to cameras, pots, and vases, all collecting a fine coating of dust. Signs and posters with curled corners adorned walls amidst paintings, originals or prints, Alice couldn't tell, hanging askew.

She spied a colourful rag rug on the floor ahead, just what she wanted, but its edges were weighed down by an antique travelling trunk on one side and a coat stand hung with stoles, ornately decorated hats, and long fur coats, on the other. An involuntary shiver ran the course of Alice's spine when she pictured the animals who'd sacrificed their pelts for the coats. Despite the warmth that the coat promised its wearer, Alice decided she'd rather stay cold. She whispered an apology to the beady glass eyes of a fox that stared at her from one of the stoles.

"I'm looking for a rag rug," she called out to the shopkeeper. "Is this the only one you have?"

"No," he replied. "A whole lot, rolled up back here."

Alice followed the voice to the rear of the shop and found a rack holding a colourful array of mats. She selected the one with the brightest colours and unravelled it, freeing the accumulated dust motes to dance up and tickle her nose.

"Achoo." She sneezed into the rug.

"One for a wish," said the shopkeeper.

"Achoo."

"Two for a kiss." The shopkeeper smiled as Fergus stood beside Alice. "And here's the man who looks like he wants the kiss."

Alice felt her face light up like a beacon. She hoped the shopkeeper would think it was the sneeze that made her blush. She felt another sneeze building and tried to suppress it so she could get her kiss. She sucked in a breath, looked at the light and then sighed when the sneeze ebbed away.

Fergus leaned across and planted a kiss on her cheek.

Beside the counter, a mahogany grandfather clock towered over Alice. It stood as tall, as straight and as strict as a school headmaster and chose the moment of the kiss to chime. Each clang as it rang out the hour sounded to Alice like the rap of the cane over her knuckles. She felt like Rangi, punished for a crime not yet committed, chastised for something that should be natural, reminded that her demise was imminent. Her relationship with Fergus was bound to be discovered and that would mean the end of everything as she knew it.

"I'll have this one please," she stammered.

"You'll have to." The shopkeeper eyed the pair over the rim of his glasses. "Nobody else will want it, now you've sneezed all over it."

Alice saw disapproval in his look, but it may have just been his normal demeanour. She checked the price tag tied to the edge of the rug and passed the rug to Fergus to hold while she handed over the correct change from her purse.

"Is that all?" asked the shopkeeper.

Annoyed at the man's tone and lack of manners, Alice forgot the other items she'd wanted for the whare, grabbed the rug back from Fergus and left the shop with nothing more than a huff.

She was in the middle of the footpath before she stopped and looked back to see if Fergus had followed.

"Well, fancy seeing you here."

Alice recognised Moira's voice immediately. She wanted to rush back into the store, wished she hadn't been so rash. Now Moira was going to see her and Fergus together and Lord knows what trouble that might lead to.

"Hello, Moira." Alice's voice cracked and she felt the familiar heat rise up her face. "Oh, and Bill. Hello Bill. I was just buying a rag rug for the floor. What brings you to town? Lovely day we're having after the horrible snowstorm. Did you have any damage in the floods? I hope not. Have you got any lambs yet? Nice dress Moira. Matches the colour of your hair."

Alice would have kept talking but she needed to breathe. And Fergus turned up beside her.

"Aha!" Moira looked Fergus up and down and smiled at Alice. "So that's why you're gibbering like a monkey?"

Having never seen nor heard a live monkey, Alice was unsure what they sounded like but knew coming from Moira, it was bound to be an insult. She stiffened her spine and wrapped her arms around the rolled-up rug as if it would save her.

"Fergus and Alice back doing what lovers should do." Moira gave Bill a coy look.

Alice tried to swallow and remain calm but instead sucked in a breath that sent her into a coughing fit.

"Alice. Alice." Fergus patted her back and wrapped his arms around her. "Are you alright?"

Even if Alice could have voiced a denial, Fergus's actions confirmed what Moira had assumed. Any rebuttal now would be futile. Moira would never believe they were just friends.

"We'd better be going, Moira." Bill tucked his hand inside Moira's elbow and nudged her away. "We've got jobs to do."

"Goodbye, you two," Moira called back over her shoulder and winked. "Don't do anything I wouldn't do, Alice."

Alice was mortified. She opened her mouth to speak but no words would come. Instead, tears threatened and that made her feel worse still.

"I should never have come!" Alice's nostrils flared. "I'll go sit in the car while you finish your jobs."

"Oh, Alice." Fergus turned Alice to face him and tucked a finger under her chin to make sure their eyes met. "It doesn't matter. It's only Moira teasing."

"And the shopkeeper," she snapped back.

"He didn't say anything."

"And the …." Alice saved herself. She couldn't admit that the clock had judged her, not even to Fergus. She could barely admit to herself how silly it sounded. She closed her eyes, inhaled deeply, and sighed loudly. "I think I'll go and sit in the car anyway. I don't think I can face the scrutiny of anyone else."

It felt as if the eyes of the entire population of Geraldine were on her, watching her cross the road to the car. Alice didn't have the courage to face up to their judgement, she kept her head down and failed to see that everyone continued about their business oblivious to her.

Alice's mind chatter didn't stop while she sat and waited for Fergus. It was no surprise she had never made the school debating teams, her arguments see-sawed backwards and forwards, neither side managing to convince her of the right or wrong of her and Fergus. For that matter she couldn't even decide what her and Fergus were, if anything.

When he arrived back at the car, the sight of him balancing paper bags, one under each arm and one in each hand, made Alice feel even more guilt. She leapt out of the car and ran around to relieve him of one of the bags just as the paper ripped under the weight of the groceries. Alice grabbed at the bag and held it tight against her body while she opened the rear door.

"That was lucky," they said simultaneously.

CHAPTER

18

"I've just got two more errands to run," Fergus announced when the supplies were safely stowed on the floor in the back of the car. "I'll be back in a minute."

There was no invitation to accompany him, and Alice was fine with that. Fergus's long stride was one she'd never be able to keep up with. He disappeared into the Pine Gould Guinness building. Alice knew them to be stock and station agents but what business he would have in there, she had no idea.

When he emerged some ten minutes later, Fergus was grinning like he'd just won the art union lottery. He turned the corner and disappeared taking his smile with him. Alice wondered what his other errand could be. It was another five minutes before he reappeared, this time carrying a piece of steel.

"You're looking happy," Alice said when he'd climbed into the driver's seat, having put the steel in the boot. "Did you get a bargain?"

"Not a bargain. I've been saving for it for months."

"What is it?"

"A part for Victor," Fergus turned the key in the ignition. "I had to save for months to be able to get it but it's the last part I need."

"Who is Victor?"

"My way out of this place, my freedom," Fergus smiled. "Don't you have dreams of something better, Alice?"

Alice froze. Fergus was planning to leave. There was no mention of her going with him. He wanted something better. He wanted to escape her. Did she have dreams of something better? Alice's childhood dreams had all been dashed by a move to a new town, by a drunken tirade from her mother, by the death of her grandfather. She saw no point in having dreams that held no expectation or even hope of being realised.

"We'd better get these supplies back to Brownie." Fergus pulled out into the traffic.

Alice sat absorbed by her thoughts as he went quiet and concentrated on driving. The car felt smaller somehow, a silent awkwardness taking up more space than it deserved. She didn't complain when his foot was heavy on the accelerator. Geraldine disappeared as an unfortunate experience to be forgotten and the sharp curves of the road arrived with a speed that would normally have frightened Alice, and caused her to grasp the armrest, but she stared out the window and fidgeted with the folds of her skirt, trying to arrange it, like her feelings, into some neat form of order.

All she could think was that Fergus hadn't even noticed she was wearing a skirt, trying to act like a lady. Did he consider her merely one of the lads? Of course, he did, why would he think anything else? She was plain, her shape and her colouring did nothing to attract men. Not like Moira, whose curves and vibrant red hair announced her arrival. It was better that way. Alice didn't want the attention of men. Even having the attention of this one man was going to get them into trouble.

She dared to peek across at him. He'd rolled his sleeves up, one tanned hand, held and controlled the steering wheel, the other rested casually at the bottom. That seemed to be how he approached life too, unlike Alice. She gripped the wheel of life with both hands and struggled to steer it in the direction she wanted. She had to sit bolt upright to have any hope of using the pedals and seeing over the dashboard to anticipate whatever life would bring her. It wasn't just because she was tiny in stature, she was small in her thinking too.

Fergus must have sensed her looking and turned. A smile curved the edges of his mouth and the dimple that was Alice's undoing, smiled at her too.

"Here," Lou spoke with his usual gruff impatience. "Brownie tells me you like looking after these things."

A lamb hung limply from Lou's outstretched hand. Its eyes were closed, its pelt still covered in the entrails of its birth. Alice's heart melted, the supplies, Fergus, her clothes; all were forgotten. She was needed. She could rescue this new-born. She reached out to take the lamb.

"You'd better get changed first." Lou eyed Alice from head to toe. "Don't imagine your white shirt would stay that way for long."

Alice rushed to the whare, annoyed that she'd even bothered to wear her blouse and skirt. It hadn't served any purpose and now, if the lamb died because she needed to get changed, she'd never forgive herself.

Back in her overalls, she hurried outside to find Lou had cast the lamb on the ground beside the vehicle while he talked to Fergus.

"Oh, poor little lamb." Alice cradled the animal against her chest. "I'll make you a bed in the whare."

"No." Lou shook his finger at Alice, so close to her nose that she worried he was going to hit her.

"I could barricade off an area in the corner," she dared to suggest.

"If they can't survive outside, they don't deserve to live," Lou growled. "There is plenty of hay in the shed and that's where the milk powder is stored. I reckon with this weather; it will be the first of many."

Lou turned and continued his conversation with Fergus and Alice knew any further protest was futile.

"What shall we call you?" she whispered to the lamb. "You can't be Lulu, Bella or Lizzy. Perhaps if there are going to be lots more like you, I'd better give you an 'A' name."

The lamb was incapable of any acknowledgement or response as its wee body absorbed Alice's warmth. There was already a makeshift pen in the corner of the shed where wooden gates had been tied to the poles. Alice pulled a wedge of hay from a broken bale and lay it on the ground for the lamb.

"You wait there, while I make you a bottle."

The shed's timber framing served as a shelf for a row of old bottles. The uncleaned teats were coated with dust. Below the bottles, Alice found a sack of milk powder hidden from the vermin inside a drum.

"I'll give these a clean and find some water for your feed." Alice spoke to the lamb as if her kind words would keep it alive.

The water in a nearby trough held a winter chill that bit into Alice's fingers as she scrubbed the teats clean. It was too cold to make the first feed for the lamb, she'd have to run back to the house and get some hot water from the kettle Brownie would surely have on the coal range.

"Please don't die on me," she begged the lamb. "I'll be back as soon as I can."

Fergus and Lou were still standing beside the car as she raced past.

"I'm just getting some hot water for the lamb's feed," she explained to Lou's inquiring frown.

She saw him shake his head and thought she heard him mutter 'Lord help us. Sentimental woman. Just what we need.'

The kettle was, as she expected, keeping warm on the coal range.

"I just need some warm water for the lamb," she explained to Brownie as she filled the bottle.

"Very well." Brownie nodded and continued getting lunch ready. "Help yourself."

Alice was back out the door before Brownie had finished his sentence.

"Slow down, girl," Lou muttered as she ran past. "You're making me feel dizzy."

Behind him, Fergus smiled at her, a soft look that said he approved of what she was doing.

The tiny lamb was still flopped on the hay where Alice had left it.

"I hope you're alive, little lamb." She sat down beside it and hugged it into her side, remembering Nel's lessons on how to feed lambs, so the milk didn't go into their lungs. "Come on, open up."

The lamb was so weak, its mouth opened easily, and its tongue flopped lazily to the side. Alice fed the teat in and wrapped her hand around the lamb's jaw to teach it to clench and release, clench and release. The lamb responded to the first trickles of warm milk by opening its eyes.

"Yippee," Alice squealed with delight. "You're going to live. What shall we call you then? What's a nice name beginning with 'A'?"

Alice ran through all the 'A' names she could think of, whispering them, testing their fit for the abandoned lamb now happily slurping away at her side.

"Annie, I think." Alice smiled as she glanced down at the lamb's belly, expanding with the milk. "Little orphan Annie."

The milk gave the lamb energy to test its wobbly legs. It pushed itself up against Alice, using her for support while its head bunted at the bottle and its tail began a contented wiggle.

"That's it, Annie, you've got the hang of it. Not too much though. Little and often is how Nel said."

Alice pulled the bottle from the lamb's mouth, and it flopped back down on the hay, satisfied and ready for a nap.

"Right, you stay there, Annie and I'll get your pen ready."

With the rest of the broken bale, Alice made a bed of hay on the floor against the wall of the shed, leaving most of the pen free for the lamb to run about when it was strong enough to do so. The string from the bale helped ensure the pen was secure, as Alice tied the gates to the poles.

"There, you should be safe and happy in here, Annie."

"Annie?" Fergus stood at the entrance to the shed with the lamb in his hand.

Alice jumped back in fright. "I didn't know you were here."

Fergus smiled. "So, you wouldn't be talking to the animals if you knew you were being watched?"

Alice could have reheated the milk in the hotness of the blush that coloured her cheeks.

"No … umm … I," she stammered, unable and unwilling to explain herself. Alice opted for attack as the best means of defence. "Don't sneak up on me, Fergus, it's not nice."

"Sorry, Alice, but this lamb is going to be grateful I did."

Alice was indignant. She'd done everything Nel had taught her. She was experienced in feeding lambs, Annie was proof of that, she was alive.

"Why?" Alice thumped her hands into her hips.

With his hand under the lamb's belly, Fergus held the lamb at arm's length, its tail facing towards Alice. With his other hand he lifted the lamb's tail.

"Because my dear, Annie can't be an Annie with these two appendages." Fergus chuckled at Alice's mistake.

All the wind went out of her. Just when she thought she had farming under control, Fergus yet again pointed out just how much of a novice she was. At least it was Fergus and not Lou.

She scratched her head. She wanted to ask Fergus if, he was sure. Fortunately, she stopped that silly question from being voiced aloud.

"I'll call him Angus then." Her frustration was taken out on an errant strand of hair that had flopped in front of her eyes. She flicked it out of the way with more gusto than required. "Put him in the pen," she ordered. "Please."

"It's an easy mistake to make, Alice." Fergus lowered the lamb into the pen.

"Mmm." Alice tried to read Fergus's face. "I think you're just saying that to make me feel better."

"No, I wouldn't do that."

His dimple confirmed to Alice that was exactly what Fergus was doing and she couldn't help but smile.

<hr/>

The rag rug brightened the whare, and Alice relished its warmth under her feet as she responded to the alarm set to wake her for the midnight feed. She burrowed her toes into its tassels while she stretched her arms above her head. They didn't protest as loud as they had been, her muscles were becoming accustomed to dragging cast sheep back onto their feet. Lambing had been in full swing for a good week now and Alice decided that despite the cold, this time of the year was her favourite. She delighted in watching lambs waggling their tails and cavorting around the paddock as if playing a game of tag with their friends, their high-pitched bleats sounding like innocent giggles.

Her heart skipped a beat whenever they came across a ewe in difficulty or an abandoned lamb. What she did mattered, determined whether a life could be saved, whether a ewe would raise her offspring or Alice would become a surrogate mother. By the end of the week, she had half a dozen mis-mothered lambs requiring regular feeds.

Alice dressed warmly, woollen jersey, hat, gloves, and her jacket as an extra insulating layer over top. With two pairs of socks on, she slipped her feet into her gumboots and left the comfort of the whare with a lit lantern.

There was a full moon to illuminate her well-trodden path to the shed where some of the lambs were already poking their pink noses through the gate in anticipation of their feed. As the numbers of lambs increased Alice had to devise a system whereby, she could feed the lambs simultaneously, otherwise their collective bleating echoed deafeningly around the shed and the bigger, stronger lambs bullied their way into more feeds than the others. She found some scraps of number eight wire hanging on a nail beside the Ferguson tractor and fashioned them into a cradle that hooked over a rail of the gate. Each one held a bottle with its teat at the right angle for the lamb to feed. She was proud of her ingenuity and that she'd been able to cut, bend and twist the wire without requiring the strong hands of a male.

Night-time feeds had to be mixed with cold water. Alice made sure she filled a bucket with water during the day; anything that limited her time out in the cold of night. She removed her gloves and blew warm air onto her hands as she rubbed them together before scooping a portion of milk powder into each bottle. A smaller bottle was submerged into the water bucket and used to fill each feeder, the teats pushed on and the powder mixture shaken until it resembled milk.

The lambs bustled to get to each of the assembled bottles and once the bottles were all in place, Alice climbed into the pen to ensure every lamb had its own teat. Angus being the oldest, and now biggest and strongest, was always first to claim a bottle. The latest lamb was no match for him and had to be lifted to the teat at the other end of the row.

"We need to give you a name." Alice still felt uncomfortable feeling between the animal's hind legs to determine its sex, but it was better than being embarrassed by Fergus again. "Mmm, a boy's name beginning with 'F'. Well, you can't be Fergus, I already have a Fergus."

"Did I hear my name?" Fergus said from behind her.

A squeal escaped Alice as her head jerked up in fright. She replayed her words over in her head, trying to fathom just what Fergus had heard. She hoped he didn't think that she had claimed him as her own. She didn't have him. She wasn't certain if she wanted to have him.

"Don't sneak up on me, Fergus," Alice growled, annoyed to have her space and her thoughts invaded.

"Sorry, I heard my name, I thought you must have seen me."

"I don't have eyes in the back of my head." There was a snap to her voice.

Fergus raised his palms in defence. "Sorry," he apologised. "Blame the full moon, I couldn't sleep, I thought you might like a hand."

Alice inhaled deeply; she had misjudged him again. "Sorry. If you can think of an 'F' name for this ram lamb, that would be a big help."

"You're certain it's a ram lamb?" His dimple let Alice know he was teasing.

She blushed; to say she was certain meant to admit she'd felt the lamb's testes. Either way he'd caught her out. Alice decided to ignore him and removed the bottles that were finished.

"How about Fred?" Fergus offered.

"Fred will do fine." Alice bent down to scratch Fred's back. "Do you like the name, Fred?" she whispered into the lamb's ear.

"Yes, I do, thanks, Alice." Fergus's high-pitched imitation of the lamb had them both laughing.

He gathered up the bottles, removed the teats and rinsed them in the bucket of water.

"There you are, all clean for tomorrow," he said as he arranged the bottles and the teats on the timber framing shelf.

"Thanks, Fergus." While Alice didn't need his help, she was grateful as it meant less time out in the cool of the night. She climbed out of the pen, rinsed, and dried her hands and pulled her gloves back on.

"Can I walk you back?" Fergus asked, offering his arm.

A quick look at the house, where no lights shone from the windows, reassured Alice that she could take Fergus's arm without their secret being exposed. She smiled up at him and hooked her arm around his.

In the light of the full moon, she could have watched every movement he made and studied every feature of his handsome face, but it was his aroma that enveloped her. An alluring scent, hints of the physicality of his day's work, the freshness of the air, the odour of an animal's pelt all combined to give Alice a sense of being cloaked in safety. It seemed counter-intuitive to being out in the dead of night with a man, but this man was Fergus, *her* Fergus, if she dared to want him.

They arrived at the whare door all too soon.

"Well, I'd best be going," Fergus said. "Morning will be here before we know it."

A tiny part of Alice wanted to invite him inside the whare, to allow him to breach the walls of her safe place, but she stayed silent.

"Perhaps a kiss goodnight." Her words were barely audible but as she tilted her head up to Fergus, she saw that words weren't necessary, their thoughts were aligned.

Fergus leaned down and covered her lips with his. It had been a week since their last kiss. Alice was mentally cataloguing them all. This one had the added frisson of the cool night fusing with the warmth of their bodies. It siphoned the air from Alice's lungs, and she relaxed against Fergus's chest, not wanting the moment to end.

"I'd better be going."

Alice heard the reluctance in his voice, felt her own in her thoughts. Did she dare to invite him to linger? Did she dare to explore the feelings simmering deep inside her? Or was it safer to leave everything as it was?

She didn't have to answer the questions. Fergus had more sense or experience than her, probably both, and walked back to the house, taking his warmth with him. The night chill brought Alice back to reality and she went into the whare. She shut the door, but for the first time, left it unlocked. Maybe Fergus would change his mind.

CHAPTER

19

"There's a letter for you, Alice." Brownie pointed to the sideboard where a white envelope rested against a crockery salad bowl.

Alice took the letter and sat at the kitchen table where Brownie had placed a steaming plate of porridge for her breakfast. Grace's familiar handwriting adorned the envelope. It had to be Grace's; she was the only one who wrote. Alice wondered what news had prompted her to write this time and carefully lifted the flap to retrieve the letter.

Dear Alice, I saw Moira in town, and she said you and Fergus were an item. I know you are a grown woman and how you choose to live your life is your business, but I also know you don't have a mother to tell you things, so I just wanted to warn you about men and their needs.

Alice gasped and clutched the letter to her chest. Damn Moira for talking to Grace and damn Grace for putting pen to paper and creating physical evidence of any relationship she may have with Fergus, who was sitting in his usual seat beside her. Alice dared not look at him.

"Is it bad news?" Brownie asked.

"What? Who? Why?" Alice's eyes bulged as she fended off Brownie's concern with more questions.

"You've gone all white." Brownie wiped his hands on his apron and placed a hand on Alice's shoulder. "Are you sure you're okay?"

"Yes!" Alice stood, forcing Brownie's hand to fall away. "Aah ... umm, ... I just forgot something. Left it in the whare. I'll be right back."

Alice was gone out the back door before anyone could respond.

Once inside the whare she made sure the lock was pushed across, strode over to her bed, and sat with her back against the wall to read the letter.

"Please know that when Moira suggests what you and Fergus have is love that she is just teasing and although she may be more experienced with men than both of us, she cannot possibly know what Fergus is thinking. Having listened in on many conversations of my brothers I can assure you that most young men have more thoughts of lust than love.

Alice slowly shook her head. It was a silent denial that she didn't have the belief to voice out loud. Grace, who Alice had trusted with her darkest secret, now thought, the very notion that Alice had been fighting hard against. Grace believed that Alice wasn't worthy of love. That because she had been a victim once, because her body had been abused to satisfy a man's lust that is all she would ever deserve. Her mother's words repeated over and over in her head – you get what you deserve.

Alice blinked back tears to read the rest of the letter.

Please do not give into temptation and do something you may later regret. Be wary that Fergus may make promises. Make sure you get to know him as a person and trust that he will honour his promises before you give anything of yourself. I know from what you've told me that you will not be wanting to compromise yourself.

Did Alice know Fergus? She knew him more than Grace who was assuming he was like every other man. She knew that he always appeared when she needed him and offered help without asking for anything in return. She knew that he had much more than her at stake if they risked a relationship anything more than platonic; he could be sent to the war to never return. She also knew that his kisses made her feel wanted, desirable and desiring of something more. This is the temptation that Grace doesn't want her to surrender to. Would she be compromising herself if she gave into her feelings? Grace was right about one thing; the decision was hers to make and not Grace's.

I hope you will feel that you can confide in me and that I will offer whatever impartial guidance I am able.

Always your friend, Grace

"Oh, Grace." Alice sighed. "You can't always fix everything. If you hadn't tried to solve my problems, I wouldn't be here at Orari Estate in the middle of all these men. You seem to deem me guilty until I can prove myself innocent."

Alice was annoyed her encounter with Moira led to the presumption that there was something between her and

Fergus. Was she guilty? Did she not want to admit thoughts of love had seeped into the empty cracks in her heart? Was an admission that her insides did things she had no control over when Fergus was around giving into lust that she would come to regret? Alice had more questions than answers.

She was certain of one thing, the evidence needed to be destroyed. Alice tore the letter into tiny pieces which she stuffed into her overalls pocket. She returned to the kitchen, went straight to the coal range, opened the door, and sent the shreds of the letter to a fiery grave.

"Everything alright?" It was Fergus checking on her this time.

"Yes." Alice sat down at the table to eat her breakfast as if nothing unusual had happened. "Thank you for asking. What work do you want us to be doing today, Lou?"

❦

Later that morning, Alice was wishing she'd never asked Lou for a job. They were at the hayshed lifting haybales, rearranging the shed so that the mould spores which had rendered the bottom row of bales inedible, didn't spread to the rest of the harvest.

By the time she arrived at the shed after feeding the lambs it was only the sodden bales that remained to be moved. She watched as the men hooked each hand under the twine holding the bales together and hoisted them to another stack. She moved to do the same, but the rotting bales were too heavy for her to lift, she tried but the twine holding them together stretched and the hay remained on the ground.

"What machine made these so heavy?" she asked. "At Whipsnade we put the hay in a stack, and it was easy to move."

217

"We get a contractor with a baler to come in," Fergus explained. "If the grass is dry, they are as light as. You need to give them a yank as you lift."

Fergus made it look easy. He pulled on the strings, with little effort at all and the bale came free from the wet earth. Even Danny with his wooden leg had no trouble. They'd rolled their sleeves up and Alice watched as their biceps flexed. Her own arms, bereft of any discernible muscle, stayed hidden beneath her shirt and jersey.

Alice knew it would be futile, but she tried again. She didn't have the strength and had to admit defeat. She stepped aside, didn't look at anyone, her cheeks burned, disappointment and anger at her inadequacies sat heavy upon her shoulders.

"Here." Fergus nudged a bale loose with his leg. "It takes a while to get the hang of it. Third time lucky, try this one."

Alice stepped up to the bale, positioned herself straight on, bent her knees and wrapped her hands under the twine. She counted to three in her head and jerked the strings. The twine stretched, then cut into her fingers but the bale came free and hovered above the mud.

"Over here." Fergus pointed to where the bale needed to go as if that would help it get there.

Alice moved, one foot at a time, each step swinging the bale to the opposite side of her body. She huffed and she puffed like the wolf about to blow the house down as step by step she carried the bale and added it to the others.

"Just like that." Fergus winked at Alice as he nudged the bale straight in the stack.

"Best you take a shovel," Lou directed. "Go around and dig out the drain at the back of the shed, direct the water away from here. By the look of those clouds out there, there's another downpour on its way."

Alice's nod was without enthusiasm. She looked from Lou to Fergus. Had Lou seen the wink? Was he suspicious of the interaction between her and Fergus? They couldn't risk being discovered.

"Do you think you can manage that?" The sarcasm in Lou's question prickled her pride.

Yes, of course she could manage a shovel. She grabbed the shovel and stomped away without replying. At least Lou's sarcasm meant he was more concerned with Alice's competency than Fergus helping her to at least appear capable.

Determined to make herself feel valued, Alice stood and surveyed the situation. There was no guttering or downpipe attached to the roof at the back of the shed, so any water ran straight off. *If you'd done the job properly Mr,* Alice silently cursed the unknown builder of the shed, *this problem could have easily been avoided.* A drain had been dug under the drip line, but it had silted up during the floods.

She looked skyward. Lou was right, the rain wasn't far away, ominous black clouds were gathering overhead. Alice set about digging out the sandy build up, carrying each shovel full over the brow of a small rise beside the shed. If it was going to be washed away by the rain it would be into the pasture and not back to the shed.

By the time she'd dug the length of the drain, welts covered Alice's fingers, the skin was red, and blisters bulged, threatening to burst at the next touch. Even the hardened skin of the callouses she'd developed on her palms when ploughing, were starting to peel.

Despite the pain, a sense of achievement boosted her.

"All finished?" Lou came to inspect her work as sporadic raindrops started. "Right then, this rain will test how good a job you've done. Best we head home for lunch before we get drenched."

Thank you, Alice. That's a great job you've done. Alice knew she wasn't going to get any praise from Lou.

The rain set in; heavy drops fell directly to the earth as if each carried its own sinker. Alice put her raincoat on and braced herself under the shelter of the eaves. She could hear the lamb's bleating for their afternoon feed so staying in the dry of the house wasn't an option. She could either walk slowly and get drenched from above or run quickly and get splashed from the puddles as well.

She pulled the hood over her head, tied the string under her chin and took off, leaping over the smaller puddles and side stepping the bigger ones. She misjudged the width of one puddle; her foot landed awkwardly, and she lost her balance, tumbling over to land on her bottom in the water. So, it was with wet overalls and bedraggled hair that Alice arrived at the shed. She giggled at herself, glad there was no mirror to see her reflection.

"Well, you don't care what I look like," Alice spoke to the lambs that wiggled their tails. "You just want your milk."

It didn't take long till they were all sucking eagerly on the teats and the bleating was replaced with satisfied slurps. Alice spread around some fresh hay and then leaned on the post to rest and watch.

A high-pitched meow had her scanning the shed for its source. In the corner, tucked in behind the milk powder drum was a tiny kitten. Alice crept closer. Its bright blue eyes were wide with fright; wet black fur stuck up in jagged tufts and a delicate pink tongue revealed itself with every meow.

"Are you hungry, little puss?" Alice bent down and reached out to pat the kitten.

Her friendliness was greeted with a hiss as the kitten arched its back and prickled its tail.

"Oh, poor little kitten, trying to be big and brave." Alice looked around for a dish to put some milk in. A feed would coax the timid kitten from behind the drum. "You're just like me."

She found the lid of an old milk can and dusted it off before mixing a small portion of powder with water.

"You look as bedraggled as I feel." Alice put the dish on the ground close to the drum to tempt the kitten but far enough away that it had to venture out into the open. "Come on, this will warm you up."

The kitten looked from Alice to the milk and back again, as if checking it wasn't a trap.

"It's alright, I'm not going to hurt you."

The kitten crept forward, crouched down on its haunches, and timidly sniffed at the dish but wouldn't drink, its blue eyes still wide with fear.

"Alright, I'll leave you alone." Alice went back to the lambs who'd finished their feeds.

She removed the bottles, glancing back at the kitten as she rinsed them and cleaned the teats. She smiled as the kitten dipped its tongue. The taste was enough to remove all hesitation and the kitten lapped at the milk. By the time Alice had finished her chores the kitten was licking itself clean, smoothing down its fur with its paws.

"You look too little to be away from your mother," she whispered as she sat on the ground close to the kitten. "How would you like to come and live with me?"

The kitten continued cleaning itself, licking its fur over and over until it lay flat and took on a healthy sheen. Slowly and quietly, Alice reached over and gently ran her fingers down the kitten's back. She felt the kitten tense but persisted until it relaxed absorbing the warmth of each pat. Alice wrapped her hands around the kitten and hugged it into her chest. Its only protest was a loud meow as the kitten stretched out a white paw and pushed against Alice's chest.

"How about I call you Socks?" Alice continued to stroke the feline. "You look like you're wearing little white socks and it won't matter if you turn out to be a boy or a girl cat."

Alice felt Socks purr; the tiny rumble that let her know the kitten was happy was drowned out by the noise of the rain on the shed roof.

"Right, Socks, let's go and see your new home." Alice put her raincoat back on, tucked Socks inside and set off for the whare.

"What have you got there, Alice?" Fergus asked as he came out the door of the house.

Alice's eyes went as wide as the kitten's as it poked its head out from the collar of her raincoat, making any denial of its presence impossible. She glanced at the door to check no-one was following Fergus.

"This is Socks. Socks meet Fergus."

222

"Cute little fella." Fergus scratched the kitten's head with his fingers.

Alice wondered if Fergus could tell the sex of the cat from just looking at it. She wasn't going to ask and risk looking foolish again.

"Brownie doesn't allow cats inside the house," Fergus warned.

"Just as well I live in the whare then." Alice could already imagine snuggling up with the cat on the cool winter nights. "Where are you off to?"

"I'm going to work on Victor." Fergus's face lit up. "Since it's raining, Lou's given me the afternoon off. Should be able to get her going now, with the bit we picked up in town."

"Fergus." Alice made sure she had his attention before she continued. "You're referring to Victor as a she. Just who or what is Victor, other than your way out of here?"

Fergus chuckled. "Victor is a truck. It used to belong to the McDonalds but hasn't worked in years and has been parked up in the back of the implement shed gathering rust. Lou says if I can get it going, she's mine."

"I thought surplus vehicles got requisitioned for the war."

"This one won't be surplus." Fergus smiled. "Not when I'm finished."

CHAPTER

20

Alice barely saw Fergus over the next week. When the essential farming tasks were done, he disappeared to Victor's shed and only the backs of his legs could be seen as he busied himself in the engine bay of the truck.

However, everyone heard his holler of excitement when after umpteen turns of the crank handle Victor's engine finally burst into life. Puffs of black smoke exploded from the exhaust as the build-up from years of disuse was cleared out.

"Yee hah!" Fergus yelled. "Who wants to come for a ride?"

Alice wanted to be the first but imagined that would raise suspicion. Why would a woman be interested in an old truck? She wouldn't. So, what was the attraction? It must be the driver. How easy it would be for someone to reach the conclusion that Alice and Fergus had been trying hard to hide.

She stayed with the lambs and watched from afar as Danny climbed in the passenger side. The two broad-shouldered men barely fitted into the tiny cab and there were no doors to stop them from falling out as Victor bounced off down the metal driveway.

It wasn't long before the chug of the engine was heard again but before Victor came into view there was a loud bang and then silence. Alice was reminded of the tractor stalling on her and wondered whether Fergus, in his excitement, had forgotten to refuel the truck. She heard Fergus cursing and decided it was best not to intervene.

When the truck reappeared, it was with Fergus and Danny walking alongside straining to push Victor back to the shed. Alice felt guilty and rushed to help.

"Thanks, Alice," Fergus said. "You made all the difference."

Alice couldn't detect sarcasm in Fergus's tone but neither he nor his dimple winked at her. She wasn't sure if her efforts made a difference or not.

"I'll leave you to it then," she said.

Fergus didn't reply before he lifted the truck bonnet again.

At dinner that evening, the talk was all about the mechanics of the truck and how Fergus should get it going again.

"Have you checked the carburettor?" Danny asked.

"It might be the wiring," suggested Lou. "Check the leads from the battery terminal."

"What about the spark plugs?" Jack asked. "They might need replacing."

225

Alice couldn't add anything to the conversation. Her lack of knowledge was yet another disadvantage of being a female. Nobody ever offered to teach her about engines. Her exasperation compounded when even Brownie joined the conversation. He could cook and he knew about engines as well.

Nobody noticed when she left the table early and went back to the whare where Socks was waiting for her. She'd tied some shreds of old newspaper with a piece of string, and it had become a nightly routine for her to drag it around the floor with Socks chasing and pouncing until they were both worn out and ready to tuck in for the night.

At least in her dreams, Alice had Fergus to herself. This time they were on the veranda of an old house, which looked across a valley flanked by steep hills. Sheep grazed the valley. Alice watched them from her rocking chair, her arms out ready to take the swaddled baby Fergus handed to her. On hearing his mother's soft cooing, the baby gurgled and smiled, revealing a dimple to match his father's. Alice felt content, more fulfilled than she had ever experienced before. Fergus left to check the flock; it was lambing time but there hadn't been any abandoned lambs for Alice to rear. Thank goodness she thought, I have my hands full. She snuggled the baby into her chest and hummed a lullaby.

Alice woke with fur tickling her nose and a contented purr humming beside her ear. It was a lovely place to be in the early morning when only a snippet of sunlight was sneaking through the sacking covering the window. There was a gentle patter of raindrops on the roof which lulled Alice back to sleep.

"Wake up, sleepyhead," Fergus called as he knocked on the door.

"Ah, what?" Alice sat upright, waking Socks as she did.

"Your porridge is on the table; it'll be getting cold if you take too much longer."

Alice grabbed her dressing gown and wrapped it around her before opening the door. Fergus filled the space, but it wasn't a Fergus that Alice had seen before. If she hadn't known otherwise, she could have mistaken him for one of the McDonalds in the portraits on the staircase. He had the air and attire of a wealthy landowner, a white shirt with a starched collar, a bow tie sitting perfectly horizontal, matching trousers and jacket with a thin vertical stripe and shoes that had been polished to such a sheen that Alice could almost see herself.

"Aren't you going to wish me luck?" Fergus asked.

Alice stood, mouth agape. Given that Fergus wasn't a landowner, she could only assume that he was off to a funeral. She didn't think luck was something you needed at a funeral but perhaps Fergus's disdain for war and killing extended to any kind of death.

"Who has died?" she asked.

"Nobody … yet." Fergus nervously scraped a hand through his hair, which had been smoothed down. He fidgeted, glanced back at the house, and then leaned in and kissed Alice on the cheek. "Better be off, don't want to be late and give the wrong impression."

"Good luck," Alice called out as Fergus disappeared down the driveway.

She heard Victor start and the engine noise fade as Fergus drove down the road. She hoped his repair job meant Victor got him to wherever he was going looking so flash. Remembering her porridge, Alice hurried back into the whare to dress for the day.

It was with a full tummy she set off on her daily check of the flocks. The ewes with their lambs at foot, mostly twins, sometimes triplets, filled her with a feeling that all was right in the world.

Nearing the end of the lambing season, only rarely now, did they come across a lamb that needed Alice's tender care to revitalise it. If the men found an abandoned lamb, unable to fend for itself they simply called out to Alice. Even Lou trusted her, appeared confident in her abilities to save the animal. He'd only visited the shed once to inspect and merely nodded as Alice went about feeding the lambs, using her number eight wire hooks to hang the bottles. Alice took the nod as approval. She knew by now that Lou would soon let her know if all wasn't up to standard.

What Lou would never discover, was today's little lamb, after Alice had checked its sex, was to be called Yolande. He had asked her at the dinner table, last night, how many she'd hand-reared. She thought of her latest, Xanthe and was quickly able to answer – twenty-four. Angus, Fergus, Molly, and Roger and all the lambs in between were out in the paddock closest to the shed. Alice had rigged up more holders for the bottles, twisting wire hooks around the middle wire of the fence but these animals had added grass to their diet and only dined on milk once a day.

Alice always came to the paddock prepared. Brownie had torn an old tablecloth, beyond its best, into square rags for dusting and cleaning. Alice kept one of the squares tucked behind the bib of her overalls. Today, she wrapped the rag

228

around Yolande's skinny frame, loosened the straps on her overalls and let the bib form a hammock that held the lamb warm against her chest. Without a ewe to care for them, the abandoned lambs were often still covered in the remnants of their birth. Once back to the shelter of the shed Alice dipped the corner of the rag in water and cleaned Yolande down.

"There, you stay here." Alice placed the lamb on a slab of hay. "I'll make you up a special bottle to get you going."

Just like she had with Angus and every other lamb since, Alice ensured their first drink was made with warm water from the house.

"Just one today?" Brownie asked when she appeared at the house with the bottle.

"Yes, there don't seem to be as many lately," she replied.

"Spring is on its way." Brownie looked out at the clearing sky. "The temperature's rising. Thank goodness. My old bones don't like winter anymore."

Alice had never considered Brownie's age. He was so tall compared to her, he just seemed invincible despite his greying hair.

The rhythm of winter had flowed comfortably through. Alice relished the short days and long nights. She wondered what spring would bring and imagined drenching, shearing, and docking would all be required. Thoughts of the physicality of those jobs and the effort required to prove her worth made her sigh with weariness.

She decided to focus on the present, the lamb that needed a feed. She filled the bottle and headed back to the shed.

Fergus still wasn't back by the time all the lambs had been fed. Alice's curiosity had her imagining all scenarios, including one where Fergus had gone to propose marriage to another woman just so that he could escape conscription. She imagined the woman would be blonde and voluptuous, everything that she wasn't. She tsked at herself, if only she'd been more like Moira, it would be her Fergus was asking to marry. She shook her head in denial, no it wouldn't, she had nothing to offer.

It was Socks who pulled Alice out of her reverie. The kitten had followed her to the shed and was now weaving in and out of her legs, meowing loudly. Alice picked the kitten up and kissed the top of its head.

"At least you'll stay with me and keep me warm."

The kitten purred in response just as Fergus drove up and parked the truck.

Happiness was etched in his broad grin and there was a bounce in his step as he came towards Alice.

"They said yes, Alice." Fergus clapped his hands. "They said yes."

"Who said yes?" she asked. "And what did they say yes to?"

"Who said you could get friendly with a stray cat?" It was Lou's gruff voice that stole the moment and made Alice jump when she hadn't heard him approach. "We haven't got time or food for such indulgences."

Alice walked outside the shed, put Socks on the ground and urged the cat to run away.

"Go hide in the whare," she whispered before Socks toddled off, tail swishing defiantly in the air.

"It catches mice," Alice defended the kitten to Lou. "And stops them getting into the milk powder."

Lou shook his head and gave Alice a look that said, 'I don't believe a word you're saying'.

"Looks like things went well, Fergus." Lou addressed Fergus with more enthusiasm than he had ever shown Alice. "Best we go and discuss where to, from here."

They turned their backs on Alice and walked towards the house, leaving her puzzled as to what Fergus was up to, something that Lou knew about, but she didn't. At least 'they' were plural, so it wasn't another woman. But … 'they' could be the woman's parents, saying yes to Fergus's request for her hand in marriage.

"Oh, stop it, Alice," she growled at herself. "Just be patient and trust Fergus to do right by you."

The questions Alice desperately wanted answers to, sat unresolved over the next fortnight. There was never a moment where she was alone with Fergus, and she didn't dare ask in front of the others and risk discovery of her and Fergus's relationship. She was beginning to wonder if they even had a relationship. Apart from sitting side by side at the dinner table, it seemed farm work was conspiring to keep them apart.

Often Alice lay awake at night or woke early in the morning, her ears peeled for any noise outside that might indicate Fergus was close by. He never came but it didn't stop her imagining what she would do if he wanted to sneak into her whare. Would she tell him to push the lock across to ensure they weren't disturbed? Would she fold down the blankets and welcome him into her bed? Alice felt a warmth emanate from deep inside when she imagined having Fergus so close. She couldn't discern if that warmth was caused by

231

the guilt of having such thoughts or something else that resembled desire.

With spring approaching, Alice's days were taken up with rearing the last of the lambs and Fergus was with the others working on repairs to the shearing shed and yards. The camaraderie of the men continued long after the working day was done and although Alice was with them, she never felt like one of them.

They joked and teased one another and used words she had no idea of the meaning of. She was too embarrassed to ask, feeling that would only highlight the differences. So, Alice sat quietly, pretended that being in Fergus's aura, being able to inhale his masculinity was enough.

For now.

CHAPTER

21

Spring's arrival was heralded by a flurry of bulbs bursting into flower, freesias in a multitude of colours brought a fragrance that made Alice sneeze when she picked a bunch for the whare. She added daffodils to the vase, their yellow frilled petals reminding her of the sun that was now shining on the Southern Alps, bereft of all but the last stubborn traces of snow.

The abandoned lambs had all been weaned. Lou was whistling for his dog to round them up and chase them to the yards for docking. The lambs seemed reluctant to go and Alice couldn't blame them. She wanted to spare them the pain but knew trying to do so was futile.

The men had brought the other mobs in from the paddocks and the yards were a hive of activity, men whistling and yelling, dogs barking, sheep bleating. The serenity of winter was a distant memory.

"Fergus," Lou called to get his attention. "You and Alice dock this pen; Danny and Jack, you split the ewes from the lambs."

Finally, Alice thought, some time working with Fergus. A pity it was the task that she least wanted to do.

"I'll hold them," she offered, not wanting to be the one to hurt the lambs she'd become attached to.

"Probably better that way." Fergus chuckled. "We don't want to confuse ram lambs with ewe lambs," he teased.

Alice caught the first lamb and held it against her chest, resting its rump on a post. Fergus reached out with a knife.

"What are you doing?" Alice cried out, pulling the lamb away from Fergus.

"I'm just going to cut the tail off."

"Don't you use elastrators?"

"Nah." Fergus shook his head. "Much quicker with a knife."

The lamb squirmed in Alice's arms, but she hugged it protectively.

"But much more painful." Her face screwed up as if she could feel the animal's pain.

"Better to be short and quick than long and drawn out. Besides, I feel three knuckles down the tail, there's no nerve there."

Alice remembered watching the docked lambs at Whipsnade, they would sit, stand, sit, unable to get comfortable for several hours. She had to trust Fergus that his method was more humane and rested the lamb back on the post. But she couldn't watch. Alice closed her eyes.

"All done. Next one."

Alice blinked. She'd expected a gushing of blood from the lamb's tail but only a small trace stained the top of the post and blotted the end of the severed tail. Fortunately, that one had been a ewe lamb so it was only a tail that was subject to Fergus's knife. There were some advantages to being born female after all.

The next lamb she caught wasn't so lucky. Alice squeezed her eyes shut as Fergus cut both tail and testes. She heard the plop as the discarded appendages fell to the ground, a pile forming at Fergus's feet.

While Alice could easily distinguish the rams from the ewe lambs, she was having more trouble telling Angus from Fred and Roger from Samuel. All bunched up in the pen together the lambs were, as Duncan had told her many a time, all looking very similar. She'd often thought their bleats were of a slightly different tone but now, when they all seemed to squeal in pain, there was no distinction, just a noise that by lunch time had given Alice a headache and didn't allow for any private conversation with Fergus.

They stopped briefly for lunch, to wash their throats clean with a cup of tea and wolf down the egg sandwiches Brownie had brought over. The afternoon was filled with the same task, repeated several hundred times as each lamb met its fate. Alice's back ached but she no longer felt the pain for every lamb's loss, there were just too many and she was too tired.

The sun that had welcomed Alice's day so cheerfully was sinking behind the Alps by the time the last of the lambs had been docked.

"We'll leave them here in the pens overnight," Lou said. "The ewes will be dry for shearing tomorrow and lambs always wean easier if they can still hear the ewes."

All Alice heard, was 'shearing tomorrow,' however was she going to find energy for another day of hard slog?

After washing up at the end of the long day, Alice slumped down at the dinner table. The aromas coming from the kitchen when she'd arrived home had exasperated her hunger pains and now oblivious to the noise of a vehicle outside, she and the men eagerly filled their plates.

"I figured you'd need all the sustenance you could eat." Brownie placed plates piled high with slices of roast mutton, potatoes, pumpkin, and beans on the table.

"It's been a successful day, especially with a man down."

Lou didn't say 'and only a woman instead' but Alice read his thoughts from the sideways glance he gave her. She was too exhausted to think of an appropriate retort.

"Did you say you were a man down?" The back door opened and in stepped Rangi, grinning from ear to ear. "I've arrived in the nick of time then."

Lou stood and turned to shake Rangi's hand. "Rangi, it's so good to have you back."

"What's happened?" Rangi asked. "You all look like you've run from here to Christchurch and back."

"Feels like we have," Jack replied.

Fergus sat up straight. "We've been docking all day."

"A record number of lambs this season," Danny added as if that justified their fatigue.

"And there is shearing tomorrow." Lou waved Rangi to a seat at the table. "If you haven't eaten already, you'd better tuck in."

"Don't mind if I do," Rangi said as he sat beside Alice. "Nice to have something different from puha and kumara."

Plates were passed, food was served, and gravy was poured. Rangi leaned over towards Alice as if to grab the bowl of beans and whispered into her ear.

"*Kia ora, wahine toa*. What have you been up to?"

Alice's cheeks instantly coloured, as if someone ran a paint brush of scarlet across her face. She felt the accompanying heat but was unsure if guilt or embarrassment was the cause. She was unable to answer. She glanced at Fergus. It was a foolish move.

"Aha!" Rangi laughed and reached around behind Alice to slap Fergus on the back. "Well done, you two, I wondered how long it would take you."

Fergus glared at Rangi. Alice hoped Rangi was smart enough to realise the look as a desperate plea to shut up or more menacingly a threat that Fergus would do harm if he didn't. It didn't matter either way, Lou had heard the comment and was looking from Fergus to Alice and back again.

"Is there something you need to tell us, Fergus?" he asked.

Pretending she'd dropped something into her lap, Alice kept her eyes downcast and fidgeted with her trouser leg.

Fergus cleared his throat.

"These two had eyes for each other before I left," Rangi announced. "By the colour of Alice's cheeks, I'd say they've managed to get together."

"Rangi," Alice growled and elbowed Rangi in the ribs. "I ... we ... have not ..."

"Well. Well. Well." Lou looked from Fergus to Alice and sighed loudly. "As if we need any more problems."

Silence engulfed the room. Everyone watched Lou, waiting with bated breath for the anticipated explosion of anger. His eyebrows drew together, hovering like a thunderous cloud above his closed eyes. But there was no storm, Lou's response came calmly.

"I suggest everyone finish the delicious food Brownie has made for us and get an early night." Lou scanned the table and settled his stare on Fergus. "You and I, Fergus, will have a chat after dinner."

"But ..." Alice wanted to be included in any decision that affected her and Fergus. What if the very outcome they sought to avoid was now forced on Fergus? Her grandfather's words rang loud and clear inside her head: Maori were trouble. Alice would never forgive Rangi if Fergus was forced to enlist.

Lou shook his finger at Alice. "This is man's business."

Yes, she thought, everything is 'man's business.' She was surplus to requirements, and it would be her sent away not Fergus. Perhaps that had been Rangi's intention all along, to reassert himself back into the fold. She ate the rest of her meal in silence, quietly thanked Brownie as she put her plate on the bench before slipping out to the whare. She didn't look at Fergus, her fate was in his hands.

It was the longest night Alice had endured at Orari Estate. Even nightmares of Jack sleepwalking in his filthy long johns didn't compare to the anguish she now felt. She cursed

Grace for ever swapping places with her. She would have been so much better off at the linen flax mill despite the stench that Grace complained of.

The single cot that had kept her warm and snug throughout winter now felt restrictive. She tossed and turned, unable to get comfortable. Alice tensed at every noise the night carried, hoots of morepork's, leaves rustling, the distant bleating of sheep but not the one noise that she wanted to hear. There was no knock at the door, no visit from Fergus telling her everything would be all right, and that nothing would change.

Socks exasperated the situation by catching a mouse, not to kill and eat, but to play with, tossing it with a paw until it attempted to escape and then pouncing with great gusto on the tiny creature. Alice couldn't decide which was worse, either a dead mouse delivered for inspection by a proud cat or an alive mouse running about the room. She lit the candle, waited for her eyes to adjust before she was game enough to put her bare feet on the floor. Socks had the mouse cornered. Alice knelt behind the growling cat and snatched the mouse up by its tail.

"Meow," Socks protested.

Alice couldn't bring herself to kill the mouse so pulled the lock back and opened the door. She tossed the mouse onto the lawn.

"Run little mouse and if you know what's good for you, don't come back."

Reflecting on her own words, Alice glanced up at the house. There were no lights on. Should she just leave, run away, and not come back? She could probably make it on foot to Whipsnade. Surely Duncan and Nel would let her stay until the women's land army placement officer could find her another position. Would the land army even want her? They might consider her trouble. Just like Rangi.

Alice's head jerked back, and she had to brace herself on the doorframe as two squabbling possums, fell from a copper beech tree and landed noisily on the roof of the whare, their war cries piercing the night. She sucked in a breath and hurried back inside, slamming the door behind her. The scraping of the possums' claws on the tin roof sounded like fingernails on a blackboard. Alice waited, wished the possums would continue their fight elsewhere but the noise continued. She had no choice. This time she put her dressing gown and slippers on before venturing back outside, candle in one hand while she searched for something to throw onto the roof. A broken branch sitting at the foot of the copper beech provided the solution. Alice put the candle down on the ground and threw the branch at the battling pests. Much to her relief, they screeched loudly and ran off into the night.

"Right, Socks." Alice retrieved the candle, picked the cat up and went inside. "No more shenanigans, it's a big day tomorrow and I need some sleep if I'm to be any use to anyone."

❦

Morning came all too soon. The mirror reflected Alice's restless night, with dark shadows under her puffy eyes and tousled hair.

"Shearing," she said to herself with a sigh as she dressed. "It might be the last job I do. I'd better give it my best shot."

She hadn't forgotten about Fergus's discussion with Lou. She was too afraid to contemplate the outcome, to worry that

Fergus might have been sent away already, with her soon to follow. But there he was, in his usual spot at the table, tucking into a plate of steaming porridge.

Their eyes met briefly. It wasn't long enough for Alice to fathom his thoughts and everyone else was at the table, stifling any opportunity to ask.

The day continued the same way. Brief glances as Alice, appointed by Lou as the rousey, collected the shorn fleeces. Fergus and the others were experienced shearers and there was a new fleece for Alice to collect every few minutes. No sooner had she removed the inferior and dirty wool, and Lou was at her side to inspect and grade the fleece. At least that was what he'd said he was doing, Alice felt like he was checking the quality of her work not the wool. The graded fleece was then bundled into the appropriate wool press and Alice was back to the shearing board where there was another fleece waiting. Even if she had the time and energy for conversation the snip snap of the hand shears, combined with the protesting bleats of the sheep created a racket over which nothing else was audible.

Any moment of rest, because the men had to sharpen their shears, was spent arching her back and rubbing her own neck and shoulders. Alice's fingers didn't have the strength to ease her tight muscles. Or the moment was stolen by Lou who needed help to stitch the full wool bales and remove them from the press and set another sack up. Even Brownie was recruited for shearing. He had the task of marking the bales with the Orari Estate stencil to ensure the farm's produce was identifiable when it was collected by the wool buyer.

By the end of the first day, a row of bales ran the length of one wall.

"Not a bad effort," Lou said, rubbing his sweaty forehead with the back of his hand. "We're almost halfway."

The dirt and dust of the day, combined with the news that they had to do it all again tomorrow, made Alice cough. The only consolation was that she wasn't out of a job yet. Perhaps that fate was awaiting her once shearing was over.

❦

Mid-afternoon on the third day the completion of shearing was celebrated with a cold beer. Apparently, it was a tradition at Orari Estate and all the men cheered as Lou flicked the top off the first bottle, which had been cooling in the water trough.

Each man smacked their lips and sighed loudly as they finished their swig and passed the bottle on. Their satisfied grins indicated the ale was like the nectar of the gods. Alice had never tasted beer before. She'd smelt it more than enough on her mother and the various men her mother brought into their lives, and she'd seen the aftereffects of imbibing too much, all too often. Amorous displays soon turned to yelling matches and if Alice's mother was really in her cups, a backhander to silence her, or a shove to get her out of the way.

Alice was at the end of the line. By the time the bottle reached her, there was very little left in the bottom.

"It's not much," Fergus said as if he'd read Alice's thoughts. "Won't do you any harm."

"You've earned it," Brownie added. "You've been working like a little trooper."

Alice glanced at Lou to see if there was going to be any acknowledgement of her efforts from him. He just belched loudly and reached into the trough to retrieve the next bottle.

She smelt the top of the bottle. Yes, it was the same odour that wreaked havoc on her childhood, but this small amount, surely couldn't hurt her. What she wanted most was to be treated like one of the men and refusing to share the celebration wouldn't help that. Alice tipped the bottle and let the brown liquid run into her mouth. It was soothing to swallow; she couldn't decide if the unique taste was bitter or sweet. It was the beer's effervescence that caught her out, a loud burp escaped before she had time to conceal it.

Fergus laughed and his dimple smiled at Alice. It was the first time she'd seen that dimple since Rangi had come back. She didn't realise how much she had missed it. Perhaps having a beer wasn't such a bad thing after all.

"Right, you two." Lou was looking directly at Fergus and Alice.

Alice gulped; now was the moment she learned her fate. Now that shearing was finished and Lou no longer had need for her, he was going to send her on her way, she just knew it. She couldn't do what the men could do. She was just as valuable, doing things they couldn't do, but Lou wouldn't see that. Alice was so busy running scenarios through her mind, she didn't stop to listen to Lou.

"Alice." Fergus tapped her on the shoulder. "Alice? Shall we go and have a talk?"

When she finally registered Fergus's voice, Alice shook her head. "What?"

"Lou suggested we go and have a chat about our future." Fergus looked worried. "Don't you want to?"

"Oh ... umm ... yes." Alice looked from Fergus to Lou, trying to fathom what they had discussed.

Fergus left the woolshed and Alice had no choice but to follow. He found a shaded spot, sat down, and patted the ground beside him. The seconds ticked by while Fergus picked at the grass as if he needed time to organise his thoughts. Alice couldn't wait any longer, she needed to know.

"What is it, Fergus?" she asked. "What do you have to tell me? Am I being sent away?"

"No, but I hope you'll leave anyway."

Alice paused to digest Fergus's remark. Even he wanted her to go, Fergus who she'd thought was her one ally at Orari Estate, wanted her to leave. She'd misjudged his feelings after all, the doubts she'd had that anyone could love her, they were valid, they were proven yet again.

"I guess I can ask the placement officer to find me another farm."

"What?" Fergus frowned. "No. Oh, bugger, I'm doing this all wrong. I want you to leave with me. I've been approved for a loan. Well, the bank will lend me a little bit and the vendors are going to leave the balance in to be precise."

"A loan for what Fergus?"

"A farm. My farm." Fergus smiled at those words and then almost coughed. "Oh, I mean our farm. Well … actually … it's a bit marginal on being a farm, but it's the only one I can afford. The previous owners have all had to sell up when the bank's foreclosed on them. But I reckon, they must have been farming it wrong. I've got lots of energy, I'll make it work. Oops, I mean, we'll make it work. That is, I mean, if you will join me."

Fergus continued to fidget with the grass and was amassing a small pile. Alice wished he would look at her, so she could garner what he wasn't saying, but the grass seemed more important.

"Where is the farm?" she asked.

"I haven't seen it yet, only the photos that the stock and station agent showed me. He reckons I'd better get in quick. He's heard rumour that the government is going to take control of all the land, keep it for the soldiers when they return home after the war. The injured ones are already arriving back. It's now or never."

"So, Fergus, where is it?" Alice imagined the property must be in the worst place possible.

"It's a small block on the hills of Mount Somers."

"Is there a house?"

"The original tiny cottage apparently. In need of a few repairs but yes there is a house."

Alice had always wanted a home of her own, a little cottage in the country where she could have a cat, a dog, a horse, where she could have a rag rug on the floor and flowers in the garden. This seemed like a dream come true, but it was Fergus's dream, and she still didn't know in what capacity she was part of it.

"I really need to do this, Alice." Fergus reached over and took Alice's hand in his. "If I'm a farmer with my own farm, I am essential services, and they can't force me to enlist."

His continual use of the word 'I' was the stumbling block Alice couldn't get past. There was no room for her in Fergus's plan. Yes, she wanted him to be safe from having to enlist but it appeared he could do that without her.

"You've gone awfully quiet, Alice. Don't you want to come with me?"

"How can I? Are you going to apply to the Women's Land Corp for a land girl?"

Fergus roared with laughter. "Oh, I really am making a mess of this aren't I?"

"I don't know Fergus. I don't know what's so funny. Why are you laughing at me?"

"I'm not laughing at you, Alice; I'm laughing at myself for being such an idiot. I'm meant to be asking you to marry me. I can't do any of this alone. The banks give lending priority to married men."

Alice swallowed. If Fergus had only left the last sentence out, she would have been on top of the moon. She would have felt wanted, not just a necessary part of a grander plan.

"Please say yes." There was a pleading tone to Fergus's voice as he stroked her fingers. "Please say you want to make a home with me."

A home. All that Alice ever wanted. A home with Fergus. Maybe he could grow to love her.

"Yes." Alice's barely audible reply would change her life forever.

CHAPTER

22

"So, she said yes then?" Lou asked as Fergus and Alice rejoined the group of men, still standing around the trough enjoying a cold beer.

Alice's balloon of excitement deflated a little more with the realisation that Lou knew of Fergus's intention before she did. Perhaps the whole thing had been forced on Fergus, Lou's punishment for their supposed relationship. Damn Rangi. Would Fergus have even proposed to her if it hadn't been for Rangi? Alice doubted it.

Fergus answered Lou by taking Alice's hand in his and leaning over to kiss her on the cheek. Alice blushed.

"Right then." Lou cleared his throat. "That'll be enough of that. Best you head into the courthouse and get things underway before anything untoward happens."

"You'll have to go to Temuka, it's closer than Ashburton or Timaru," Brownie added. "They burned the Geraldine courthouse down a few years back, eyesore that it was."

"I've got a whole list of things to do in Geraldine now too." Fergus sighed but it was a happy sigh. "Visit the stock and station agent, finalise the loan with the bank and sign the papers for the property at the solicitors."

"Since we've all worked so hard, once we get the sheep back to the paddocks, you can all have tomorrow off."

There was a collective 'yay' and Danny and Jack clunked their beer bottles together in a cheerful toast.

Alice felt like she was caught in a whirlwind, her world was spinning, everything was happening so fast. Her only anchor was her tiny hand cocooned in Fergus's. She hoped it would always stay that way.

"Right." Lou demanded everyone's attention again. "Danny and Fergus, you clean the hand shears, make sure they're oiled up for storage. Rangi and Alice, you can take the horses and get the sheep out to the paddocks. Jack, you, and I will deal with the lambs."

"I'll go and get the dinner on," Brownie said. "See what I can wrangle up to celebrate."

"There'll be plenty of time for that when the deal is done," Lou said.

Fergus released Alice's hand and was gone before she could react. She was still stuck on Lou's words. She was a deal to be done. If she'd ever hoped for a romantic marriage proposal, she wasn't going to get it. Perhaps she was more like Moira than she realised.

"Come on, Alice." It was Rangi that drew Alice out of her reverie. "Let's go get the horses."

"And no broken legs this time," Lou cautioned. "The sheep have finished the crop. They can go out the back paddocks again."

The sheep, having been deprived of food for twenty-four hours, were eager to get to the paddock, so once Rangi and Alice had herded the sheep into the race, they merely had to amble along behind the flock. The slow clip clop of the horses' hooves and the rocking motion with each step was just the tonic Alice needed to regain her equilibrium. It was as if she absorbed some of the horse's strength. She felt powerful sitting up so high, the reins giving her control to direct the horse. If only the rest of her life was so easy.

"I hope Fergus asks me to be his witness," Rangi said.

"Witness?"

"Yeah, to get married, you'll need two witnesses."

Alice had only ever thought of bridesmaids and groomsmen, not witnesses. Another term making the whole arrangement feel like a business deal.

"Who are you going to have?" Rangi asked.

Who could Alice choose? She didn't have any sisters. She didn't have any childhood friends. Her only friends were Grace, Betsy, and Moira.

"Grace, I think." Alice hoped Grace would say yes. She'd have to, Grace had got her into this whole situation.

Alice wanted to direct the conversation away from her own dilemma.

"How would you get married?" Alice coughed. "I mean, umm, on the marae."

"Well, Alice, Maori can get married in churches and at registry offices too." Rangi chuckled at her awkwardness. "But we don't have to, we just get the *hapu* to agree."

"So, there is no signing documents, exchanging rings, nothing official?"

"It's as official as it needs to be among our people. Remember we didn't have paper before you Pakeha arrived." Rangi looked across at Alice. "What are you smiling at?"

Alice had reached the conclusion that Rangi and her, weren't so different. They were both bastards. Both born out of legal wedlock. She had to smile. Her lack of a named father had plagued her, but now, knowing that most Maori never had their parentage officially recorded either, lifted a weight off her shoulders.

"We're both bastards," she said with a chuckle. "No paper record of our parents getting married."

"We survived for centuries without paper," Rangi continued. "Sometimes tribes exchange *taonga* and have a big feast to celebrate."

"*Taonga*?" Alice asked for a translation.

"Treasure," Rangi replied. "If the woman is Rangatira, then a *taonga* will be demanded if the marriage is intertribal. In the old days, most marriages were arranged, promises made when babies were born. It's all about the strength of the family."

"So, you don't get to choose who you marry?" Alice felt a little that way. She had feelings for Fergus, but this marriage seemed to be being forced upon her.

Rangi laughed. "They can't think I'm worth much. I haven't been promised to anyone yet. Times are a changing."

"I don't think we will have a big feast," Alice said. "Not with all of the rationing and we don't have any money."

"I'm sure Brownie will rustle up something. We'd better hurry or we'll miss out on whatever he's preparing for tonight."

❦

Alice must have been exhausted. She slept late into the next morning. Fergus was already returning from Temuka when she emerged from the whare.

"I've got it," he announced, waving a folded piece of paper above his head. "A week today and we will be husband and wife."

Alice's mouth opened and shut repeatedly. Like a goldfish, no noise came out, only air that she was struggling to breathe. One week. One week, and she would be married.

"Are you alright Alice?" Fergus came closer and wrapped his arm around her shoulder.

What could she say? No, I'm terrified that then you will discover the real me. She couldn't admit that. She needed to look at it as a business deal, just like everyone else was. An arrangement that would give her a permanent home and save Fergus from having to enlist.

She sucked in a deep breath. "Yes, I'm fine. There's just so much to do between now and then."

"There sure is." Fergus's excitement was almost palpable. "I'm heading into Geraldine now; did you want to come?"

"I do need to catch up with Grace. I'm going to ask if she will be my witness, but she'll probably be at work."

"We could stop off at the mill," Fergus suggested.

"Don't you have lots of jobs to do though?"

"Yes." Fergus kissed Alice on the cheek. "But anything to help you become Mrs Buchanan."

"Mr and Mrs Buchanan." Saying the words out loud made Alice feel very grownup. She'd never imagined herself being called Mrs anything. It sounded important, like it came with responsibilities that she hoped she was ready for.

"Come on then, we'd better get going. I need to put some more fuel in Victor. He's a bit of a gas guzzler."

"I'll just get my purse." Alice ducked back into the whare. "In case there is anything I need in town."

It was Alice's first ride in Victor out on the open road. She tucked herself into Fergus's side, not for any reason other than fear. Victor had no doors, and the tar seal was rushing by in a blur that she didn't want to become part of. It was too noisy for conversation, so Alice sat quietly contemplating her options if Grace said no.

They arrived at the flax mill and Fergus pulled up in front of the office just as Mr Cresswell stepped outside. He stared at them with a blank face, until he must have remembered who they were.

"You two," he said. "Have you made an honourable woman of this girl yet, young man?"

"That's why we're here sir." Alice climbed out of the truck. "I was wondering if I could speak to Grace. I need to ask her to be witness at our marriage."

Mr Cresswell turned his wrist and glanced at his watch. "She'll be on a break in ten minutes. You're welcome to wait in the women's lunchroom until then."

"I'll go on in and do my jobs and pick you up later," Fergus suggested. "That way you girls can have a good chat."

"Thank you, Fergus."

❦

"Alice! What a lovely surprise." Grace wrapped her arms around Alice and squeezed until Alice coughed. "Oh sorry, I'm so excited to see you I got carried away."

"It's more your …." Alice didn't want to insult Grace in front of the other women in the lunchroom. "Umm … scent."

252

Everyone, except Alice, laughed.

"You mean stink," Grace said. "I know, I've been in the retting room. You get used to it after a while."

"It's worse than the pigsty at Whipsnade."

"What brings you here?" Grace ushered Alice to a table a little separate from the others.

"I want to ask a favour." Alice fidgeted nervously, unsure what she'd do if Grace said no.

"Well spit it out. You know I'll always help you if I can."

"I'm getting married." Alice announced before she lost courage. "I need you to be my witness. Oh, I mean, will you please be my witness, Grace?"

"Oh, Alice, that's wonderful news." Grace's face lit up. "What are you going to wear? Have you got a dress picked out? Do you need me to alter anything for you? Who would have thought that you'd be the first of us to get married? Well, I suppose, Betsy sort of is, but not officially. How exciting. I assume Fergus is the lucky man?"

"Yes, Fergus is the groom," Alice answered the last of Grace's many questions. "I don't know about being lucky, but the arrangement serves us both well."

"Arrangement?" Grace looked puzzled. "Alice, I've seen you two together, it's more than an arrangement."

"Well, anyway, you haven't answered my question, will you be my witness?"

"Yes, of course, I will," Grace said. "When is the big day?"

"Friday next week."

"Friday next week!" Grace's eyes went wide. "That's a workday, I suppose Mr Cresswell will give me the day off. He was the one who wanted you and Fergus married. We'll have to hurry though, there's so much to organise. Your dress, flowers, a reception, a going away outfit."

"Grace!" Alice put her hand up. "It's a registry office wedding during war time rationing. There is no need for any of those things."

"What are you going to wear then?" Grace asked. "You're not planning to go as you are, are you?"

Alice looked down at her farm clothes. "No. My skirt and blouse will do fine."

"I'll ask Betsy to lend you the dress you wore to the dance." Grace appeared to ignore Alice's solution and powered on in her usual fashion of organising everyone. "You've got to have something different, it's your special day. There's a lovely flower garden at the boarding house where I'm staying. I can get you a posy of flowers from there."

"No need to go to any trouble," Alice said.

"Nothing is ever too much trouble for a wedding. What about the reception?"

"I think we're leaving straight after," Alice replied.

Grace nudged Alice with her elbow and winked. "Eager to get going on your honeymoon, Alice? Where are you off to?"

"You sound like Moira." Alice blushed and glanced over at the other women to check none of them had heard Grace's teasing. "Fergus is buying a farm. We're moving to the farm straight away."

"You're moving away?" Grace asked. "Not too far I hope."

"Over at Mount Somer."

"Mmm, a bit far for me to ride on my bicycle. We'll have to get Moira to borrow Bill's car and we will all come for a visit. If you're going all that way, you'll need to eat beforehand. We can have a lunch somewhere, a few sandwiches, a cake. You've got to have a wedding cake. It'd be bad luck not to share something."

"Thank you, Grace." Alice tried to temper Grace's excitement. "But please don't go to any fuss."

"I'm not going to any fuss Alice. You're lucky my mother isn't here. She's been waiting to organise my wedding all my life. She'd have a guest list a mile long by now."

Alice's face dropped.

"Oh, Alice, I'm sorry. I shouldn't have mentioned mothers, should I?" Grace winced. "Will your mother be able to come?"

Alice shifted uncomfortably in the seat and lowered her voice to a whisper. "My mother won't even know that I'm getting married. I don't have an address to contact her, and she'd probably be too drunk to make it."

"We'll have to get Duncan to come with the camera and take some photos," Grace suggested. "One day, your mother might like to see the pictures. You are her only daughter."

Alice shook her head. Perhaps asking Grace was a mistake. The simple ceremony at the courthouse seemed to be growing into something elaborate, far too grand for Alice. Grace must have sensed Alice's reticence.

"Don't you worry about a thing," Grace said. "Just leave everything to me."

"Excuse me." Miss McPherson approached Alice and Grace. "I hope you don't mind me interrupting but I heard you talking about a wedding, and you can't have a wedding, wherever it's going to be, without 'something old, something new, something borrowed and something blue'. It might be an old custom but if you want a good and happy marriage, it will pay to heed it."

"You'll be borrowing Betsy's dress so that takes care of that one," Grace said. "You could buy some new lingerie for the day. I'm sure Fergus would appreciate that." Grace giggled.

Miss McPherson cleared her throat. "I'll leave you to it then. Five more minutes Grace, then you need to get back to the factory. I'll recommend to Mr Cresswell that he gives you the day off. You might have to come in on the Saturday to make up for it."

"Thank you," Grace said.

"Yes, thank you," added Alice.

"Mmm." Grace scratched her head. "We still need to find something old and something blue. A pity Betsy's dress wasn't blue, then that would kill two birds with one stone. We've still got a week, I'll come up with something, don't you worry."

Thoughts of the impending nuptials and what would follow plagued Alice's night. Sleep eluded her while images of everything that could go wrong played like a horror movie; the truck breaking down on the way to Temuka, her drunken mother stumbling through the courthouse door, Moira outshining the bride with her natural glamour, Rangi calling her a bastard and causing Fergus to look at her with dismay, undressing on her wedding night into her plain white serviceable bra and undies. How unsexy that would be, but it wouldn't matter, Fergus wouldn't be expecting her to be sexy, he just wanted her so that he didn't have to go to war. That's what she had to do, treat it like the arrangement it was.

But snippets of memories of her grandparents' wedding photo, that sat proudly on the mantlepiece above the fire, brought a promise of something better. Alice couldn't remember the detail of the photo, what the young couple wore or who else was in the wedding party, just the emotion between them that was captured by the photographer. She hoped that, perhaps one day, she and Fergus might develop some of that emotion that Alice assumed was love.

She wondered about the farmhouse where they were going. Did it have a fire? Would she be able to warm her house the same way her grandparents had, make a house into a home? Would there be children? Alice finally found comfort with that notion. An opportunity for her to give unconditional love to a child that was part of her. How she could love that tiny person with all her heart and make sure he or she never had any doubts about belonging. Alice felt her heart open, pictured a tiny bundle being placed into her arms. She looked into the baby's eyes and saw her own reflected back at her. With this image Alice finally drifted into a blissful oblivion.

Alice found herself assigned to the tractor for the next few days. The eaten-out crop paddocks needed to be ploughed for resowing into grass. So instead of spending time with Fergus ensuring the arrangements for their marriage and relocation to the farm were complete, she spent her days on Ferguson, the tractor, going in ever decreasing circles around the paddock.

The tractor's steel seat was no less uncomfortable and jarred her in the very places she didn't want to be before her wedding night. Alice imagined the look on Fergus's face if he was to see her black and blue. That look of disgust. Alice knew she couldn't avoid their marriage being consummated but she'd have to ensure it was dark when it happened. It was one thing to imagine his disgust, it was another to bear witness to it.

Turning her thoughts to more mundane issues, she doubted they'd even have a tractor at the farm they were going to, so it seemed her time was wasted. She would rather have been learning other farming skills that would be useful. When Lou then entrusted her with the task of planting the grass seed, she knew he was just trying to keep her, and Fergus separated. Alice half expected to see a guard posted outside the whare each night or perhaps it was easier to keep an eye on Fergus and ensure he never left the house after dark.

While Alice was nervous about the marriage, it couldn't come soon enough. Grace phoned her on the eve of the ceremony and confirmed that everything was under control.

"We'll make sure your big day is special," Grace promised. "Don't you worry about a thing."

With the men sitting at the table behind her, Alice couldn't discuss her worries, the expectations that usually a mother would have advised her daughter of.

"Thank you, Grace," was all she could say. "We'll see you tomorrow."

CHAPTER

23

It was a quarter-hour drive south to Temuka, a journey that would change Alice's life forever. She and Fergus were once again in the front and only seat of Victor, and Rangi was on the tray of the truck, his back against the cab.

Fergus was dressed in the same smart striped jacket and trousers, starched shirt and bow tie he had worn the last time he'd gone to town for something important. The bank manager had obviously been impressed by his appearance then and Alice was equally as enamoured now. If she had to marry anyone, she could have done much worse than Fergus.

She hadn't seen Grace or Betsy to get the blue dress so put her white blouse and skirt on. She didn't feel like a bride, but it was wartime, and this was an arrangement that would provide her with a home. She didn't have to be dressed in white for that to happen.

They drove through Temuka and turned left onto Domain Avenue. On their right the courthouse stood like a temple at the end of a wide concrete path. It was a grand building with stained glass windows and spires painted in cream to contrast the red brick façade. Above the ornate double front doors, panes of glass fanned out like rays of sunlight. Alice hoped the sun would shine on them today and for the rest of their life despite the ominous black clouds that were scuttling south.

"There you are." Grace ran up to Alice. "We thought you'd chickened out."

Alice glanced nervously at Fergus before replying in a shaky voice. "No."

"Hello, Fergus." Moira purred as she and Betsy joined the group. "We're just going to kidnap your bride for a while and make her beautiful."

The land girls whisked Alice away towards the courthouse before she could protest.

"We'll meet you inside," Grace yelled back to Fergus.

They passed through the lobby and into a side room. Alice managed to catch the sign on the door which said, 'witness room.' She felt like a witness to her own life as Grace did what Grace always does and took control.

"Take your blouse off." Grace's hands were already on the front of Alice's blouse.

"I can do it." She pushed Grace's hand away and undid her buttons.

"We haven't got much time." Grace moved behind Alice and pulled the zip down on her skirt.

As soon as the blouse was gone, Betsy slipped the dress over Alice's head. Alice was made to step out of the skirt which lay in a puddle on the floor.

The room had a fire, but no flame rose from the wood neatly arranged like a tepee. Despite the chill, Alice felt perspiration welling in the pores of her armpits and breathed the odour of fear enveloping her.

"Take your shoes off," came the next command, this time from Moira. "You can't wear those sensible things. I've brought you some of mine. Nothing like a bit of heel to glam everything up. They might be a bit big, but they'll be alright for the ceremony and photos."

"But I ...." Alice wanted to protest. She'd never worn heels before; however was she going to walk in them?

"And this is from Nel. It was her mother's, so it's very old." Betsy stepped forward with a gold chain, at the end of which dangled a deep blue sapphire. "Just to borrow. She'll get it back from you when we go to Whipsnade for lunch."

"We're going to Whipsnade for lunch?" Alice asked. "But Fergus and ....."

"I told you I'd organise everything. Don't worry. Just smile. Fergus and the others are invited too."

Alice remembered her manners and thanked Betsy as she put the necklace around Alice's neck.

"It's beautiful," she said.

"And you will be too." Moira stepped in close to Alice's face and wound up a tube of lipstick. "As soon as I give you a bit of makeup."

"Not red!" Alice stiffened and readied herself to escape Moira's ministrations.

Moira laughed. "You've already got your man, well nearly, you're not trying to catch another one. I think an innocent pink is more appropriate for you. Now part your lips just a bit so I can get this on."

The word 'innocent' hit Alice in the chest like the lie it was. How was she ever going to convince Fergus she was innocent? How was she going to prevent the disgust he would most surely feel when he discovered someone else had been where he alone should go?

"It's okay, Alice." Grace must have sensed Alice's panic and placed a comforting hand on her arm. "Everything will be all right. You have something old, something blue, something borrowed and with this, you will have something new."

Grace handed Alice a parcel. It was an oblong gift box in the palest of pinks with a white satin ribbon.

"It looks expensive. What on earth is it?" Alice asked.

"It's a present from all of us to ensure on your wedding night you have something new."

Moira giggled as Alice's mouth fell open. "Dab your lips together."

After a stunned moment, Alice did as she'd been instructed and then pulled on the ribbon and lifted the lid. Inside a white silk nightie with shoestring straps was neatly folded. A rose in delicate shades of pink had been embroidered so that it would sit in the hollow between her breasts. Alice put the box down on a table in the corner and held the nightie out in front of her. The silk fabric cascaded like a waterfall from her hands, and she gasped at the beauty of it, more elegant than anything she had owned before.

262

"Well, I won't need to put any rouge on your cheeks," Moira teased. "You've gone as red as a beetroot."

Alice fumbled with the nightie and nearly stumbled ungracefully from the high heels when a knock at the door interrupted her thoughts.

"Are you girls going to be long?" Rangi yelled. "The court is ready for us."

"Coming," Grace replied taking the nightie from Alice. "I'll take that and keep it in the box until you need it."

"Or don't need it." Moira laughed at her own humour.

"Thank you, Grace. Thank you all of you. I don't know what I would have done without you."

"Here you are, Alice." Betsy passed the bride-to-be a small posy of flowers. "Nel collected them from the Whipsnade garden."

Alice had to blink away tears. So many people were making an effort for her. She'd never experienced such support before. She glanced down at the posy and saw the smiling face of a pansy. Just like the day Alice had arrived at Whipsnade the happy face of the flower carried a feeling that everything would be alright.

"And just in case there's not enough perfume in the flowers, I'll give you some of this." From a dainty scent bottle, Moira dabbed perfume on Alice's wrists and behind her ears. "For later," she teased as she put a final dab just below the sapphire.

The women left the confines of the witness room. Walking through to the main courtroom in high heels made Alice feel she was teetering on the edge of a great precipice, with an ungraceful fall imminent.

The high ceilings and dark stained timber fittings of the courtroom reminded Alice of a church, its loftiness creating a grandeur befitting of a special occasion. She took every step cautiously, determined not to destroy the ceremony.

Fergus and Rangi stood in front of the magistrate's empty bench. Beside them was the court registrar, an older gentleman with a stern nose and square chin.

"We just need the bride and the witness up here please," he said. "The rest of you can be seated in the public gallery."

Alice and Grace walked between the dock and the witness box to stand beside Fergus and Rangi. With every step, the heel of Alice's shoe resounded on the wooden floor, like the fall of a hammer, hitting nails into a coffin.

"The law requires that each of you declare before me." There was a tedium to the registrar's voice that indicated this ceremony was just another chore in his long day, one that he wanted to occur according to schedule. "And at least two other witnesses that you are freely entering into this marriage, and you take the other person to be your lawfully wedded wife or husband."

The quick glance that passed between Fergus and Alice reflected their nervousness and apprehension.

"Fergus, please repeat after me." The registrar turned towards Fergus. "I vow that I do not know of any legal objections to this marriage between myself, Fergus Alexander Buchanan and Alice Victoria Clarke."

Alice heard Fergus's voice repeat the words, but her mind had wandered. Fergus's middle name was Alexander, she hadn't known that simple fact. A stark reminder that there was so much she didn't know about the man standing beside her, the man she was about to bind herself to for the rest of her life.

"Alice, please repeat after me." The registrar now looked directly at her. His piercing eyes seem to ask the very question she was asking herself – are you sure you know what you are doing?

No, was the answer that came to her mind swift and fast, but she didn't say the words. She knew the alternative was not one that either of them wanted. She repeated the words of the registrar, the same words that so many before her had said, and so many more in the future would do.

"I'll now invite you to exchange rings," the registrar continued.

Alice's gasp was audible. She looked at Fergus, afraid to ask whether they had rings. Rings cost money, something they didn't have much of and something that could be better spent on animals and equipment for the farm. Rangi's outstretched palm provided the answer, a platter upon which two thin gold bands sat. Under the registrar's instruction, the smaller of the two was placed by Fergus on Alice's finger. She had to hand her posy to Grace so that the giving could be reciprocated.

"These rings serve as a symbol of your love and the vows you have made to each other."

Love. Four letters that hold so much within their lines. There was certainly something between Fergus and Alice, but was it love she wondered. If it wasn't, would it grow into love?

"I now pronounce you husband and wife."

Alice glanced down at the ring, shining on her finger, and twisted it around. It was there for all to view, a symbol of life going forward. When she looked up it was to see Fergus leaning in for a kiss. There was no love conveyed in the short perfunctory joining of their lips.

From the back of the courtroom, Moira and Betsy clapped and hollered their congratulations. The registrar gave them a disapproving look and cleared his throat, as he moved towards the table in the centre of the courtroom.

"It's not official until the paperwork is signed," he said, placing a fountain pen beside the two marriage certificates. "Bride first."

Alice's fingers trembled as she picked up the pen. The form had been typed up with most of their details. She noted Fergus's birthday was the thirtieth of September and he was two years older than her. His parents were Russell, a stevedore, and Marion, whose maiden name was Pollock. She also discovered that her address was going to be Winterslow Road, Staveley. She wondered what sort of life they would make there.

As Fergus's parents had been recorded, so were Alice's but of course, her father was listed as unknown. Alice sucked in a breath and straightened her spine. It didn't matter, she told herself, she was a bastard just like Rangi. Her mother's name was repeated twice for she had never married. Seeing it written didn't conjure happy memories of her mother but rather a sense of calm when she thought of her grandfather, his voice echoing words of wisdom inside her head, *'you're strong Alice, you can do this.'* She looked up. Everyone was watching her, Fergus, Grace, Rangi and the registrar.

"Is there something wrong?" Fergus asked.

"No," Alice said too fast. "No, nothing at all," she repeated trying to emulate her grandfather's calmness.

She signed her name and stepped back to let Fergus do the same. They then stood side by side while Rangi and Grace added their signatures.

"You look beautiful." Fergus whispered to Alice as he took her hand in his.

She looked up at her husband. They smiled at one another, and Fergus's dimple smiled too.

Once back outside, the marriage licence neatly folded and tucked into Fergus's jacket pocket, Alice learned of all the arrangements that had been made while she had been stuck on the tractor, ploughing.

Unbeknown to her, Grace and Fergus had had several phone conversations, and in turn, Grace had spoken with Betsy and Betsy had discussed matters with Duncan and Nel, so it was all decided. A wedding breakfast, actually lunch but called a breakfast being their first meal as a married couple, was being readied at Whipsnade. The men from Orari Estate had been invited, and Bill and Moira.

"But I thought we were leaving for Mount Somers straight away?" Alice queried.

"We'll spend tonight at Whipsnade," Fergus replied. "Load Victor up in the morning and then say our goodbyes. Hopefully, the rain will pass through overnight and we'll be able to get everything moved without getting saturated."

"Where will we sleep at Whipsnade?" Worry etched a line in Alice's forehead. "The rooms are all taken up with land girls."

"Not Captain Boyle's room," Betsy said.

"And it is your wedding night, Alice." Moira chuckled. "I don't think your husband will have sleep on his mind."

Alice felt the familiar heat rise, all the way from her toes to the tip of her head. She wished at least that could be something that changed with marriage, that she wouldn't blush so easily with a ring on her finger.

Fergus made a noise that was half-laugh and half-cough, fidgeted awkwardly and then announced. "We'd better get going, we don't want to keep everyone waiting when they've gone to such an effort for us."

"I'll go with the ladies," Rangi said. "Let you lovebirds drive together without a chaperone, now that you can."

Fergus took Alice's hand as they walked over to the truck and helped her into the passenger side. Alice appreciated his gentlemanly ways. They made her feel special, more special than she had ever felt before. So many people were doing so much for her it was almost overwhelming. Alice breathed deeply, stemming the tears that prickled at her eyes.

"Do your parents know about me?" she asked as they left Temuka.

"I've written and told them we were to marry and that we were moving to Staveley."

"Perhaps they could visit us one day."

"Not likely." Fergus's tone was abrupt, and he went quiet, a brooding cloud settling over his face.

The silence seemed to drag on and Alice felt the need to fill it. Surely Fergus's parents couldn't be any worse than her own.

"My mother is an alcoholic," she admitted. "And I don't know who my father is. Russell and Marion surely can't be any worse than that."

"At least your father would want to know you if he knew you existed."

"What do you mean?"

"My father has disowned me."

Alice couldn't imagine her husband could do anything to warrant that.

"Why would he do that?" she asked.

"He thinks I should be away fighting." Anger tarnished Fergus's voice. "That I am just a yellow-bellied coward."

"Perhaps if we visited them. If they saw us together."

"Alice, that's not going to happen. He threatened to shoot me if I set foot on the place."

Alice gasped.

"Let's not ruin our wedding day with threats from my father." Fergus patted Alice on the leg.

She nodded in agreement, happy to travel the rest of the way in silence.

❦

"You're shivering, lass." Nel walked up to greet Alice and Fergus as they pulled up at the Whipsnade house.

"It was a little chilly in the truck." Alice wasn't certain of the reason for the trembles that shook her body. Was she terrified of what she had just committed to? Was she excited by what would grow between her and Fergus? Or was she simply cold from the drive, in the truck without doors, dressed in a dress meant for a party.

"I'm sorry, Alice," Fergus apologised. "I should have given you my jacket. What sort of husband am I?"

"One that I hope will look after this dear girl." Nel tutted. "Oh, my mother's necklace looks beautiful on you."

"Thank you for lending it to me, Nel. It is beautiful." Alice reached to remove the necklace.

"Not yet." Nel stopped Alice. "Duncan! Where's the camera? We can have some photos in the garden before we all go inside."

Nel bustled the couple towards the garden and Duncan took so many photos that Alice imagined her mouth would be cast permanently like a smiling clown in a sideshow. There were photos of just her and Fergus, side by side and facing one another, photos with Grace and Rangi, photos with Nel. Then they were separated for photos of Alice with the land girls, and photos of Fergus with his mates.

"We'd better have one for Orari Estate," Lou said. "Have it on record that we had a woman in our midst."

Alice wasn't sure if Lou wanted it recorded as a warning to others or a recognition of her good service. She didn't want to spoil the day by asking. She was squashed in the centre of the line-up, Fergus on her right and Brownie on her left. Brownie was so tall she fitted under his armpit and cringed as she felt his arm across her back and shoulders. Another benefit of being married and leaving with Fergus; she wouldn't have to be subjected to the unwelcome advances of the other men, real or imagined. She would just have to deal with the advances of Fergus.

"We'd better have one last one with you kissing," Moira suggested.

And so it was that their second kiss as a married couple was recorded in black and white for all to see.

CHAPTER

24

The group made their way inside.

"Just in time," Nel said. "Those rain clouds look set to bless your wedding with a downpour."

She headed toward the kitchen and Alice went to follow.

"No, no." Nel pointed Alice towards the sitting room. "You're the bride. You're the guest of honour. You're not working in the kitchen today."

"But you'll need a hand." Alice felt guilty and wanted any excuse not to be the centre of attention which never sat comfortably with her.

"I have the new land girls," Nel replied. "They're already there and will have everything nearly ready."

"Thank you, Nel." Alice did as she was told and headed to the sitting room. She entered to find the men from Orari Estate had enclosed Fergus in their midst.

"You've ticked another one off the list, Fergus," Lou said.

"The list?" Fergus looked puzzled.

"Yes, the list of criteria that will put you further down the conscription roll." Lou's comment gained everyone's attention including Alice's. "You're a landowner, now you're married. Now you've got to farm the land successfully, which I know you will."

"Thank you for your confidence in me." Fergus smiled at the compliment, but Alice was still stuck on the fact that she was simply part of a list, something that had to be done, not something that was wanted or desired. The beauty that she had felt, dressed in Betsy's dress, wearing Nel's mother's necklace and glammed up in Moira's makeup, was washed away in an instant.

Jack's malevolent laugh caught her attention. "You just need to become a father now," he said as he slapped Fergus on the back.

"Is everything alright, Alice?" Grace must have seen Alice's distress and came to her side.

"I think I'll go and change back into my own clothes," she uttered the first excuse she could think of to leave the room. "I'd hate to drop food on Betsy's dress."

"Would you like a hand?" Grace offered.

"No. No." Alice wanted to be alone with her thoughts. "I just need to know where my clothes are."

"Betsy put everything up in Captain Boyle's room," Grace replied. "Are you sure you are alright? You look a little pale."

Alice gave a half-hearted giggle. "Yes, I'm fine, just wedding jitters, nothing more."

Despite her short legs, Alice took the stairs two at a time. She almost expected to see Ben propped up in Captain Boyle's bed, just as he had been when she'd last entered this male domain. But the room was empty, still, and quiet. She imagined the escaped soldier was wishing he was enjoying the comfort, instead of the prison cell he now wallowed in. These were problems that Alice didn't have to deal with. What she did have to do was be able to find her own comfort in this bed that was to be hers for the night. Not the single bed in the dormer room at the far end of the landing, nor the narrow cot back in her whare, this double bed where tonight she wouldn't be alone. She would have to share the bed with Fergus.

Alice sat down on the corner of the bed, ran her palm over the brocade bedspread. The pink gift box, that held the silk nightie the land girls had gifted her, sat within arm's reach. She tried to picture herself in the lingerie, the feel of silk against her skin, with the embroidered rose sitting between her breasts. To wear it would be an invitation for Fergus, that Alice didn't feel quite ready to offer. Not if she was just another criterion on a list. She couldn't not wear it; it was too expensive not to honour her friends' gift.

The sound of men and women chatting and laughing merrily echoed up the stairs.

"The meal is ready." Nel rang a bell to get everyone's attention. "Please come into the dining room."

Alice quickly changed back into her white blouse, fawn skirt, and flat-soled practical shoes. She didn't need to look beautiful if all this was simply an arrangement.

❦

The land girls had never used the dining room, eating their meals with Duncan and Nel at the farm manager's house. It was grand. An oak dining table, capable of seating at least twelve had been moved to the side and the chairs placed around the walls, with more added so that there was a seat for everyone. The table now held a selection of cold

273

meats, and potatoes that Alice imagined had been freshly dug from Nel's vegetable garden. Warm sliced bread lay like fallen dominos on a platter, exuding their yeasty smell. There were carrots, beans and beetroot that made Alice feel thankful she had changed, lest she stained Betsy's dress with its blood-red juice.

To the side of the main table was a smaller version bestowed with the honour of displaying the wedding cake. Alice gasped. She'd never had a cake made for her. A miniature bride and groom adorned its ivory top, standing amongst a bed of tiny flowers shaped from icing and tinged pink with cochineal.

Given that Duncan was the closest person to the owner of the property he took on the role of master of ceremonies. When crystal glasses of fruit punch had been handed around to the ladies and glasses of beer to the men, he chinked the side of his glass with a spoon to gather everyone's attention.

"I'd like to propose a toast to the bride and groom," Duncan began. "I don't know you Fergus and have only recently met Alice, but I know she has a natural affinity for animals which I hope will stand her in good stead and a dedication to getting the job done. I wish you both the best for the farming life you are about to embark on. And ..." Duncan chuckled at his own humour before he delivered it. "I hope your house doesn't become home to more abandoned animals than babies."

Everyone laughed and Alice blushed, of course she did. This time she blamed it on the punch. Fergus took her hand in his and returned the toast.

"Alice and I thank each and every one of you for your help and support on our special day and beyond," he said giving her hand a gentle squeeze. "I am so fortunate to have found in Alice, someone with whom I can achieve my dreams. We hope you will all come and visit us once we are settled in our new home."

Standing at Fergus's side, her hand enclosed in his, Alice felt empowered, as if some of Fergus's energy had flowed to her. She wanted to believe Fergus's toast to be genuine, born of the magic that comes with dreams, that their new home would be filled with love. She wanted to believe.

"Hear, hear. Hear, hear." The cheers echoed around the room accompanied with the clinking of glasses.

All too quickly the delicious food was eaten, the large punch bowl nearly drained and numerous bottles of beer emptied. Someone whistled, as if they needed a dog to round up the herd of sheep, to quieten the room. The volume of the banter had increased as the supply of beer diminished and now, as the noise abated, Alice found herself again standing beside Fergus, this time behind the cake, smiling with knife poised for Duncan to capture the last of the day's photographs.

"Good to see she's got her hand on top," Moira said.

"Why?" Betsy asked. "What difference does that make?"

"Means she's going to be the boss of their relationship."

"I should certainly hope so," added Grace.

"Girls, girls." Nel tutted and lowered her voice. "The secret is, you've got to let them think they're in charge, that they come up with all the good ideas when all the while it is you getting what you wanted all along."

The land girls giggled at that, knowing full well that was exactly how it was in Duncan and Nel's marriage.

As was custom, the cake was cut, and a piece offered to all the guests. Those who were already full, wrapped the cake in a paper serviette and took it with them as farewells were said.

"Bill and I are leaving now." Moira announced as she stood at Alice's side.

"Thank you for your help today, Moira," Alice said. "Your makeup and your shoes."

"You surprised me, Alice. Who would have thought you'd be the first to get married? To get married at all." There seemed to be a hint of envy in Moira's voice as she glanced back at Bill, deep in conversation with Duncan.

"It'll happen for you too one day."

Moira snorted. "Huh! A white picket fence and babies were never on my shopping list."

Alice thought she detected a crack in Moira's façade of bravado but who was she to judge. She had secrets of her own, that were inching their way closer, and with every person that left the room, to being revealed.

Every time she'd glanced over at Fergus, he was grinning like all his dreams were about to come true. Alice was happy, it was just that she'd be happier when tonight was over, when she had got over that barrier, invisible but mammoth, that kept her from believing that anyone would ever desire her.

By the time the last of the guests had departed, darkness was closing in, hurried along by a sky of black clouds. Realising the time, Alice couldn't stifle a yawn.

"I saw that yawn," Grace said, coming to her side. "It's been a big day, you'd better head upstairs and refresh yourself before you're too exhausted to enjoy your wedding night."

Alice sucked in a breath as fear gripped her. "I'm scared," she whispered to Grace.

"Fergus is a kind man, you can see by the way he looks at you, he'd never hurt you."

"I hope you're right." Alice wiped her clammy hands on a serviette. "I hope you are right."

Grace gave Alice a hug.

"It should be you going upstairs with Ben," Alice said. "Have you heard any more? Is he still in prison?"

Grace's face lit up. "He's been moved to the Balmoral Detention Camp."

"Balmoral." Alice recognised the Christchurch suburb. "That's by Mount Pleasant in Christchurch, isn't it?"

"Next suburb over but I don't think it's pleasant there. Apparently, they spend their days cutting firewood but are well-fed and the living conditions are better than prison."

"Will you be able to visit him?" Alice asked.

"I'm going to try." Grace looked hopeful.

"Are you ready to go, Mrs Buchanan?" Fergus approached them and rested his hand on the small of Alice's back.

The warmth on her back was soothing, stimulating, yet confusing.

"Yes, I'm ready." Alice's voice quivered but at least she'd been able to utter the words.

Fergus ushered Alice from the room and then took her hand.

"Show me the way, Mrs Buchanan."

She led Fergus to the stairs but took them slowly, one at a time, pausing on the landing.

"Have you forgotten which room it is?" Fergus asked.

"No, no, it's this one." Alice opened the door to Captain Boyle's room, their room, for tonight at least.

Once inside Fergus closed the door. Someone had been in the room since Alice. The curtains were pulled, a lamp on the bedside table was on, the bedcovers turned down and Alice's silk nightie had been removed from the box and spread on the bedcover.

"Mmm, I'd like to see you in that." Fergus smiled and pulled Alice into his arms. "Actually, I think I'd like to see you in nothing at all."

Alice couldn't speak, she had no words to respond, no experience to draw on. It didn't matter, Fergus's lips on hers prevented any reply. He tasted of beer but that didn't matter either. Remembering to breathe while his mouth devoured hers was all that mattered.

Thunder boomed overhead, like a warning of what was to come. The clouds finally opened, and the resultant downpour pounded the iron roof. It was if an entire symphony orchestra was playing a concerto for the newlyweds.

Fergus broke away and Alice wanted to damn the storm for making him. He took her hand and encouraged her towards the bed.

"I want to be able to see you," he said as the bedside lamp cast a glow.

His big fingers fumbled with the tiny white button at the top of Alice's blouse.

"They don't make it easy, do they?" Fergus chuckled as the first button came free.

Alice considered she should help but revealing herself, she wanted to delay that as long as possible. When Fergus realised, she wasn't perfect, the look in his eye, that she'd judged to be lust, if not longing, would certainly change.

She inhaled sharply as the second button came free, and again with the third and the fairness of her skin revealed itself. She waited for Fergus to step back but instead he leaned in and touched his lips to her skin. He pulled the collar of the blouse aside and continued a trail of kisses up her neck until his warm breath brushed her ear.

"Mmm, you smell lovely, Mrs Buchanan," he whispered.

Moira. Moira's perfume. It was her smell that he was attracted to, not Alice.

The trail of kisses circled Alice's face and arrived at her mouth with a tongue that teased her lips apart.

"Mmm, you *taste* delicious, Mrs Buchanan."

That wasn't Moira. Only Alice could taste like Alice. Perhaps. Maybe. Just possibly, Fergus did find Alice attractive.

The blouse was soon discarded, and Fergus's hands moved to the zip of Alice's skirt. Another clap of thunder and it fell to the floor. Alice's heartbeat was echoing the thunder, pounding so hard she imagined Fergus could see and hear it.

She gave an involuntary shiver.

"Oh, I'm sorry." Fergus shook his head. "I'm wanting to savour each moment and now you're freezing to death."

"No, don't hurry," Alice squeaked. "I'm not cold."

Alice didn't want Fergus to hurry but whether it was because she wasn't cold or because she wanted to delay the inevitable moment of disappointment, she wasn't sure. She'd worn her best bra and undies, but they were still plain and practical, hidden beneath her only white petticoat, all that stood between her and the consummation of her marriage.

Fergus ignored Alice's plea to not hurry. He quickly undressed, cast his clothes aside and stook buck-naked in front of her. Alice's eyes went wide as Fergus's member rose proudly between them.

"What's wrong, Alice?"

"Can we turn the light out?" Alice glanced at the bedside lamp. It was the only way she could cope with Fergus's masculinity. He was handsome, *all* of him.

"Ah! You are shy." Fergus chuckled. "I understand. This is your first-time making love." Fergus reached over and turned out the lamp. "I want to see you but there will be plenty of chances for that."

'*Making love*', Alice wouldn't have been lying if she'd said yes to it being her first time. What had happened to her, in the confines of the changing room, wasn't making love, it was destroying everything that was good.

Fergus didn't need light to see. His hands deftly found the hem of Alice's petticoat and lifted it up over her head. He knelt on the floor in front of her, tucked a finger either side of her undies and drew them down, planting tiny kisses on Alice's thighs as he did.

She couldn't breathe. It was as if all the oxygen had been sucked from the room. She thought she would faint when she felt Fergus's breath at the juncture of her thighs. How could a man make her body respond with the slightest of touches? If this was making love, she liked it. She ran her fingers through Fergus's hair to encourage him.

Alice felt the heat rise within her. She imagined her cheeks would be scarlet and was grateful for the darkness. Yet, at the same time it felt as if all the blood had rushed to her most tender bud, like a torrent of water surging her towards a precipice. She wasn't afraid, she welcomed the feeling and when it came, she cried out to Fergus.

Her trembling body crumbled into Fergus's arms when he stood and carried her to the bed. What happened on the softness of the mattress; Alice would remember forever. All memories of anything prior were erased.

Fergus was gentle and tender as he entered her. He seemed to wait for Alice's cue, only releasing his own passion when Alice's body urged him on. And she had no way of stopping her body from seeking what it desired. To be joined with another made Alice feel complete.

When finally spent, their bodies remained entwined, cocooned together as if each were what the other had been searching for.

The cry of a rooster roused Alice. She sensed the half-light through her closed eyes and waited for the memories of yesterday to replay before she dared to open them. She could smell Fergus and the carnal evidence of their wedding night. She could taste him, his maleness still on her. What she wasn't yet brave enough to do, was look at him or more importantly see the way that he looked at her.

"Hello, Mrs Buchanan," he whispered into her ear. "I think I'd like to have you for breakfast."

Alice giggled. They had made love twice more during the night. Despite the tenderness between her legs, she wasn't going to say no to starting the day in the most perfect way. That Fergus still wanted her, was all the encouragement that she needed.

She opened her eyes and saw Fergus smiling at her. His dimple smiled too, but just for a split second before he disappeared under the covers to explore Alice's body once more.

CHAPTER

25

The aroma of bacon and eggs lured Alice and Fergus to the farmhouse for breakfast; the night's activities had left them ravenous.

"Good morning." Nel smiled. "You two look like marriage agrees with you. Look at you, grinning like Cheshire cats. Have a seat, you're probably starving."

Alice blushed. Could people tell what they'd been up to or was Nel just assuming?

"Good morning, Nel," she answered. "Is Duncan about? I wanted to thank both of you for hosting our wedding breakfast and letting us stay."

The smile fell away from Nel's face, and her eyes glassed over. She put the frying pan down on a placemat on the table.

"Excuse me," she muttered as she sniffed and left the room.

"Duncan's gone to see when William will be arriving," Betsy explained.

"Oh, Betsy how exciting for you."

"I am engaged to Roland. Remember."

Alice wasn't sure if Betsy was reminding Alice or herself.

"Do you know what his injuries are yet?" Alice asked. "Is that why Nel is upset?"

"No. There have been a couple of letters, but it appears William doesn't want to speak of the war."

"You'd better eat up, Alice." Fergus was busy tucking into a hearty breakfast. "We've got a big day ahead of us."

Socks was safely stowed in a wooden crate tied onto the back of the truck along with Fergus's and Alice's belongings. The wedding gifts had been carefully packed into cartons, a dinner set left wrapped in tissue paper, serving bowls swathed in the linen. Alice was grateful for the practical gifts; she'd never expected to marry and had no glory box. It wasn't much to be starting a life together with, but they'd make do, they had to.

Their wedding night had given Alice the most precious gift. She'd overcome her worst fears. Her secret, which she feared would be revealed to Fergus last night, remained concealed. Nobody need ever know, other than her and Grace. She had been damaged, but now with Fergus as her husband she was ready to move on.

Rangi, Lou, and Brownie came outside to farewell them.

"You're not out of the woods yet, Fergus," Lou warned. "They might yet extend the ballot to married men you know. Being part of essential services has kept you out of the war

284

thus far, but that excuse mightn't be acceptable to the Armed Forces Appeal Boards if your farm isn't productive."

"And some will always argue that every young man should have to join the fight," Brownie added.

The tone in Brownie's voice hinted that this was his view too. It wasn't the type of farewell that Alice had been hoping for.

"We'll make it productive." Fergus sounded sure of himself. "I'll work from dawn to dusk every day if I have to."

"And with a *wahine toa* at your side." Rangi nudged Alice with his elbow. "You'll be fine."

"I hope you're right, Rangi," Fergus replied.

Alice just smiled. She wanted to say, it'd all be Rangi's fault if they couldn't make a go of it. He was the one who'd disclosed their relationship. It didn't seem fair he was excused from fighting just because he was colour blind. On the outside, he appeared and was just as physically strong as the rest of the men. Once again, it was men who were making the rules that affected Alice's life. She wondered if there would ever be a day when women were in charge. If that ever happened, at least they'd be assured of no more wars, women didn't need to prove their power like men.

"Right, we'll be off then." Fergus shook hands with the men and climbed into the truck. "You've got the address, make sure you visit when you're in the neighbourhood."

Rangi gave Alice a quick hug. "Take care, Alice. You've got a good man there."

"Thank you, Rangi."

Next Alice found Brownie's arms wrapped around her.

"Bye, Brownie." She squirmed and wriggled free, smiled at Lou and hopped into the truck before he could attempt a hug as well.

Alice looked back at the Orari Estate house and her little whare as Fergus drove off. She saw Rangi double over laughing as a ruckus started at the back of the truck.

"Bloody hell!" Fergus pulled on the hand brake. "Not now, Victor."

"What is it?" Alice asked. "Have we broken down?"

The noise stopped, but Rangi kept laughing. Fergus drove a little further and the noise started again. This time Fergus got out of the truck and lifted the bonnet. Finding nothing amiss he walked around the truck.

Attached to the towbar was a handwritten 'just married' sign and a baling twine trail of tin cans.

"Very funny, Rangi." Fergus removed the twine and threw the cans back towards his friend.

"Just wanted to let everyone know the good news." Rangi slapped his thigh and continued to laugh at his own humour.

They headed west towards the hills, leaving behind the familiar and onwards to whatever the next episode of their lives would deliver. Alice sat snuggled into Fergus's side, absorbing his warmth and revelling in the memories of their naked bodies, thoughts which brought a welcome heat to her insides. Even the thoughts were enough to make her blush and giggle.

"What's funny, Alice?" Fergus patted her thigh.

Alice swallowed. Was she brave enough to tell her husband she'd been thinking about sex? Would he welcome her newfound enthusiasm, or would he think her brazen?

"I'm just excited for our adventure."

"Adventure?" Fergus moved his hand back to the steering wheel as he turned the vehicle around a sharp corner. "I'm thinking it might be a little more arduous than an adventure."

"What's it like?" Alice was curious to know about her new home. "The farm where we are going."

"I've never been there, only seen the photos. A bit hard to tell from black and white images but there's grass, animals, and a house for us to live in."

"A house that we can make into our home."

Alice rested her head against Fergus and let her thoughts wander to what she would do to make the dwelling their own. She remembered all the houses that she'd lived in over the years and what, from each one, had made her feel safe and warm. Lace curtains at the windows, a fire in the hearth, rag rugs and sheep skin pelts on the floor, fresh flowers from the garden and healthy vegetables on their table. Still tired, Alice drifted off with these happy thoughts.

The truck jolted as the tar seal road became a narrower gravel track, waking Alice with a fright.

"Are we there?" she asked, like an impatient child.

"Not yet, sleepyhead." Fergus chuckled. "Did I wear you out last night?"

Realisation of the innuendo of Fergus's question brought another blush to Alice's cheeks. She glanced up at him and was glad to see his eyes were on the road and he didn't witness her embarrassment.

"It was a big day." Alice smiled.

While she'd slept, the terrain had changed and so had the weather. Hills, hung with ominous clouds, rose sharply either side of the road. From inside the truck Alice couldn't see their peaks. It was a stark contrast to the wide-open plains of Canterbury. Whether the hills looked ready to welcome or smother them, Alice couldn't decide.

On the steepest faces, native trees still flourished, towering Kauri, Rimu and Kahikatea that had escaped the pioneers' saws, rose majestically among the Ponga and fern. Alice remembered childhood stories and imagined the fairies and goblins that must call the woods their home, showering in the dew drops from the spiders' webs.

Where bush had been cleared, grass and bracken coloured the hillsides which still looked too steep for animal or human to walk.

"It's steep," she said.

"Ermm, it is, isn't it?" The laughter had gone from Fergus's voice, his question not requiring an answer.

As much as Fergus tried to dodge the potholes, it was impossible to miss them all. Alice sucked in her breath each time the truck lurched, silently praying that the ropes securing their belongings would hold. She imagined the dinner set fragmented into a million pieces, incapable of holding the food Alice wanted to prepare for her husband.

Socks meowed loudly.

"Not much further Socks," Alice called out, hoping her comforting words to the cat were true. "Is it much further, Fergus?"

"We've turned onto Winterslow Road," he replied. "We're the last property on the right."

The road straightened after the next corner and on the left was a small homestead with smoke rising from its chimney. Yesterday in Temuka, Alice had been wearing a short-sleeved dress and now she was venturing into an area where fires were required in the middle of the day. She shivered. She wasn't cold but the realisation that there were no power lines travelling the road with them and a fire was to become the lifeblood of her existence, brought a chill to her new reality.

"That must be our neighbour's house." Fergus gave a toot and a wave to the man sitting on the veranda smoking his pipe.

Alice imagined the man to be as ancient as the hills among which he lived, among which she was going to live. His shaggy grey hair was long. Where it ended and his beard began, Alice couldn't see. He raised his hand in acknowledgement and smiled a toothless grin, his lips hidden beneath a nicotine-stained moustache. Her own smile was forced. Instead of wishing they were nearly home, Alice hoped for distance between her and this neighbour.

"I'll have to come back tomorrow and introduce myself," Fergus said.

"Why?" Fergus didn't react to the raised pitch of Alice's voice.

"He has a house cow and a horse for us." Alice didn't share the enthusiasm that peppered Fergus's reply. "I bought them off him through the stockbroker. I'll need to get them home so we can start working the farm."

The further they travelled, the lower the clouds seemed to descend, shrouding them in a mist that lowered the temperature, showered them in tiny droplets and brought a musty odour to the air. Alice rubbed her thighs to generate some heat and then folded her arms across her chest to keep warm.

Victor wasn't blessed with wiper blades and Fergus had to hang his head out the door to see where he was driving. Fortunately, he saw the large ram standing defiantly in the middle of the road around the next bend and was able to stop. It raised its head and looked curiously as if it had never seen a vehicle before. Quite likely hadn't, thought Alice.

Horns spiralled out from the ram's head daring anyone to defy its superiority. Its long shaggy fleece, which must have avoided a woolshed for several years, sheltered the beast from the rain.

"That fleece will be worth a bit." Fergus licked his lips at the thought of the money to be made.

"He must have got through the fence." Alice pointed to the roadside where broken moss-covered battens and stretched wires left a gaping hole ripe for escape and, added another job to the workload which appeared to be growing with every mile they travelled.

Fergus tooted the truck horn. *Ooga ooga* resounded around the hills and the ram slowly ambled off to munch on the grass at the side of the road, allowing them to continue their journey.

The downpour became torrential and soaked Fergus to the skin. He had to slow the pace or risk driving off the winding road. Even though it was still daylight, Fergus turned the truck headlights on. They acted like spotlights and Alice waited for them to shine brightly on the main attraction, the treasure that had brought them so far away from the life they had known. Finally, just when Alice was beginning to despair that Fergus had been duped and no farm existed, the truck crested the brow of a hillock and at the end of the beams of light, a small building emerged.

As they approached, a part of Alice wanted the building to grow, to be a substantial homestead where they could raise a brood of children, but it remained a tiny cottage with one window and a door along the frontage. Perhaps cottage was too kind a description, the structure, patched with corrugated iron, was more like a converted shed. Alice sucked in a breath. She wanted a home to call her own and now she had one, it didn't matter what it looked like, it just needed to be somewhere for her heart to land, to bed itself in and find contentment.

Fergus turned the truck into the driveway, a muddy track that stopped outside the front door.

"Stay right there," he said to Alice as he turned the key off and leapt out of the truck.

Before Alice could move, Fergus appeared on the passenger side with his arms outstretched, wet hair plastered against his forehead but the biggest smile on his face.

"What are you doing?" Alice asked.

"I'm going to carry my wife across the threshold." Fergus reached in and wrapped his hands under Alice's legs and behind her back.

"But it's raining," she protested with a giggle.

"I'm already wet." Fergus stated the obvious. "This way I can keep your little toes nice and dry."

Before Alice could protest further, Fergus slid her across the leather seat and hoisted her up into his arms. He turned and dashed across the short distance to the cottage, climbed the single step onto the veranda and stopped to catch his breath.

"You'll have to open the door." Fergus lent down so Alice could reach the door handle.

She had a sense of deja'vu seeing the round brass doorknob, it was like the entry to the factory that she'd dreamed of so many months ago. This handle held no fear for her. This doorhandle didn't even hold the door as it came off in her hand and the door swung open.

From the dark of a short passage, a startled sheep bleated loudly at them, nearly unbalancing Fergus as it rushed past, out into the day, leaving behind a trail of small dark odorous pebbles.

"Maybe this is the sheep shed and there is another house further along." Alice hoped so.

Fergus stepped inside and lowered Alice to her feet.

"I don't think so," he said, pointing to a bed frame in the room off to the right of the passage. "Welcome to your new home, Mrs Buchanan."

A sense of dread seized Alice's insides. Her feet felt leaden. Should she drag them on further or should she turn and run? Outside was rain, torrential rain and cold. Inside the temperature was marginally warmer but there was no rain, only the sound of it pounding the iron roof. She shivered.

Fergus took her hand and encouraged her forward. The passage opened to reveal a space no bigger than Alice's whare. A coal range stood central on the back wall. A leaky roof had allowed its surface to colour orange with rust. To one side sat a table, its chairs upended, no doubt by the sheep. Behind the table was a wooden bench with wall-mounted shelves above and below. Alice imagined the tree that had surrendered its life to allow whoever had built this abode to create the serviceable features. She felt she owed it to the tree, to not wallow in the self-pity that threatened.

"I'll find some wood and light the fire." Fergus left Alice with her thoughts and hurried outside.

It was dark inside, but Alice knew it was pointless to search for a light switch. The curtains that hung at the small windows either end of this living space, were rotted and frayed, hanging like lifeless vines. Deciding to let in what little natural light there was, Alice walked to the window beside the bench and pulled the curtains back. The faded fabric, with just a hint of flowers to indicate a woman once lived here, came away in her hand. A cloud of dust followed as she pulled the remainder of the fabric from the wooden rail that had held them in place. She screwed the curtain up and used it as a rag to wipe away the cobwebs covering the window and filtering the light.

"At least there is running water." Alice tried to be positive as she turned the tap on the kitchen sink. The pipes creaked, water gurgled, and air hissed before a brownish liquid spluttered from the taps. Alice held her breath until finally the water ran clear. Her sigh of relief was quickly followed by the urge to use the toilet. She looked around the space and her heart sank a little further with the realisation that there was no inside lavatory.

"I found some dry wood." Fergus came back inside with his arms loaded. "There's a whole shed of it out the back."

"Is there a toilet out there too?" Alice dreaded the answer but reminded herself it was only in recent times that she'd lived with the luxury of indoor facilities.

She watched Fergus's face, saw him picturing all he had discovered at the rear of the house, and wished she could share some of his excitement, knew that she needed to.

"Yes," he replied excitedly. "There's another little lean to with a hand basin, bath, and a small room to one side. That's probably the toilet."

"Good." Alice said the word but barely believed it to be true. "I need to go."

"Watch where you walk," Fergus warned. "It looks like we've got wild pigs on the farm too."

"Wild pigs?" Alice squealed.

"They're not wild, wild, they're just not domesticated ones and they're not out there now. I can see they've been here rutting at the ground. There are holes that I wouldn't want you to twist your ankle in."

Fergus's caring words gave Alice some courage, knowing that she wasn't in this alone, that she had Fergus to protect her.

"You go and I'll have the fire lit by the time you get back. I just have to find the carton the matches are packed in."

Alice opened the back door to a waterfall where the guttering had separated, and the rain ran off the end of the roof to create a puddle she jumped over. She dodged the ruts and the rain and reached the lean-to. There were still traces of white on the sides of the basin and bath but the murky brown water that sat in the bottom appeared to be growing a fungus that Alice dared not get too close to.

The rusty hinges of the toilet door strained and creaked as she pulled the door over the grass that had grown in front. Alice had expected the spiders that made this dry spot their home, but not the density of the cobwebs that she had to brush aside. Luckily, she found a shepherd's crook leaning against the wall to use instead of her hands.

Squatting over the wooden seat, Alice carefully held her clothes, terrified that they would drop into the deep, dark hole which at least, from lack of recent use, held no stench. Her eyes darted from side to side, alert to an angry spider wanting to persecute the invader. Relief came as her bladder emptied.

"I don't think the ballot will ever find you here, Fergus Buchanan," she whispered.

CHAPTER

26

By the time Alice made it back inside, Fergus had the room opposite the bedroom filled with their cartons. He'd freed Socks from her crate, and she meowed loudly as she explored their new home. Alice picked the cat up for a cuddle.

"What do you reckon, Socks, are you going to be happy here?" Alice asked as much of herself as her pet.

"There's certainly going to be no shortage of food for the cat," Fergus said.

"Why?" Alice cringed, imagining the house wasn't so different from the factory and rats abounded. "What have you seen?"

"Looks like some mice may have made a home in the kapok mattress."

"Mice …" Alice's eyes went wide, "or rats?"

"No, not rats, the trail of droppings is too small for rats."

Alice righted one of the chairs and sat down. She felt a weariness in her bones that she knew she should try and shake. She took a deep breath and closed her eyes to imagine the house clean and fresh smelling.

She opened them again when the smell of smoke assaulted her nostrils as it billowed from the coal range. Fergus was crouched, blowing into the open fire to encourage the flame.

"I think the chimney might be a little blocked," he said. "Probably a bird's nest. Hopefully the flame will just burn it away and not the house as well."

Alice laughed, she had to, it was that or tears. The only thing worse than being stuck in the back of beyond in a shack was being stuck in the back of beyond with no shelter at all.

"You go find the kettle," Fergus suggested. "We'll have a cuppa and decide where to start first."

Alice carried the carton labelled 'kitchen' into the living area and began unpacking the contents onto the table. Staying active was the easiest way to keep her thoughts from wandering. She waited until the tap water ran clear again before filling the kettle and putting it on top of the coal range. Next, she found a teapot, the caddy with tea leaves, the tea cosy Nel had knitted for them and two cups and saucers. At the bottom of the carton was a cake tin, which held the remainder of their wedding cake. Alice's grandmother would have said it should be saved for the christening of the first child, but Alice doubted it would last that long without a refrigerator. There was a safe in the corner, a cupboard that was vented to the outside, with netting to stop the flies but allow the cool air to flow.

However, one of the hinges had rusted and the cupboard door hung askew, and it looked like vermin had scoured the cupboard for any remnants of food.

Before long the fire was roaring, the smoke had dissipated, and the kettle was whistling its readiness to brew the tea.

"Well, we're finally here," Fergus said as they sat at the table waiting for the tea to draw.

"We don't have any milk."

"We will tomorrow," Fergus replied. "When I visit Mr McGregor, the neighbour."

"You've thought of everything." Alice was filled with admiration for the man sitting opposite her, her husband.

"I tried to. We've got to make this a success, Alice." Fergus reached across the table and held Alice's hands in his. "It's literally a matter of life and death. If we aren't successful farming this land, I might as well be dead."

It was the jolt Alice needed to get out of her self-pity. This situation was Fergus's escape from the war. The war office wouldn't find him out here, and those who sneered at and bullied the conscientious objectors wouldn't find him either. And if they made a living off the land and contributed to the war effort by supplying meat and wool, then even if found, Fergus wouldn't be sent away. He couldn't be sent away; he was Alice's husband.

"I think we should set up the bedroom first," she suggested. "Then at least we'll have somewhere to sleep at the end of the day."

When Alice looked across at Fergus, his dimple was winking at her and his eyes had a sparkle, she'd seen a lot recently.

"I like how you think, Alice," Fergus chuckled. "I'm not sure we'll just be sleeping though."

Alice almost choked on the mouthful of tea she was trying to swallow and coloured scarlet. Fergus just laughed at her embarrassment.

"To the bedroom it is then." Fergus downed the last of his cup of tea.

The mattress leaning against the wall was carried out onto the veranda and whacked with the broom handle until the cloud of dust particles abated. Where the fabric had been chewed and the kapok moulded into a warm nest, Fergus made sure the inhabitants were long gone. Fortunately, the holes were at one end, which they put at the foot of the bed. Alice found the carton packed with linen Fergus had brought from the second-hand store. It was still in good condition, and it was clean.

As Alice smoothed down the faded candlewick bedspread, Fergus grabbed her from behind, picked her up and dumped her face up on the bed.

"Not now, Fergus, not now." Alice giggled as she half-heartedly protested. "It's daytime and someone might see."

Fergus laughed, before planting a kiss on Alice's cheek. "In case you haven't noticed Alice, our nearest neighbour is about two miles back up the road."

He stifled any further protests by smothering Alice's mouth with his. She surrendered. Being pinned beneath her husband was a nice place to be. Tasting him, feeling his desire for her, she listened to the sounds of the rain, like a symphony on the roof to accompany them, while they made love for the first time in their new home.

❤

Later that day, a westerly breeze rattled the windows in their frames and blew the rainclouds over the hills at the back of the cottage but also took with it the daylight.

"We might have to go to bed early," Fergus said with a mischievous grin as he lit the gas lamp and sat it in the middle of the table. "Just to preserve our supplies of kerosene."

Alice giggled. After their earlier dalliance, they'd worked hard all afternoon and almost had the house looking like a home, but thoughts of their lovemaking were never far from her mind. If this was what marriage was like, she quite enjoyed it.

They ate a simple meal, stewed mince with onions and potatoes all cooked in a single pot on the coal range. Alice had often had to prepare meals when her mother was too inebriated to do so. Her skills didn't extend to anything fancy but there wouldn't be time or money for that.

Nel had given them a freshly baked loaf of bread. Another skill Alice was going to have to master, it was a long way to drive for fresh supplies.

"It's good the rain has gone." Fergus wiped the last of his gravy with a crust of bread. "We'll be able to get outside tomorrow and see what needs to be done."

Alice didn't want to be a killjoy, but it seemed like everywhere they looked there was another job to add to the list.

"I'm so glad I've got you," Fergus said. "There's too much to do for one person."

The words Fergus spoke didn't match the loving look he was giving Alice, so she tried not to think of herself as only here as an extra pair of hands. She told herself she was both wanted and needed by Fergus and wrestled back the tiny niggle inside that dared to say otherwise.

The flickering light from the lantern danced shadows across the walls. Where once wallpaper had been neatly hung, dampness sagged the sarking and tore the faded wallpaper to leave it hanging in lifeless strips. The curtainless windows were now frames to the blackness outside. Alice didn't like to think of what or who lurked beyond, able to see them but remain unseen.

Standing to take the dirty plates to the sink, Alice glanced out the window. Two beady red eyes stared back at her. She gasped and thumped the plates back down on the table.

"What's that?"

Fergus's eyes followed her pointed finger.

"It's just a possum. You must have seen a possum before, surely."

"Yes," Alice said defensively, "but not one staring in the window at me. And why is it making that clicking noise. Is it going to attack us?"

Fergus laughed. "I might have to attack it. It appears the possum wants to mate with you as much as I do. Possums click when they're trying to attract a partner."

"Well, I'm already taken." Alice stomped her foot, picked up the plates and went to wash them up.

❧

It was pitch black when Alice stirred, an undeniable need to toilet having woken her. She had no choice; it was venture outside to the toilet or wet the bed. She wished they'd thought to bring a chamber pot.

Beside her Fergus slept soundly, his breath came in extended huffs as his belly rose and fell. Alice climbed quietly out of the bed and reached under her pillow for the silk nightie the land girls had gifted to her. She'd hardly worn it; Fergus liked the feel of her soft skin against his, so the nightie was soon removed if she bothered to put it on at all. Alice found her slippers before daring to leave the room in search of the lantern.

Without her bearings in the unfamiliar surroundings, Alice splayed her arms out in front, feeling first for the door frame and then the table. She yelped when her knee found the table leg before her hands. Luckily the box of matches lay beside the lantern, and she soon had a small flame to light her way outside.

The night air still carried the dampness of the rain, but it was silent except for the distant hooting of a morepork. Alice held the lantern aloft and checked the over-friendly possum had moved on. Happy that there were no eyes looking at her, she crossed the yard to the long drop. A quick search for spiders showed no new cobwebs had yet formed but Alice still wasn't game enough to shut the door.

She hung the lantern on a hook, so her hands were free to hitch her nightie up. She laughed at the irony of the nightie; it looked lovely but offered no protection or warmth at all. A frost had settled on the wooden toilet seat and Alice gasped as it bit into her skin. She jumped back up and opted to squat above the long drop. When she was finally able to urinate, her relief was short-lived. A snuffling sound had Alice on high alert. She was not alone.

Alice strained her eyes, searching the darkness for the source of her terror. She imagined the ground plagued with rats, baring their teeth at her, then told herself not to be so stupid. The noise wasn't loud enough for a mischief of rats.

Using newsprint, they had recycled from packing to toilet paper, ripped into strips and hung from a nail on the wall of the toilet, Alice finished her business and grabbed hold of the lantern again.

"What do you want?" she asked trying to sound fiercer than she could ever be.

The snuffling continued, unperturbed by her aggression. Alice swung the lantern, shining its light around the yard. There were no rats, but a small hedgehog stopped, raised its prickles, and looked at her. Just as fast, the hedgehog must have assessed Alice as no risk whatsoever, its protective spines lowered and it continued on its way, snuffling as it sniffed out its dinner.

Alice's sigh of relief was audible. She wondered if she'd ever get used to living on Winterslow Road. A shiver ran the length of her spine.

"Get out of the cold, you silly girl, or you'll catch a cold." It was Alice's voice, but the words were her mother's, telling her yet again she would get everything she deserved. She hurried back inside eager to snuggle into Fergus's warmth.

With no curtains on the bedroom window, daylight came all too soon. Alice sensed it on her still shut eyelids. She wanted to roll over and go back to sleep but felt someone was watching her.

Hoping it was just her imagination, she opened one eye to check.

"Good morning." Fergus smiled at Alice and pulled her close. "You're looking beautiful this morning."

"Do we have to get up already?" Alice murmured in a sleepy voice.

"Not just yet." Fergus chuckled and his erection pulsed a silent invitation against Alice's nakedness.

The subtle move was all that was required, Alice's body stirred, a warmth emanated from deep within and she parted her legs. She felt brazen. How could she have gone from fearing to be with a man to being wanton, desiring of sexual contact with so little encouragement? Was it love? Had she fallen in love with her husband already?

Fergus's lips found hers, meshing as he manoeuvred himself above her. She welcomed their joining, revelled as their bodies found a natural rhythm and moved together as one. Again, she felt as if someone was watching her. It was one thing to receive pleasure from another person, another entirely to have that person witness your pleasure.

If Fergus was watching her, she would distract him, bury her face where her emotions would remain secret. But Fergus nibbled on her earlobe. It couldn't possibly be him looking at her.

She felt a shadow settle over them. Alice opened one eye again and saw a silhouette at the window. The shape of a beast with shaggy hair. She felt sick. With all the strength she could muster she pushed Fergus off.

"What's wrong? What's wrong?" His face screwed up, annoyed at being interrupted, and worried why.

"The window …" All the blood drained from Alice's face as she pointed.

Fergus turned towards the window. "Mr McGregor! Bloody hell! A bit early for a visit, isn't it?"

He didn't wait for an answer, leapt from the bed, quickly stepped into his underpants and trousers, and went to the front door.

"I've delivered the horse and cow." The neighbour dispensed with any greeting and sniggered. "I thought you might like to milk the cow this morning, but I see you're busy. Nice to be newly married."

Alice cringed and pulled the covers up over her head at the news that the neighbour had witnessed their lovemaking. Top of the list of jobs for today, make some curtains for the window.

Fergus cleared his throat. "That's very kind of you, Mr McGregor. We'd best find a paddock for them."

"The wife gave me this for you too." The neighbour pulled a dented cake tin from a rucksack slung over the horse. "She'd deliver it herself but she's poorly. The cold has crept into her bones, left them gnarly and arthritic."

Alice heard the conversation from the bedroom. It was reassuring to learn there was a woman living nearby. Perhaps she'd misjudged Mr McGregor by his appearance. He couldn't be all bad if he had a wife. She found her dressing gown hanging on a hook on the back of the door and pulled it tight around her body, heeding the warning to not let the cold seep into her bones before she started the day's chores.

CHAPTER

27

"I'm going to have to fix the fences around here first." Fergus had one eye on the window, ensuring the horse and cow didn't wander away while he ate his toast. "Or Jericho and Daisy will disappear back to the neighbours."

Ooga ooga! A horn blast echoed around the hills, startling the horse and cow who charged away down the paddock.

"Bloody hell!" Fergus jumped up from the table. "Who the hell is visiting us now?"

They both went to the front door to find a truck pulled up beside the rusty letterbox nailed on top of a post at their front gate.

"You'll have to fix this flap if you want to keep your mail dry," suggested the mailman as the door of the letterbox fell in his hand.

"I'll add it to the list of jobs to do," Fergus said. "I've got to go and catch my animals first. No need to announce your arrival in future."

"Sorry. Long time since I've been here. Thought I'd better catch up with you. First to deliver this parcel." The man handed over a parcel wrapped in brown paper, tied with string, and addressed to Mr and Mrs Buchanan. "Secondly, to let you know I'll be out this way once a week if you need any supplies brought out, or letters taken back for posting."

"Thank you." Alice stepped up and took the parcel. It was the first mail they'd received addressed to Mr and Mrs Buchanan, the black ink brought Alice a certainty, evidence, and ratification that they were married. Everything was happening so fast, it barely seemed real. "If you could bring us a loaf of bread each week, that would be wonderful."

Fergus went to the paddock with a handful of hay and called out to Jericho and Daisy. Alice farewelled the mailman and took the parcel inside. She saw the sender was M Buchanan, her mother-in-law and was eager to tear the brown paper open. Like an impatient child she squeezed the parcel, trying to discern what treasure it held. There was something small, hard, and square in the centre; maybe a book thought Alice, protected by a soft outer layer. She glanced out the window to see that Fergus had the animals tethered to the fence beside the cottage. She wouldn't have to wait long to have her curiosity satisfied.

"Haven't you opened it yet?" Fergus poked his head in the back door. "Hurry up, we've got work to do."

Alice didn't need prompting again. She found the scissors and cut the string close to the double knot so that it could be re-used later. Unfolding the brown paper revealed a patchwork quilt, squares in florals and checks, all colours of the rainbow carefully handstitched together.

"Oh, it's beautiful." Alice sighed, wishing she'd had someone to teach her needlework.

Fergus laughed. "Mum's been at it again. She made one for every bed at home. What's the pattern on it? She always forms a picture with the patches."

Alice spread the quilt over the table and stood back to admire her mother-in-law's creation.

"It's a heart," she exclaimed with delight. "And there is an envelope."

She bent down to pick up the envelope that had dropped to the floor. Alice pulled a card from the envelope and read the message aloud.

'Fergus and Alice, Congratulations on your wedding. May there always be love and understanding in your marriage. Know that you are always in my thoughts. I wish you well, your loving Mother.'

"Hmmph," Fergus huffed. "Nothing's changed then."

"What do you mean, Fergus?" Alice felt confused by his reaction to his mother's beautiful message.

"The old man," Fergus replied as if those three words were enough.

Alice re-read the message and realised it was from Marion alone.

"I'll put the quilt on the bed, and I'll be right with you," she said as she disappeared to the bedroom.

♥

There was no further mention of Fergus's father while they spent the morning fixing the fences in the paddock beside the house. They pulled the wires tight, replaced battens that were broken from a pile of used fencing material they found behind the hayshed, and re-stapled others to hold them in place.

Alice worked as hard as she could, trying to anticipate Fergus's next step, to be able to hand him a batten or a staple, whichever was needed, and to brace the batten with the head of the axe when he was ready to nail in the staples.

The wooden gate at the roadside was too rotten to fix.

"We'll pull this out, some of it we can use for firewood, and I'll rig up a Taranaki gate," Fergus said.

"What's a Taranaki gate?" Alice asked. "Do we have to get it sent down from Taranaki?"

Fergus's laugh told Alice she'd asked a dumb question.

"Well, I don't know," she pouted defensively.

"Sorry, Alice. Of course, you don't know. I forget you've only been farming for a few months. You're so good at it."

Alice looked askance at Fergus. Was he teasing her or was his praise genuine? His dimple wasn't winking, maybe her husband appreciated her efforts. She hoped so.

"A Taranaki gate is a gate made with battens and barbed wire, strung between two posts so when it's shut it just looks like part of the fence."

"Why do you call it a Taranaki gate?"

"I think the dairy farmers use them a lot up in that province," Fergus replied as he dismantled the rotten gate. "You go get the wheelbarrow for this lot and I'll make up the new one."

It was hard work pushing the heavy wheelbarrow through the long grass, even more so when Alice had loaded it up with wood. She felt the blisters forming on her palms. As the sun arced its way across the sky, Jericho worked his way closer to Alice, following her about the paddock. Where the horse went the cow was not far behind. Alice felt something tickle her cheek and a hot breath beside her ear. It wasn't Fergus; he was on the other side of the fence. She turned to see the horse's nostrils, heard a friendly whinny, and felt a slobbery nibble at her chin.

"Hello, Jericho." Alice reached up and scratched the horse's neck. "You're a friendly old chap, nice to meet you."

"Hopefully he's not too old to get us up them hills." Fergus assessed the hills that rose steeply behind the cottage. "After lunch we'll go and see what the rest of the property looks like."

After a simple lunch of eggs on toast, Fergus and Alice set out on Jericho to explore the property, assess the condition of the livestock that came with the farm and make a mental list of what needed to be done. If the rest of the fences were anything like the roadside ones, there might be no stock left on the property.

Out to the side of the hayshed, was an overgrown track that wove its way up the hillside. It was a slow trek, not because Jericho was too old but because the poor condition of the track made it dangerous to go at anything faster than a slow amble.

Fergus insisted Alice sit in front of him on the horse. His arms wrapped protectively around her body to hold the reins. Her back was cocooned against his chest, and they rocked together, from side to side with each lift of the horse's hooves. It was a rhythm Alice found soothing, a closeness that brought a smile to her face.

Bracken fern grew haphazardly over the track, the green fronds of the fresh new shoots formed a soft blanket while the old hardened brown shoots created a barricade Fergus had to push the horse through.

"A pity we don't have a bulldozer," Fergus said. "I could clear this in a day. It's going to take me months with a slasher."

"I'll help you," Alice offered. She looked at the palms of her hands. They were already blistered from the wheelbarrow. She'd have to harden up if she was to be of any use to her husband wielding a slasher.

Halfway up the hill, Fergus reined the horse in and turned so they could admire the view. The valley spread out below them, one flat paddock either side of the road on which they'd arrived. Although the rain had stopped overnight, clouds still clung to the tops of the higher hills only allowing shafts of sunlight to filter through.

"It's ours Alice. It's ours." Fergus rested his chin on Alice's shoulder and sighed with pride before he kissed her cheek.

Alice's insides melted. She wasn't religious but she felt those shafts of sunlight were straight from heaven. Some higher power was blessing her, bringing this gentle, loving man into her life, providing them with a home and a farm that they could work together. It would be hard work, but Alice felt the sacrifice would be worth it. She just had to keep Fergus safe from the military, to not let the war permeate their far-flung valley.

They continued up the track. Fantails flitted along beside them, chirping happily as they feasted on the insects disturbed by the horse's hooves. Tufts of sheep's wool snagged on the bracken provided evidence that sheep had once taken the same path. They smelled the first of the sheep before they saw it. The hawk that was pecking at its intestines flew off as they came into sight but circled overhead awaiting their departure.

"Damn," Fergus cursed. "We're too late to save that one. It must have got cast and died."

"Smells like it's been there for a while." Alice pinched her nostrils to block out the stench as Jericho passed the carcass.

Eventually, where the land plateaued, they came across the first of the live sheep, a small herd of a dozen animals whose fleeces hadn't seen the shears for some time. Dags rattled at their behinds; wool hung down over their eyes. The fleeces of the older sheep hung in shreds, ripped off by the bracken that grew just as tall in the paddock as on the track. The sheep bleated loudly at the intrusion but didn't move off. Amongst the flock were several of this year's lambs. Alice wondered how they would have ever found the ewe's udder for a feed. Memories of all the lambs she'd rescued at Whipsnade and Orari Estate flooded back. She hoped they hadn't missed saving any lambs here.

"What are we going to do with this lot?" she asked.

"Ermm." Fergus rubbed his forehead and frowned. "We'll have to fix up the yards before we can get them in for shearing, drenching, docking …."

"Hopefully, they'll survive until then." Alice tried to muster some positivity. While she disliked the cruelty of docking and ringing lambs, it was surely better for the sheep than being left in the condition of these animals.

Fergus clicked his heels into Jericho's side, urging the horse on. They found a trough, or what should have been a trough. A million flying midges hovered over the black stagnant water. Water dribbled over the broken concrete rim, spilling down the side in a green slime trail. Whether the water source was from the rain, a spring, or a water pipe, they couldn't tell through the thick grass that grew up to meet the slime.

Fergus headed towards the back of the property, where the scrub and bracken gave way to native bush. A rickety boundary fence threaded its way through the gorse bushes that would have originally been intended as a hedge. Yellow flower buds were forming, ready to burst open with the warming temperatures.

"I'd better come chop these down too," Fergus said. "Before the flowers open and seed."

"Look at the size of the trunks." Alice pointed to the gnarly branches rising from the grass like arthritic hands. "They must have been planted decades ago."

"Perhaps the first farmers were settlers from Scotland," Fergus suggested. "They thought gorse would grow like it did back home, not go rampant like it does in New Zealand."

"I don't think the slasher is going to get through those," Alice said. "Oh, Fergus. It seems like everywhere we look there is something else to be done."

"At least, Alice, whatever we do, we are doing for ourselves."

Alice leaned back into Fergus's chest, absorbing his energy, letting her heart fill with his words, words that made her feel wanted, loved. Did Fergus love her? Did she love him? If what they had wasn't yet love, Alice felt it soon would be.

Skirting along what should be the back boundary, they found several narrow but well-trodden paths heading into the darkness of the dense forest.

"Are we losing animals into the bush," Alice asked. "Or are animals coming out to feed?"

Fergus jumped down off the horse to inspect the droppings littering the path.

"I think it might be deer," he said. "I can come shooting and get us some venison to eat and a nice skin for a floormat."

Alice cringed at the thought of a deerskin on her floor, but she knew out here, life was going to be survival of the fittest and strongest and she needed for her and Fergus to be the survivors.

On the way back down the hill they found a track that branched off to the right. It had been hidden from sight on their ascent by the scrub but led to an opening with a small pond on which a pair of Paradise ducks paddled. Another flock of sheep grazed behind the pond. These ones appeared in no better condition than the others but there were more of them bringing the total herd up to a productive number, enough to make a living from if they were able to keep them from running away.

"Well, Alice, it's going to be all hard work from here on in." Fergus dismounted again and held his arms out to help Alice do the same. "I think we should stop for a cuppa before it all starts. It might be our last chance to catch our breath."

Fergus held Alice in his arms and leaned in for a kiss, a kiss that took Alice's breath away. At this hour of the day, the disappearing sun seemed to summon the stubble to Fergus's face. Alice felt its roughness but didn't pull away.

Jericho's neigh broke them apart.

Fergus laughed. "All the animals seem to want you as much as I do, Alice."

Alice blushed, giggled, and squirmed with delight as that newly discovered warm feeling called desire bubbled inside her. She glanced around the paddock. Could they make love outside? Her brazen thoughts reminded her of Moira; would Moira do it out in the paddock? Was she becoming like Moira?

"Alice! Alice!" Fergus waved his hand in front of her face. "You look like you're a million miles away."

She shook her head, the heat from her body rose to her crown and coloured her cheeks scarlet like a beacon signalling her desires. She couldn't possibly give them voice, could she?

"Didn't you promise me a cup of tea?" Decorum overruled desire.

Fergus pulled the corked beer bottle from his rucksack and two tin cups. He'd filled the bottle with boiling water and tea leaves before they'd left, the woollen sock he'd stowed it in protected the bottle and kept the well-stewed tea warm.

A fallen log beside the pond provided a convenient seat and Fergus draped his jacket over the log which was still damp from yesterday's rain.

"Well, what do you think Alice?" Fergus cupped his tin mug to absorb the last of the warmth. "Can we make a go of this? You and me?"

Although merely questions, the thoughts behind them made Alice's heart swell so much she thought it would burst from her chest and land in Fergus's lap. Wanting to sound like a competent farmer rather than a swooning sop, she tempered her words.

"It'll be a lot of work. Hard work but together I think we can give it our best efforts."

"Our best efforts better be enough," Fergus replied. "Or that darn war will catch up with me."

❦

"We'll just do a quick walk around this mob before we head home," Fergus suggested as he stowed the empty mugs and bottle back in his rucksack. "I see that hawk circling again. Perhaps there is another dead animal over here."

They left the horse grazing and skirted the side of the pond. A small white hump, tucked behind a mound of tussock caught Fergus's attention.

"Looks like we've got a dead lamb," he said. "I'd better bury it to keep the scavengers at bay."

"Wait!" Alice pulled at Fergus's shoulder as he bent to pick up the carcass. "It's still breathing."

"I don't think so, Alice."

"Yes!" she insisted. "I saw its stomach move. Just a little bit but I know I saw it."

Fergus moved aside. "You're the expert on saving lambs. Do what you can. We'll need every animal we can."

Alice knelt beside the lamb. She watched its limp body to be sure her imagination wasn't playing tricks on her. The sunken stomach moved again, it was feeble, but it was movement. She scooped her hands under the lamb and hugged it into her body.

"It's alive." She smiled at Fergus. "It just needs a feed and to warm up by the fire."

Fergus laughed. "At least with our rundown old house, it won't matter if you have animals inside. Come on then, we'd best get you home so you can work your magic."

CHAPTER

28

Alice stretched and reached her arm out to Fergus's side of the bed. The sheets were cold and the imprint of his head on the pillow long gone. On the bedside table, the hands of the clock formed a single vertical line; it was six o'clock.

"Fergus." Alice called out as she wandered the cottage putting on her dressing gown.

The only audible reply came from the lamb huddled on some hay in one of their packing boxes in front of the coal range.

"Are you hungry, Angel?" Alice stirred the embers in the coal range and added some more wood. She'd named the lamb as a reminder of how blessed she felt. She didn't need reminding, everywhere she looked she felt a sense of pride, of belonging and of love; all the things Alice had wanted for so long.

Out the back window she saw the other reason for her contentment. Fergus. His body looked miniature on the hillside, thrashing away at the bracken. Fires of smouldering

318

debris showed his progress up the track. Alice's thoughts wandered. She pictured Fergus naked, his muscles flexing, the smoothness of his skin, how it felt when their bodies meshed, the taste of his mouth on hers. She cursed the farm for taking her husband from their bed before she got to turn her desires into reality.

The lamb bleated meekly but enough to make Alice blush at the risk of her thoughts being discovered.

"Right. Right. I'll make you a bottle."

Alice mixed the last of Daisy's milk with some hot water from the kettle. The beer bottle that had sufficed as a thermos, now became a lamb feeder with a teat Angel latched onto with eagerness.

After the lamb was fed, Alice fed herself while making a mental list of the chores to be done today. Top of the list was milking Daisy.

There was no milking shed on the farm. A concrete pad with protruding broken posts the only sign that one may have existed. Still unsure of Daisy, Alice decided she'd first attempt to milk the cow in the paddock where at least there was no risk of her running off. Jericho and Daisy stood at the fence as if expecting her visit.

"Good morning, you two." Alice stood between the horse and cow and simultaneously scratched their necks in greeting.

Daisy was an old Jersey cow who looked like she'd been dipped in golden syrup, apart from her black eyelashes which curled as if her morning routine included the application of mascara. Without a stool, Alice had to squat beside the cow, the bucket only just fitting beneath Daisy's full udder. She had to trust that the animal wasn't a kicker as she began the squeeze and pull motion to encourage the milk flow. Alice was beginning to doubt she'd remembered her training from Whipsnade when finally, the milk made its welcome spirt into the bucket.

"Thank you, Daisy," she whispered, resting her forehead on the cow's side, listening to the gurgling of the animal's stomachs.

Above, the clouds seem to hang on the hills like a blanket this sleepy valley was reluctant to remove. The smoke from Fergus's bonfires whorled its way skyward to merge with the clouds, darkening the sky and only allowing the merest of sunlight to seep through.

When Daisy's milk was safely stowed in a jug in the cooling cupboard, Alice decided her next job was to establish a vegetable garden, hoping she'd remembered enough of Nel's good advice to grow a garden as plentiful as the one at Whipsnade. At the back of the house was a patch where the previous owners must have attempted the same. Spires of seeded silver beet plants rose above a mat of weeds, yellow flowers of broccoli looked pretty but Alice was unsure if they were edible. She pictured the rusty wire mesh strung between two posts, now entwined with dead woody tendrils, as a frame supporting a bountiful harvest of runner beans or maybe a crop of peas that she could eat straight from the pods. She could almost taste the fresh peas and eagerly grabbed the fork to begin clearing the area.

The remnants of an orchard stood beyond the weed patch. Several trees whose bark resembled the wrinkled skin of an old witch, were attempting to blossom once more. Fresh green leaves and tiny white flowers adorned the ends of the branches that were out of reach of the animals. Alice imagined a swing, tied with rope, hanging from the strongest branch. A place where she could relive the freedom of her childhood. A place where her own children could play, and she would listen with delight to their giggles.

Children? Alice stopped. Where and how had children crept into her thoughts and dreams? Was it because she now felt like she had a home? Was it because her body wasn't doing what it would normally be doing at this time of the month?

By the time Fergus arrived back for lunch, Alice had a mound of weeds to compost, and a patch of freshly dug earth for her efforts.

"Looks like we've got ourselves some fertile earth, Alice." Fergus ran a handful of dirt through his fingers allowing the worms to wriggle free.

"It will need to be." Alice straightened, wiped her brow on the back of her sleeve and leaned on the fork handle to catch her breath. "It's got to feed us."

"Well, we've got enough food for lunch," Fergus replied. "Have a rest and come and eat."

Alice needed a rest. She was determined to carry her weight, do as much as Fergus in bringing their property into shape but the morning's efforts had seemed more draining than she'd expected.

They dined on cold meat sandwiches washed down with a cup of tea. Angel sat up in the box watching them, the pinks of her ears shining forward as if she was taking in every word of their conversation.

"Looks like you've saved another one." Fergus smiled at the lamb. "You're a good mum."

Alice blushed. Was it her reluctance to accept praise or did she think there was a chance she might be a mum already? She held her teacup in two hands, raised it to cover her face as she took a sip of tea and hid her thoughts and emotions from Fergus. Alice wasn't ready to reveal what might or might not be happening. Another week and she'd know for sure. She'd always been regular, so regular she could almost set a clock by her cycle. Perhaps, with everything that had happened over the past fortnight, her clock was just running a bit behind time.

"A few more days…" Fergus sighed.

Alice's head shot up and her eyes bulged. Had Fergus read her mind? Was she thinking out loud?

"A few more days and I reckon I'll have enough of the track cleared that we can get the sheep down safely, get them in for shearing and a drench," he said.

"That will be good." Alice smiled. Her secret was safe, for now. If she was with child, Fergus would be the first to know, it wouldn't be a secret Alice would keep for long.

"We might have to fix up some yards to put them in too. Maybe put a roof on that concrete pad so it can double as a cowshed and a shearing platform. I found a stack of old sheets of iron. It's covered in blackberry but I'm sure it'll do the job. We can't afford any new stuff."

Alice nodded in agreement as if she was intently hearing Fergus's every word, not a million miles away lost in her own thoughts.

❦

Several days later and some of the seeds Alice had planted in the vegetable garden had sprouted and dared to poke their tender shoots through the earth. Inside Alice's own body she was now certain a seed had also been planted. Her and Fergus's seed to be nurtured and grown with love. Alice felt a joy and a trepidation all at once. To be a mother would be an honour but to have responsibility for caring for a tiny person, Alice wasn't sure she was up to the task. She hoped the skill of motherhood wasn't something determined by your genes. If she was like her own mother, Alice feared for her baby.

As Fergus and Jericho herded the sheep down the track, Alice waited to shoo them away from the garden and into the makeshift yards they had constructed. There was no time for her hopes and doubts of motherhood to linger, she needed to focus on the task at hand. The sheep were their livelihood, the source of income that would make the farm profitable and keep Fergus from having to enlist. If the war claimed him, took him away to fight on the other side of the world, then Alice would become a solo parent, just like her mother. She could cope with that temporarily but what if ….? Alice shuddered.

The sheep came hurtling down the hill towards her, their dags rattling like maracas. Alice whistled and waved her arms, urging them towards the yards. Fergus dismounted and tethered Jericho to the fence with the reins so he could shut the sheep in with another Taranaki gate he'd built. The sheep jostled and bleated at their confinement.

"I'd say it's been a while since they've been shut into anything," Fergus said. "Best we keep this short, or these yards mightn't hold."

They'd spent the previous afternoon repairing what was left of the stockyards, removing the boards that were broken or too rotten to be of any use and replacing them with used rails that would hopefully hold until Fergus had time to mill some trees.

Fergus hooked his hand under the jaw of the biggest sheep and sat it on its bottom. They pulled the sheep's wool free of snagged bracken twigs before Fergus leaned the sheep back against his thighs.

"Pass me the shears, please," he asked holding his other hand out. "Careful, I've already sharpened them."

Starting at the sheep's belly, Fergus's steady hand clipped the wool away from the breast, around the teats before he snipped off the dags.

Alice waited until he'd finished before she dragged the turd infested wool away with the garden fork. It would be a great addition to her compost pile but would devalue the fleece if allowed to contaminate the good wool.

Fergus shore the rest of the sheep with ease. Alice wondered if she would ever master the procedure that looked simple in the hands of an experienced farmer. She gathered up the fleece and took it to the concrete pad to remove any remaining imperfections before bundling it into the woolsack they'd nailed to the railings. There was no wool press, like everything else on this farm, they had to improvise.

"I think this one might be a late lamber." The udders of the next sheep were swollen and the teats protruding.

"It's not Angel's mother, is it?" Alice asked with genuine concern. Although she loved rearing the lambs, she admitted the best place for them was with the ewe.

Fergus inspected the sheep's vulva. "No, this one doesn't look like it's lambed yet."

It was simply a matter of observation and fact, but Alice's cheeks coloured a deep red. Could you tell by looking down there whether she'd had a child or not? What did Fergus see when he disappeared under the covers and made her feel so good? She'd imagined he, like her, had his eyes closed but now, she dreaded to think, maybe not.

She refocused her thoughts on keeping a tally of the flock. All up there were forty-four ewes, a mixture of two tooths, which hopefully would lamb for the first-time next spring if they could capture the ram they'd passed on the way in, and some old ewes whose neglected feet meant they would be destined for the abattoir before too much longer. There were another ten lambs that had been born this year and thankfully had survived thus far without human intervention.

"We'll have to dock these lambs and ring the ram lambs," Fergus said as he finished shearing the last of them.

Alice straightened up, wiped her brow, and yawned. It had been a big day already and the thought of docking and ringing lambs exhausted her remaining energy.

"We'll leave it for tomorrow," Fergus said. "Let them calm down in the paddock overnight before we give them another shock."

Alice's sigh was audible. She hoped this wasn't what pregnancy did to expectant mothers. How was she going to be any use to Fergus making the farm profitable if she was exhausted by the smallest of jobs?

"I think we deserve a bath after all our hard work." Fergus must have seen Alice's yawn. His own face was dirty but painted with a mischievous grin. "Do you want to head back and stoke the fire up, so we've got plenty of hot water? I'll tie off the wool bale and clean the shears and be right behind you."

Although Alice had spent hours cleaning the bath, removing the fungi growing in the bottom and scouring the stains from the cast iron sides, it still wasn't a sterile white colour. Beggars can't be choosers she recited to herself as she turned the taps. It was several seconds before the water cleared the scum built up in the pipes and ran clean, so Alice was able to put the plug in.

After loading the coal range and opening the damper, Alice kept dipping her fingers in the rising bath water, adjusting the hot and cold taps to ensure the water temperature was just right. She'd closed the lean-to door to keep the heat in and now the bathroom was steaming like a sauna.

"Just what I need." Fergus came into the bathroom with nothing but a towel in his hand and a big grin on his face.

Alice jumped at the sound of his voice and nearly swallowed her own tongue when she saw his nakedness.

"Don't look so shocked." Fergus chuckled. "We can't bathe with our clothes on. Do you need me to help you get undressed?"

Alice's eyes darted about the room as the realisation of Fergus's intention dawned on her. She looked at the bath, she looked at Fergus's nakedness and then she looked down at her own dirty clothes.

"We'll both fit," he said as if anticipating her offering that as an excuse. "Come on, the water will be getting cold. I can scrub your back and you can scrub mine."

There was truth in everything Fergus said but Alice still couldn't make her feet move.

Fergus's eyebrows knitted together in a frown. "Is there something you're trying to hide from me?"

"No," Alice replied a little defensively.

"Well, I'm getting in." Fergus dropped the towel, climbed into the bath and sunk down into the water with a satisfied sigh. "I don't want to waste this heat."

Alice imagined the water lifting the weight from her aching body. The anticipated relief was enough to overcome whatever decorum she was trying to maintain. There was no reason to be embarrassed, this man was her husband, he was not ashamed of his body, why should she feel the need to hide hers? Despite all that, Alice turned her back to Fergus and slowly undressed, careful to be ladylike as she stepped out of her clothes and hid her undergarments. She glanced down at her breasts. She'd felt their tenderness under the buttons of her overalls all day. Had they grown already? Would Fergus be able to tell the subtle differences in her body? Ones that she was only just discovering. Should she tell him, or should she wait until her pregnancy is confirmed by a doctor? Perhaps it is all just in her imagination. Will Fergus be angry at her if she is pregnant and can't work the farm? It's the farm that is going to keep him from the war, not a baby.

She sought confirmation in the mirror, its chain looped over a nail high up on the wall. Even if her height had allowed Alice to glimpse more than the tip of her collarbone, the cloudy de-silvering mirror was protecting its secrets.

Alice felt the chill seeping through the wooden floorboards into her bare feet. "You move forward, and I'll wash your back first," she offered, knowing that way Fergus wouldn't be looking at her.

When she was tucked in behind Fergus, he passed Alice the soap and flannel which she lathered up and ran up and down his back, noticing every contour of muscle, the smooth lines, the indentations of the strong frame that carried him, and the freckles she itched to trace a line between as if to identify a faraway constellation. She rinsed the flannel and rung the water out so that it ran like rivulets from his neck down.

"Your turn." Fergus grabbed the discarded soap and stood to turn around in the bath.

Passing the flannel brought Alice face to face with Fergus's manliness. She blushed, gulped, and almost choked at the closeness of his groin before she hitched her knees up and spun herself around in the bath, grateful for the advantage of being small.

Fergus laughed again. He seemed to delight in shocking her or was it just that he was so relaxed with his body and Alice should learn to be the same? She didn't know but her heart ticking like a time bomb in her chest, told her something was about to change.

The water level rose as Fergus lowered his body back into the bath and began washing Alice. It was another first for her. The gentle hands of a man gifting her a simple action that carried so much more. Alice surrendered herself.

CHAPTER

29

It was Friday again by the time the lambs' tails had been ringed and the ram lambs' testes removed. Knowing that the lambs would soon recover didn't help Alice find the task any less cruel. She cringed as she watched the lambs restlessly sit, then stand, then sit again searching for relief.

Friday brought the mailman who remembered not to toot his truck horn.

"Look who I found walking up the road," he yelled as he pulled into the driveway. "A friend of yours."

Sunshine reflected off the truck windscreen hiding whomever the mailman was delivering.

"*Kia ora*." The Maori greeting gave Rangi's presence away before his curly black head and wide smile emerged from the passenger door.

"Rangi!" Fergus rushed forward to greet his friend with a handshake and a *hongi*. "What? How? You didn't walk all the way from Orari, did you?"

"No." Rangi raised his thumb as his lips curled into a happy grin. "Hitched a ride most of the way. I got dropped off at the end of your road. Thank God for the mailman, or I mightn't have got here until tomorrow. It's a long way in and there ain't much traffic."

"Sorry, if I'd known you were coming, I could have come and picked you up in the truck." Fergus took the mail and farewelled the mailman.

"A bit hard. I would have been here before any letter arrived and it doesn't look like you have a telephone." Rangi pointed skyward. "Hell, it looks like you don't even have power."

"No, not yet," Fergus replied.

"I hope you haven't lured the lovely Alice here on false pretences." Rangi winked just before he wrapped his arms around Alice and squeezed her tight.

Too tight for her tender breasts. "Ouch!"

"Oops, sorry Alice." Rangi released her and stepped back to study her face. "I didn't mean to be rough. You certainly look like this place agrees with you." Rangi laughed and nudged Fergus with his elbow. "Or is it married life that's got you fair blossoming?"

The predictable heat rose, colouring Alice's cheeks a deep red, no matter how hard she tried to breathe deep, to calm herself, to pretend she wasn't embarrassed, her body gave her away. Her concern this time was what exactly was she giving away? Was Rangi just teasing or could he know of her condition? What if this was the way Fergus was to discover his impending fatherhood? Alice couldn't let that happen.

"You'll be wanting a cuppa after your long trip then." She turned and headed for the cottage. "I'll go and get the kettle boiling."

"So, what brings you all the way out here?" Fergus asked as they followed Alice inside.

"Thought I'd better come and see where you were before I leave."

"Leave? Where are you off to?" The heightened pitch of Fergus's voice echoed the surprise Alice felt but kept to herself.

"I've enlisted." Rangi dropped his bag to the floor in the passage.

"What!" Fergus and Alice exclaimed in unison.

"Well, not actually enlisted." Rangi made himself comfortable at the table. "They still won't take me with my colour-blindness, but I can volunteer."

"But I thought you and I were on the same page as far as fighting went?" Fergus looked like his toes had been trampled by an elephant.

"We are. We are," Rangi reiterated. "I'm not going to fight. I'm going to help those that have no choice but to fight. The poor buggers who are getting shot and blown to bits. I'm going to be a porter at one of the hospitals they ship them out to."

The kettle's piercing whistle was like an alarm reverberating around the room, echoing the misgivings held for Rangi's decision.

"But they are right on the front line too." Fergus rubbed his forehead as if Rangi's news were giving him a headache.

"I'm not going to a field hospital," Rangi explained. "In England, they've got hospitals where soldiers go to get full medical care after the patch-up jobs they do at the front. It's where they recuperate before they either get shipped home or sent back to the frontline."

Even a hospital in England sounded far too close to the fighting for someone Alice knew. She steadied herself against the bench, while she added the tea leaves to the pot, poured in the hot water and encased the pot in its crocheted cover.

Fergus sat across from Rangi, nodding his head. The gesture terrified Alice even more. Was her husband merely trying to understand Rangi or was he now in agreement with his friend's thinking? Would Fergus think volunteering at a hospital was the way to help his fellow countrymen without going to war? Would he be wanting to do the same? Alice took a deep breath and tried to conceal the tremble in her fingers by carrying each cup and saucer to the table separately.

"But there have been air raids in London too." Alice turned the teapot three times and carried it to the table. "Even Buckingham Palace is all boarded up."

"The hospital I'm going to is in Worcestershire." Rangi struggled to get his Maori tongue around the ancient English county name. "It's north of London and away from the fighting."

"At the moment." The war that everyone thought would be over in a matter of months was dragging into years and Alice feared it would never end.

"I'll be fine," Rangi said with his usual grin, but Alice saw the quiver in his lips as he reached for his cup of tea and a piece of cake. "Nice cake, Alice."

"It's the last of our wedding cake." Alice looked at Fergus and smiled at the happy memories of all that had happened since that day.

"I thought you Pakeha had some weird custom of saving that for your firstborn." Rangi chuckled. "Is there some news you want to share?"

"Give a man a break, Rangi." Fergus punched Rangi lightly on the arm. "There's plenty of work to be done around here before I start thinking about that."

Alice couldn't look at either of them. She fidgeted with her fingers in her lap. Fergus wasn't ready for children. What would he do when he found out it was already too late?

"You'd better show me what you've been up to then." Rangi gulped down the last of his tea. "I'm only here overnight. If there's anything I can help you with, I'm happy to."

"I've found a recently fallen tree. Thought I could saw it up for timber to rebuild the milking shed and yards. It will save Alice if you get on the other end of the saw."

"Lead the way." Rangi pushed his chair back and stood. "Alice saved me when I needed it, anything to repay the favour."

"I could saw," Alice protested.

"Yes, but you don't have to while I'm here." Rangi put his hand on her shoulder to stop Alice from rising.

"I could come and collect the offcuts for firewood," she offered not wanting to feel useless.

Fergus lent down and kissed her on the cheek. "You deserve a day off, Alice. We've been working hard since we arrived. If you want to come up later, you could bring some sandwiches and a drink, then we won't have to stop for long."

The men headed to the door before Alice could protest further. She jammed the lid of the cake tin on, thumping it down with her fist as her cheeks reddened again. This time, with the heat of anger. Another man on the property and Alice was relegated to domestic duties. It wasn't fair that Rangi had come between her and Fergus again. Why did men always do that? He might be bigger and stronger than her and they'd probably get through the job twice as fast but all that was beside the point, Alice wanted to be treated as an equal. And she didn't want Rangi planting seeds of volunteering in Fergus's mind, she needed her husband here to care for her and the seed he had planted in her. Alice placed her hands on her flat belly.

"We won't let him go anywhere, will we, little one?" Alice whispered. "We won't let that Maori make trouble for us."

Perspiration beaded Alice's forehead by the time she reached Fergus and Rangi with a basket of food for lunch. It was the finest day they'd had since moving to the valley, and it felt as if the hills had captured all the sun's rays to beam down on her as she climbed the track on foot.

She heard the men's laughter before she found them and the stack of timber they'd already created. The long lengths with slivers of wood in between to allow the air to circulate and the timber to dry, gave off a pleasing aroma.

The laughter stopped abruptly when Alice rounded a mound of bracken that hadn't yet been cleared and came into their view. She sucked in a breath, filled her lungs with doubt as she watched the men exchange glances across the saw, its blade wedged into the log. Was that guilt she saw on their faces? What had they been talking about? Her?

"I've brought your lunch," she said with as much dismissiveness as she could muster.

"We'll just finish this one," Fergus replied.

He nodded to Rangi, the men repositioned their hands and feet and the saw moved through the wood, backwards and forwards in a smooth rhythm as its teeth chewed a line and deposited a pile of sawdust either side of the log.

They'd discarded their shirts, white singlets that were no longer white but covered in dirt, saw dust, and sweat revealed biceps flexing with each pull of the saw. Alice stood and admired and had to concede that she didn't have the muscles this work required.

A stand of totara trees with dense spiny leaves provided Alice with some welcome shade and dry ground to sit and unpack the sandwiches. A tauhou flitted about the lower branches, its forest green head bobbing from side to side as it blinked its silver eye at Alice. She tore a piece of crust from the sandwich she'd made for herself and held it out to the bird.

"Come on, little wax eye," she whispered. "You can trust me."

The bird puffed out its grey breast as if to say it was big and brave but stayed out of reach. When her arm tired, Alice conceded defeat and cast the crust onto the grass. The tauhou flew in and pecked at the bread as its eyes remained alert.

The crust was abandoned when Fergus and Rangi joined Alice in the shade and flopped down onto the grass to rest.

"Phew!" Rangi lay back and stretched. "When I said make the most of me, I didn't mean wear me out completely."

"You'd better eat some of Alice's delicious sandwiches then," Fergus replied. "We've got the rest of the log to get through yet."

"You're getting lots of good timber," Alice observed. "By the looks of that pile."

Fergus grinned with excitement as he grabbed a sandwich. "We'll have a proper milking shed for you and Daisy, and a set of yards, and I might be able to build a shed for Victor or extend the hayshed."

All these plans for the farm brought a sense of calm to Alice. Fergus couldn't do all of that and join Rangi in volunteering.

"I have to get things shipshape." Fergus's excitement drained away; his serious face looked like one of the stern portraits on the staircase wall at Orari Estate. "In case …"

"In case what?" Panic rose in Alice's voice.

"In case something happens to me." Fergus patted her on the thigh.

She glared at Rangi. Had he already convinced Fergus to volunteer? They were already doing their part for the war effort. They were producing food and wool. Perhaps Alice should do more. She could learn to spin, knit socks and singlets for men at the front. One thing she would have to do, is tell Fergus about the baby. Tonight. The first chance she got for a private conversation.

♡

That chance didn't come until the lights were out and she could hear the rumble of Rangi's snore through the bedroom wall.

"Are you awake, Fergus?" Alice whispered into the darkness.

"Mmm, just." Fergus pulled Alice to his side. "It's been a big day. Sorry, don't think I have any energy to make love. I'll be right as rain in the morning though."

Alice giggled. The thought tickled her insides. She'd have to ensure Rangi was still snoring in the morning for that to happen. She'd be mortified if he heard her and Fergus, the satisfied whimpers and sighs that always escaped.

"I need to tell you something." Alice ran her hand over Fergus's chest and rested it on his belly.

She felt his body tense before he spoke. "Yes …. is there something wrong?"

"Hopefully not."

Fergus rolled away, reached for the matches, and relit the candle on the bedside table. Its flickering flame cast ominous shadows around the walls. Across the passage, Rangi was silent, his snoring interrupted. Was he now awake and Alice's moment lost? She held her breath and silently urged him back to sleep.

"Alice?" Fergus turned to her and searched her face for answers.

She stayed silent, tried to show her love for this man with her eyes, the touch of her hand on his heart, until she finally heard Rangi's loud breathing again.

"You're not thinking of going away, are you? You can't. Not now. It wouldn't be fair. There are people here who need you. More than the people you don't know on the other side of the world. Well, you might know some of them but not as well as you know us. Will know us."

Fergus stopped Alice from talking in the most effective way. He kissed her and didn't stop kissing her until her body relaxed beside him.

"Alice," he said gently. "Please calm down. What is it you're trying to say? You're not making much sense to me."

"I'm pregnant," she blurted.

In the light of the candle, she watched as the whites of Fergus's eyes grew whiter. His lips parted, but nothing but air left his mouth. Slowly, the news registered and found its way from his head to his heart, wrinkles on either side of his eyes were the first signal of his happiness.

"Yippee!" yelled joyously into the night was the only proof that Alice needed to know her family and her home were safe.

"Shh, Fergus, you'll wake Rangi." Alice warned despite hearing the continuing rumble of Rangi's snore.

"I don't care if the whole world hears me. I'm going to be a dad. We're going to be parents. Oh Alice, this is wonderful news."

Fergus tucked a strand of Alice's hair behind her ear, baring her neck where he planted a row of kisses from her collarbone to her earlobe.

"Why did you think I would go away?" he murmured into her ear.

"You seemed to want to follow Rangi's lead and volunteer to help the Allies."

"Alice, you're the only ally I want and need, my ally for life."

Love flowed into every corner of Alice's being. She could never be happier than how she felt at this very instant.

Fergus chuckled and rested his hand on Alice's stomach. "And I'm suddenly feeling very energised so if this little baby doesn't mind, I want and need all of my Ally right now."

Husband and wife became one in the moment.

AUTHOR'S NOTE

Any woman who finds her inner strength to overcome challenges on her life journey is my heroine.

The late Doris Wilson, a real-life land girl, was the inspiration for Alice's character. *Diane Bardsley* in *The Land Girls, In a Man's World 1939-1946* quotes an eighty-nine year old Doris as saying 'Whatever men could do, I aimed at doing better. I was a faster crutcher than both the men I worked with.' She worked with eight men at Orari Estate, living in a whare behind the four-storied homestead, without electricity.

I sincerely hope Doris was never subjected to any sexual molestation and my heart goes out to any person that has. I hope that you have found your inner strength to move on in whatever way you can.

While I have endeavoured to remain true to the facts of the era and location, I'll have to claim poetic licence in a few instances. I'm sure avid readers and historians will be aware the Ferguson brand name was first applied to a tractor in 1946 but I couldn't have Fergus teaching Alice to drive anything other than a Ferguson. There is a Winterslow Road in Staveley, where I imagine the seasons pass slowly but whether there is a small tin cottage at the end of the road I do not know. I will leave the remainder of my tweaking of the truth for you to discover.

There are so many to thank in bringing this second book in my Kiwi Land Girl series to you – not only the courageous land girls that inspired the story but Annie Seaton for her editing skills, Kura Carpenter for cover design, Dixie Maria Carlton for her marketing advice, my writing buddies – Ami, Bruce, Frances, Joan, Robert, Shona, and Stella who offer valuable advice, inspiration, and motivation along the way. My heartfelt thanks to you all.

To you the reader, thank you for making time to read Alice's story. I hope you have enjoyed watching her grow as a person.

If you would like to read more about the Kiwi Land Girls, you can subscribe to my newsletter through my author website to get updates and receive a free look at Fergus and Alice's life 10 years on.

www.taniarobertsauthor.co.nz

Facebook: Tania Roberts Author
Instagram: taniarobertsauthor

Below is an excerpt from book three in the Kiwi Land Girl
series - Battle of Hearts.

William heard the comforting sound of female voices. He
couldn't make out the words, but it had been a long time
since he'd heard anything feminine. A long time since he'd
left home. Mum? Was he back home? What would his
mother say when she heard of the mess, he'd got himself
into? She'd growl; that fake growl she had for Dad's benefit.
She'd want to hug him, to wrap her arms around him like he
was the most precious thing in the world, like she did when
he was a boy and he needed somewhere safe to cry. He's
not a boy now though. He's a man. A soldier. He can't cry
now. Never again. If he was to give into crying, the
floodgates would open, and he would never stop.

There were other women at home, land girls. What were
their names? William couldn't remember. A pretty one,
whose name starts with 'b'. Why couldn't he remember?
What was wrong with him?

There were other noises too, unfamiliar sounds that left
William unsure where he was. He should open his eyes and
look. If only it was that easy. Everything appeared black,
his eyes unwilling to see. His head pounded, his entire body
ached, and an incessant throbbing radiated from his right
hand. Female voices continued a conversation that he
couldn't join.

"Welcome aboard, or should I say below. Your first shift,
isn't it?"

"It's strange being thirty feet underground. At least the
Germans won't find us here."

"Ermm. Don't be deluded by the muted sounds of the bombs. They're still close enough to get us, but we've been lucky so far."

'Lucky.' William could make that word out, but he didn't feel at all lucky. It seemed as if he was pinned to the ground, it was more comfortable than what he'd been sleeping on for the last few nights but still his body ached. He thought he could relieve the pain if he rolled over. William willed his body to do as his mind wanted. A spasm tore through his abdomen, and he howled in agony but remained lying exactly where he'd been placed.

"Sounds like he's coming around now."

"Well, you never can tell, some of them scream the whole way through. Fearful nightmares they must be having after what they've seen. We only see the results. Imagine what it is like to actually be in the midst of it."

Dust. Grit. Rats. Blood. Death. William had been in the midst of it. He could smell it. War had a stench all its own. It had seeped its way into his pores and there didn't seem to be any escape. There was another odour now, added to the mix, barely discernible but comforting, clean and offering a glimmer of hope. Perhaps William was lucky. The thunder of bombs seemed muted, the screams of his mates no longer a constant. There were no commands being yelled at him. He didn't have to get out of the trenches, scramble on his belly, squirm under coils of barbed wire into no-man's land, fearing with every breath the bullet of a sniper.

He didn't have to look at the big brown, pleading eyes of his mate, hold his hand and lie to him. Tell him that he was okay, as life ebbed from him, his lower limbs blown to pieces. William groaned. The pain of his memories, the pain of his physical injuries, which was worse, he didn't know.

A warm hand touched his arm. "I'll sit with him a while."

Yes, please he wanted to say but he couldn't move his mouth to form anything more than a grunt.

"You won't have time to do that, we're full up. There are thirty soldiers in here, each one needing dressings changed, pain relief and feeding if they can't feed themselves, before they get shipped out and the next lot arrive."

The hand was gone and William, unable to protest was left to drift back into a fitful sleep.

He stirred again late in the night when a nurse placed her hand on his arm in a comforting gesture. The same nurse or a different one, he couldn't tell.

"Hello, soldier, welcome back," she said.

"Back ... back where?" William croaked, his voice little more than a raspy mutter.

"Welcome back to the land of the living."

"My eyes .... my eyes ... I can't see." William clawed at the bandage covering his eyes. "Where are my eyes?"

"They're still there." The nurse pulled William's hand away. "Calm down and I'll remove the bandage so we can have a look."

William hoped she was right, that he could have a look. If he couldn't see, life wouldn't be worth living. His frustration grew as the nurse carefully unwrapped the bandage and no brightness edged its way through the gauze.

"It's dark!" Anguish gripped at William's insides. He see-sawed between anger and despair. He needed to leap out of bed and kill the Huns that had put him there but if he never saw another battle, he would be eternally grateful.

"It's okay, soldier. It's night-time, it should be dark. The gas lamps have been extinguished so you can sleep. Gas is a precious resource out here, not to be wasted." The nurse had hung her dimly lit lantern from a hook at the head of the cot so she could see. "There, bandage removed, how does that feel?"

William blinked his eyes several times, hoping the action would clear the blurry images that confronted him.

"I can't see!"

"Nothing?" The nurse held her finger out from William's face and moved it from left to right.

"Blurry. It's all blurry." He sensed a movement in front of him. Instinct told him to dodge. Don't let the bullet hit you, he yelled to himself as he tried to move.

"Calm down, soldier. Be patient. It might take a while to refocus. I'll reapply the bandage to your right eye and the doctor can have a look in the morning."

Another soldier howled in agony on the opposite side of the ward.

"Here; have a sip of water before I go and see to the other fellow." The nurse helped William lift his head up enough to take a drink from the glass she held to his lips. "That's it. Now rest up. It's the best means of recovery."

Recovery. The word bounced around William's head like the shrapnel that had put him here. Of course, he wanted to recover. Being blind and with a hand he couldn't seem to make work wasn't an option that sat well with him. But what did recovery mean for a soldier? Did they turn around and send you back to the front, back to the heat that parched your skin and throat, the flies that landed on every bare surface devouring whatever open flesh or food that lay in their way and the sand and grit that ground into every bodily orifice. All that to deal with before even imagining the fearful scream of the Sukas dive bombing at speed, the rattle of the Messerschmitts machine gunning the convoys or worst of all the sight of a fellow soldier less fortunate than you.

Or did recovery mean he would be sent home? What would be there for him? Who would have use for a man with no sight and a useless hand? No woman, not even the pretty land girl, would want to look at him, marred with battle scars. The prospect of recovery was grim either way he considered it.

www.ingramcontent.com/pod-product-compliance
Lightning Source LLC
Chambersburg PA
CBHW011219120626
46545CB00010B/3068